Bibliographic Performances & Surrogate Readings

Janelle Rebel

Bibliographic Performances & Surrogate Readings

Janelle Rebel

Table of contents

11–12   Preface
14–17   Introduction

Bibliographic Performances and Surrogate Readings

19–31   Bibliographic Performances and Surrogate Readings
33–71   The Visio-Bibliographic Turn in Art and Design
73–78   Scope of the Catalogue

Catalogue of Bibliographies

80–83   52 Transactions — K. Slade
84–88   336 Pages 336 Books — T. Prill, A. Vieceli, S. Cremers
89–91   Africanismus_12469 — J. Cyrus
92–94   All: The Books I Never Wrote or Wrote and Never Published — J. Drucker
95–101 The Artist's Novel & The Book Lovers — D. Maroto, J. Zielińska
102–104 Atlas of Punctuation — H. Neilson
105–109 The Author of This Book Committed Suicide — A. Krach

110–113	Barcode Cornel West & Barcode Oprah — S. Blake
114–119	The Best American Book of the 20th Century — Société Réaliste
120–125	Bib., Rev. Ed. — T. Lin
126–130	Bibliographic Sound Track & The Ph.D Sound — T. Lin
131–134	Bibliography of Architecture Theory — J. Rebel
135–143	Bibliomania — S. Morris
144–148	Bibliozines — Sitterwerk
149–153	Bookcatalogtest — T. Tamm
154–158	The Bookshelf Project — L. Davidson
159–164	Bulletins of the Serving Library ★Test★ — S. Bertolotti-Bailey, A. Keefer, D. Reinfurt
165–171	Coth • A Commonplace — A. Hamilton
172–176	Common Threads — C. Hicks
177–184	Cyberfeminism Index — M. Seu
185–189	A Die With Twenty-Six Faces — L. Lüthi
190–193	Difficult Times: Every Book About Spirituality I Own — M. Mills
194–198	The El Saturn Research Library — C. Smith
199–203	Exhibition Takeaways — J. Rebel for B-SSCC
204–211	A Final Companion to Books from "The Simpsons" in Alphabetical Order — O. Lebrun
212–215	Further Listening — C. D. Dworkin
216–220	Hidden Histories — T. Strachan
221–226	Human_3.0 Reading List 2015–2016 — C. Smith
227–232	Ideal Syllabus — J. Saltz & Frieze
233–235	Irma Boom: The Architecture of the Book — I. Boom
236–241	Juxtaposed — Mike and Maaike

242–245	Kentifrications: Convergent Truth(s) & Realities — K. A. C. Hinkle
246–249	Lonely Books — J. MacPhee
250–257	The Mary Shelley Facsimile Library — Werkplaats Typografie
258–261	Meanwhile, the Surrogate for the Presently Absent Gets a Proxy — J. Rebel
262–266	The Missing Pieces — H. Lefebvre
267–273	A People on the Cover — G. Ligon
274–278	The Perverse Library — C. D. Dworkin
279–280	Pile of Books — A. Mellegers
281–287	PM Tables, Visitor Tables, Your Tables — Printed Matter
288–291	Poet-Saints of July 06 — J. Rebel
292–297	The Queen's English — M. Syms with C. Roif and J. Cain.
298–300	Reading Trayvon Martin — M. Syms
301–304	Saints & Guides — Are Not Books & Publications
305–311	Someone Else – A Library of 100 Books Written Anonymously or Under Pseudonyms — S. Gupta
312–315	Sorted Books — N. Katchadourian
316–317	A Stack of Books, A Book of Stacks — T. Tamm
318–321	Strike and Riot — C. Lee
322–327	Study Room Guides — Live Art Development Agency
328–333	Wherein the Author Provides Footnotes and Bibliographic Citation for the First Stanza Drafted after a Significant and Dangerous Depression Incurred upon Being Referenced as a "Hack" Both by

Individuals Unknown to the Author and by Individuals Whom the Author Had Previously Considered Friends[*][†][‡][§] — J. Verlee

334–335   Works from Stack 655 — A. Desjardin

337–338   Acknowledgments
340–343   Reproduction Credits
345–350   Index
353   Author Bio

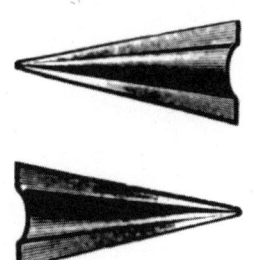

preface

One can never be quite sure what the motives of an author are even if they attempt to tell it to you plainly. Even if they attempt to understand it themselves, it might not be entirely clear. The question that pursues me and has been asked of me with quizzical suspicion over the years is "Why bibliographies?" Some people like red. Some people prefer blue. Does it need justification? I am interested in bibliographies, full stop. It doesn't strike me as particularly strange but it doesn't strike me as entirely ordinary either. So one reflects.

I did grow up in the woods of rural Wisconsin on the outskirts of a small village. Our house had a tv antennae on the roof and depending on the weather, we could dial into anywhere from zero to five fuzzy networks. So among other activities, reading took place. I remember exhausting the village public library and outgrowing our school library. Then we got cards at the nearest city public library which was a bit of a trek in the evening, but thank God, had shelves of books on multiple floors.

I kept lists of titles and authors I wanted to read. An author's best known works were never on the shelf—checked out or lost—so I'd read everything else by them and their friends instead. The forgotten stuff, the unfavorably reviewed stuff. The titles central to a milieu or movement escaped my reach. I knew they were out there though. I'd encounter them again and again in the very dry books I would skim to build out my lists, in those lovely sections for "suggested reading," in minuscule footnotes and other paratextual material.

I did not consider my work then as creating a personal bibliography—such a term would have been too abstract. But through my inquiries, list making, and reading, I had come into contact with the excitement of the inexhaustible. I was just scratching the surface and I knew it. There was more to discover beyond the bounds of my geography, beyond any limitations of my present circumstances. It's hard to describe that feeling. It's an awareness, a freedom of being of self, found in books read and books not read, but familiar.

Why bibliographies? Why not bibliographies.

Take heart, dear reader.

Introduction

!

While much has been written in the art press on the archival turn and the indexical, *Bibliographic Performances & Surrogate Readings* delves into the imaginative realm of books and libraries. It is about the impulse to show reading, the circulation of information, the power of recommendations, subject formation as resource curation, and the interpretive structures of experimental subject bibliographies. It hones in on a niche territory that has blossomed in recent history, reviewing over fifty compelling visio-bibliocentric projects. No book to date has been expressly dedicated to artistic and poetic practices in bibliography.[1] It will be the first monograph of its kind to historicize, theorize, and survey two decades of what I refer to as contemporary visual bibliography or experimental subject bibliography.

I initially wrote and designed a draft of *Bibliographic Performances & Surrogate Readings* in 2016 with the support of Joseph Grigely, Patrick Durgin, and Johanna Drucker in culmination of my masters degree in Visual and Critical Studies at the School of the Art Institute of Chicago. At the time, it was a way to survey the field and create a platform for my own artistic practices.[2] In the intervening years, I have presented on portions of this project, expanded my thinking, located additional examples, and kept the conversation going. My scholarly work in special collections librarianship and exhibition making problematizes staid constructions of the canon and the masterwork. In 2021, I staged a small exhibition at the Brizdle-Schoenberg Special Collections Center at Ringling College of Art and Design which allowed me to work out new project descriptions, reach out to some artists, and garner feedback.

At the outset, this project thinks in terms of the politics of history and history writing—who garners scholarly attention and who doesn't, who gets represented in a canon and who doesn't, and how emergent work and work by underrepresented creators fall by the wayside. It counters cultural gatekeepers stuck in unimaginative ruts that advance the same figures or the same ideas or the same artifacts year after year.

The book you now read has been reorganized, revised, and expanded from my earlier work—adding more front matter, project entries, new images, and an index—plus skillfully reimagined and redesigned by Arnaud Desjardin (publisher) and Margherita Sabbioneda (designer) at The Everyday Press. Two essays—a theoretical essay that draws on architecture theory, modeling, and "design's desire," and a historical essay that defines a genre with roots in conceptualism and literary experimentation—precede an inclusive catalogue of visual bibliographies from the past twenty years. The examples that have been selected for this survey are created by diverse, international cultural workers pushing the boundaries of bibliographic possibility and design experimentation. The project acknowledges bibliography as a site of knowledge production as well as draws attention to the visual and phenomenal forms that influence such production.

The objective of *Bibliographic Performances & Surrogate Readings* is to define a new genre, survey the field, and learn from a host of voices. It connects the fields of textual studies, library science, and graphic design, informed by a healthy dose of writing from art and design history, geography, literature, book arts, and poetry. As an exhibition in book form, this published catalogue, I hope, will be engaging to the reader and serve as a precursor to future exhibitions or symposiums.

(1) The following titles may be of interest. They focus on the intersection of art and reading, libraries, and/or archives whereas *Bibliographic Performances & Surrogate Readings* is expressly dedicated to artistic and poetic practices in bibliography: Simon Morris, *Reading as Art* (York, [England]: Information as Material, 2016); Ariane Roth and Marina Schütz, *The Dynamic Library*, trans. Alta L. Price (Chicago: Soberscove Press, 2015); Tate Shaw, *Blurred Library: Essays on Artists' Books*, (Victoria, TX: Cuneiform Press, University of Houston—Victoria, 2016); Anna-Sophie Springer and Etinne Turpin, *Fantasies of the Library* (Cambridge, MA: MIT Press, 2016); and Garrett Stewart, *Bookwork: Medium to Object to Concept to Art* (Chicago: University of Chicago Press, 2011).

(2) Yes, I've shamelessly included several of my own projects in this catalogue. See entries for "Bibliography of Architecture Theory," "Exhibition Takeaways," "Meanwhile, the Surrogate for the Presently Absent Gets a Proxy," and "Poet-Saints of July 06."

***

***

***

*

*

***

***

Bibliographic Performances & Surrogate Readings

"The arrival of a station at the train."

— Charles Bernstein

BIBLIOGRAPHIES AS MOBILE HUBS

A bibliography is a performative place of changeable references with the capacity to exhibit research and serve as a site for interaction. Charles Bernstein's line "the arrival of a station at the train" is a somewhat strange but appropriate analogy to capture the double movement of a bibliography.[1] Acting as a mobile hub, a subject bibliography is constituted by and for a set or sets of resources-in-motion. "Bibliography," as D. C. Greetham notes, "literally means 'the writing of books.'"[2] There is action implicit in the noun.

Bibliographies are both portable and expandable—progressive places with dynamic characteristics. They have the ability to bridge discontinuous collections, describe heterogeneous bibliographic units, and accumulate new works on a given topic as they are written. Bibliographies actively gather assemblies of thought, bringing written works into conversation and debate with one another. The shifting relationships within a bibliography are akin to those of a geographic place where "specificity" is "constructed out of a particular constellation of social relations, meeting and weaving together at a particular locus."[3]

A subject bibliography, sometimes referred to as a pathfinder, finding aid, or research guide, is "strictly speaking, a systematic list or enumeration of written works by a specific author or on a given subject, or that shares one or more common characteristics (language, form, period, place of publication, etc.)."[4] It may strive to be "comprehensive" or opt to be "selective" but in either case, the intellectual work of the bibliographer is present—for example, in the determination of its scope, the organization of its selections, the mode of annotation, and the formatting of its resources.[5]

Researching and selecting works to include in a bibliography is an act of model-making, of knowledge production. Partial knowledges come together in a bibliography to form an evolving body of knowledge, to make a new model. In relation to our present cultural moment, Olafur Eliasson writes:

> Models have become co-producers of reality. Models exist in various forms and sizes: Objects such as houses or artworks are one variety, but we also find models of engagement, models of perception and reflection. . . . models of thought and other experiments that add up to a model of a situation. Every model shows a different degree of representation, but all are real.[6]

Following the logic of Eliasson, if the bibliography is a model, then it performs its role as a "co-producer of reality."[7]

In action, subject bibliographies can introduce a reader to new works and help a researcher gain expertise beyond or outside of formal educational structures. Historically they have been necessary for assessing library collections and indispensable for getting alternative literature into libraries. In other words, these thought models have an outward-facing personality, responsible to a variety of individual or institutional publics.

"Facts, facts everywhere but not a drop to drink."
—C.B.

BIBLIOGRAPHIES AND TWENTY–FIRST CENTURY DISCOVERY

Why bibliographies, why now? Locating and consulting a relevant subject bibliography may seem like a less attractive option to many twenty-first century researchers accustomed to the speed and deluge of search. Search query results are produced on the spot. Immediacy and quantity are a boon. Hit return and Google, for instance, replies with millions of results time-stamped in a fraction of a second. Carefully created bibliographies, on the other hand, may entail a slowness of labor and manual updates on the backend, but its arrangement of curated resources may ultimately save the time of the user. Search results exist to disappear, while bibliographies portend a longer shelf life.

Though advancements continue to be made, bibliographic search systems, specifically, tend to operate in the realm of "complexity reduction"—using subject headings, controlled vocabularies, and keyword and Boolean searches without lemmatization or homonym detection.[8] Querying a bibliographic database or library catalog to find resources is a heuristic process—a process of trial-and-error that leads to success only gradually.

In a 2016 survey, *How Readers Discover Content in Scholarly Publications*, "search accounts for approximately 40–45% of [article] discovery" but as Roger Schonfeld points out, "the other means of discovery specified [by respondents]—everything from personal recommendations and social media to alerts and citations—collectively add up to drive more traffic than search."[9] While the study focuses on a single topic, that is finding an article from a scholarly publication, it points to directions other than search. It challenges notions of search as the end-all-be-all of discovery mechanisms.

Given that subject bibliographies are put together by bibliographers of all stripes—subject specialists in libraries, individual scholars and scholarly associations, non-profit organizations and fringe groups, amateur experts, bibliophiles and book dealers, etc.—they can demonstrate a tremendous range of interdisciplinary, transdisciplinary, postdisciplinary, and nondisciplinary thinking. The specialist and the enthusiast are not so dissimilar in this context. The labor of the bibliographer is one that includes many micro-acts of interpretation and judgment, effectively engaging in a form of critical editing at the level of subject construction.[10] Subject bibliographies wrench resources out of search-driven systems and into the realm of spirited recommendations, troubling arrangements of resources, challenging canonical norms, countering algorithmic suggestion loops, and constituting new thought models.

> "   Even the Pacific Ocean has a bottom,
> but you'd be hard pressed to get there with even strokes.   "
> —C.B.

BIBLIOGRAPHIES AND TRADITIONS IN TEXTUAL SCHOLARSHIP

Taking a step back, it might be helpful to look at subject bibliographies in relation to longstanding bibliographic practices within textual scholarship. In Greetham's overview, textual scholarship encompasses "all the activities associated with the discovery, description, transcription, editing, glossing, annotating, and commenting upon texts."[11] Whether trying to excavate a text's history or produce an edited text, textual scholars use several procedures to understand both the "process" and the "product."[12]

To do this research, the first few steps are to find the appropriate source material (enumerative bibliography), "list and adequately describe these documents" (descriptive bibliography), understand their technical production (codicology or analytical bibliography), and "chart the history of the transmission of the text" (stemmatics).[13] The information captured in these forms goes well beyond what is typically featured in a library catalog record and, as with descriptive bibliography for example, comes with a set of "very exacting standards."[14]

The takeaway for this essay is that the waters of textual studies are concerned with "the historical investigation of texts *as both artifactual objects and conceptual entities.*"[15] It takes a deep dive to explore the artifactual and the conceptual specificity of a written work through the various means mentioned above.

Subject bibliographers, like textual scholars, examine or attempt to examine each item in their bibliography firsthand. Entries in a research guide may take a lighter touch toward the written work, however, and may not be descriptively worked through to the same depth as practiced in some corners of textual studies. Since the emphasis is largely placed on the discovery of a written work rather than on its history and origins, bibliographic units are intentionally treated as mobile entities with a public-facing charge. The reader of a research guide should be able to ascertain enough information to chart their own path through the entries and locate the written works represented therein. Bibliographic methods in textual studies tend to circle around notions of authority. Subject bibliographies, generally speaking, have less fidelity to such aims—unless perhaps the author is organizing a bibliography of their own works. At any rate, research guides deal and trade in surrogate objects—objects that crib authorial legitimation and stem from the bibliographer's vision.[16]

"Not the flow but the flows of perception." —C.B.

SURROGATE READINGS

A surrogate is an approximate representation of a thing, a stand-in, a proxy. In the *Oxford English Dictionary*, a surrogate is variously "a person or (usually) a thing that acts for or takes the place of another" and "a person appointed by authority to act in place of another."[17] Within the frame of a subject bibliography, the representation of a written work—that is, as a surrogate object—is precisely what the reader encounters.[18] Representation takes on a heightened importance in this context.

To take an example from the world of libraries, the catalog record is often referred to as a digital surrogate because it serves as a proxy to an item. Text-based descriptions, which are sometimes supplemented by cover images, approximate the physical and digital items held by the library. Item information regarding materiality, summary information, table of contents, cover art, etc. help patrons narrow or make selection decisions at the level of the catalog record.[19] The bibliographic surrogate is usually an abbreviation, an opportunity to preview or evaluate a resource without reading the written work in full.

Similarly, the role of the subject bibliography is not one that is limited to description (an explanation, a narrative, a report) but one that has a stake in representation (a drawing, a picture, a portrait) as well. The bibliography is a constellation of surrogates—and these surrogates by nature are poised to act on behalf of the works they represent. This idea goes back to an earlier point. The subject bibliography is a model. The bibliographic units represented within are surrogate objects. The model and the surrogate both have their own artifactual value. Moreover, they both have a stake in reality.[20]

Alberto Manguel states that in literary traditions "surrogate reality" denotes that "the representation of an experience is equivalent to itself."[21] Through interactions with surrogates, readers gain a familiarity with written works. After all, many a bibliophile are known to delight in reading booksellers' catalogs.[22] *By encountering a curated set of surrogates, doesn't the reader get a sense of the greater themes and subjects being portrayed in the bibliography? In what ways does the bibliography embody or perform its subject? In what ways are the surrogates read and understood?*

> "The structural problem is how to foster counter-hegemonic perspectives, including aesthetic ones."
>
> —C.B.

DESIGN'S DESIRE

Too little attention has been paid to the visual materiality and graphic textuality of subject bibliographies, as well as to the exploratory potential of model-making. *In what ways might the bibliography be more than or other than a research tool that directs you to information?*

Design's desire could be formulated as a hospitable and critical act. As once described by Stuart Bailey, the highest achievement of graphic design is like "form and content having great sex, mutual and inseparable, or at least French kissing."[23] The desire in nonmodern terms might be to reconcile *nous* (spirit) and *aesthesis* (physical senses) in the same body.[24] A great design is a suturing of the artifactual with the conceptual.

Subject bibliographies are intended as pathways for independent users "to acquire, browse and gather information on their own terms."[25] They promote open-ended rather than predetermined outcomes, which is an interesting task to appoint to design. A well-designed subject bibliography is one that the reader can perceptively skip across to locate and comprehend compelling and relevant information. *In addition, what ways might the bibliography as a designed pathway foster the tychic element within research, that is, court the unexpected?*

Richard Shiff, recognizing the benefit of the tychic element or role of chance in the organization of his books, writes:

> The books in my library are as much arranged by time and space as they are by subject matter or the alphabet. The destabilized arrangement encourages stray thoughts to interrupt a developing pattern—it's like an outside party introducing a healthy moment of doubt into an argument by asking a somewhat irrelevant question.[26]

To what degree can design facilitate flexible narrative structures or offer ways to get to know resources at a glance? As Are Not Studio points out, "today, many graphic designers understand their primary function as . . . asking questions and making inquiries into the nature of post-industrial cultural needs and contexts."[27] Information science is one such need and opportunity. Experimental subject bibliographies or visual bibliographies as conceived of here are projects that explore artifactual, intellectual, spatial, and design possibilities simultaneously.

Readers and researchers are confronted with an enormous amount of choice, what Lucy Lippard has called "being immersed in a veritable tsunami of decontextualized cultural knowledge."[28] Bibliographic projects that incorporate critical annotations, novel methods of graphic representation, inventive juxtapositions between written works, or conceptual themes for discussion and debate offer lively ports of entry, identifiable places in the vast waters of "information."

All epigraphs from Charles Bernstein, "Brief and Indeterminate Glimpses," in "Models," ed. Emily Abruzzo, Eric Ellingsen, Jonathan D. Solomon, special issue, *306090* 11 (2007).

(1) Bernstein, "Brief and Indeterminate Glimpses," 40.

(2) D. C. Greetham, *Textual Scholarship: An Introduction* (New York: Garland Publishing, 1992), 6.

(3) Doreen Massey, "A Global Sense of Place," in *Space, Place and Gender* (Minneapolis: University of Minnesota Press, 1994), [7].

(4) Joan M. Reitz, *ODLIS*, s.v. "bibliography," accessed October 11, 2015, https://products.abc-clio.com/ODLIS/odlis_b#bibliography.

(5) Reitz, *ODLIS*, s.v. "bibliography."

(6) Olafur Eliasson, "Models are Real," in "Models," ed. Emily Abruzzo, Eric Ellingsen, Jonathan D. Solomon, special issue, *306090* 11 (2007): 19.

(7) Eliasson, "Models are Real," 19.

(8) Paul Michel, "Organizing Knowledge," in *The Dynamic Library*, ed. Ariane Roth and Marina Schütz, trans. Alta L. Price (Chicago: Soberscove Press, 2015), 35.

(9) Roger C. Schonfeld, "How Readers Discover Content in Scholarly Publications," *The Scholarly Kitchen* (blog), March 30, 2016, https://scholarlykitchen.sspnet.org/2016/03/30/how-readers-discover-content-in-scholarly-publications/.

(10) Thanks to Joseph Grigely for suggesting that the construction of a bibliography is a form of critical editing.

(11) Greetham, *Textual Scholarship*, 2.

(12) Greetham, *Textual Scholarship*, 2.

(13) Greetham, *Textual Scholarship*, 4.

(14) Fredson Bowers, *Principles of Bibliographical Description* (New Castle, DE: Oak Knoll Press, 1994), 3.

(15) Greetham, *Textual Scholarship*, ix–x; emphasis added.

(16) Following the logic of Gerard Genette's definitions of the paratext, could the subject bibliography perhaps be something like a public epitext? See Gerard Genette, *Paratexts: Thresholds of Interpretation*, trans. Jane E. Lewin (Cambridge: Cambridge University Press, 2001).

(17) *Oxford English Dictionary*, s.v. "surrogate," accessed May 1, 2016, http://www.oed.com.proxy.artic.edu/view/Entry/195052?rskey=wRxxbG&result=1&isAdvanced=false#eid.

(18) Exceptions in this catalogue might include "Juxtaposed," "The Queen's English," and "Works from Stack 655" which exhibit hard copies of books.

(19) These digital surrogates are valuable when an item is unavailable and cannot be examined in person and indispensable to researchers who want to request materials from a closed-stack non-circulating library, special collections, or archive.

(20) Bibliography could learn something from conceptual art in this regard. Boris Groys writes: "Conceptual artists shifted the emphasis of artmaking away from static, individual objects toward the presentation of new relationships in space and time." Boris Groys, "Introduction—Global Conceptualism Revisited," *e-flux Journal* 29 (2011): 1, https://

www.e-flux.com/journal/29/68059/introduction-global-conceptualism-revisited/.

(21) Alberto Manguel, *Curiosity* (New Haven, CT: Yale University Press, 2015), 266.

(22) Umberto Eco writes that "they get as much pleasure out of this as a reader of Jules Verne gets from exploring the deeps of the silent oceans and encountering terrifying sea monsters." Umberto Eco, *The Infinity of Lists* (New York: Rizzoli, 2009), 377.

(23) Discussions about form and content are usually yawn-inducing for the present author, with this notable exception. The full quote is: "The majority of what passes as graphic design doesn't really stick to any reasonable notion of form following function. On the contrary, I would say form generally *fucks* function. And to proceed with such a dubious line of thought, I'll turn it around again and say that contrary to this, the examples here show form and content having great sex, mutual and inseparable, or at least French kissing." Stuart Bailey in *Dutch Resource: Collaborative Exercises in Graphic Design* (Amsterdam: Valiz, 2005), 211.

(24) See any account of Philo of Alexandria's ideas about the first human. Briefly mentioned in Manguel, *Curiosity*, 38.

(25) The full quote from Murial Cooper addresses design rather than bibliography specifically: "This new world demands a new kind of designer who will provide opportunities, pathways and processes for a more independent user, a designer who will create rich structures for users who will be able to acquire, browse and gather information on their own terms." Markus Weisbeck, "This New World," *Frieze*, March 2014, 136–39.

(26) Richard Shiff discusses the tychic as, "the chance element, the luck in a turn of thought, whether good fortune or bad fortune. [C. S.] Peirce argued that intuitive thinking took a good turn more than it took a bad turn, but there was no rational, statistical reason that this should have been so." "Richard Shiff with Katy Siegel," *The Brooklyn Rail*, May 6, 2008, https://brooklynrail.org/2008/05/art/richard-shiff-with-katy-siegel.

(27) Are Not Studio, *Publishing as the Critical Practice of Graphic Design* (Wheaton, IL: Art Not Books & Publications, 2014), 12.

(28) Lucy Lippard, "Ghosts, the Daily News, and Prophecy: Critical Landscape Photography" (lecture, MFA Art Criticism and Writing Program, School of Visual Arts, New York, NY, April 7, 2011). Video podcast.

The Visio-Bibliographic Turn in Art and Design

This catalogue reviews a sampling of projects from a twenty-year span, approximately from 2000–2020, a malleable range that isolates a flurry of visio-bibliocentric activity for closer study. Some historical precedents are noted within individual entries; however, I wanted the opportunity to tease out more connections through a multifaceted approach.

What are the possible origins of what I call "experimental subject bibliography" and "visual bibliography"? How does one account for a proliferation of artistic and poetic bibliographic experimentation over the last two decades? As such seemingly novel practices have gained momentum, what may have led up to this moment? Reader, I stake no claim at being a historian nor have I set out to find one tidy history. Several related and intersecting constellations of activity are of particular interest to me. This essay is a bibliographic sketch, a collage of possible precursors to experimental subject bibliography and visual bibliography, and a notepad of related examples that didn't fit neatly elsewhere in the book.

1. THE DEMATERIALIZATION OF ART

(A) The dematerialization of art in the 1960s and 1970s ushers in conceptual art, instruction art, mail art, happenings, the book as art, and the publication as exhibition. Artists are newly driven to reach "an audience larger than that which has been interested in contemporary art" in the foregoing decades.[1] Some are taken by information, the burgeoning deluge of communications, and looking to the graphic textuality of "the index, the catalogue, the dictionary definition, the philosophical proposition, the list, and other such serial structures" with fresh eyes.[2]

✷ 1970: Kynaston McShine captures a segment of this making and experimentation, curating an international survey at the Museum of Modern Art, New York, called *Information*. Simon Morely underscores that the show "mark[s] a significant moment of recognition of the new idea art."[3] As an extension of the gallery exhibition, participating artists respond to an invitation to create their own contributions to an exhibition catalog. In this instance, the idea-generating museum exhibition collides with the vehicle of the book, a form which has successfully circulated ideas for centuries. Here newly conceived artworks rather than reproductions of existing works reach beyond the confines of the museum.

✷ 1968: Two years prior, Seth Siegelaub and Jack Wendler sidestep the traditional gallery show altogether to realize a group exhibition in catalog form. Known colloquially as the *Xerox Book*, and officially published as *Carl Andre, Robert Barry, Douglas Huebler, Joseph Kosuth, Sol LeWitt, Robert Morris, Lawrence Weiner*, this catalog famously loosed the gallery exhibition from the walls and onto the printed page. The art exhibition is no longer bound by a calendar of opening and closing dates, but in this case, by a glue-bound spine.

Exhibition catalogs like this perform the work of art and/or are themselves artists' books, i.e., democratically conceived works of art.[4]

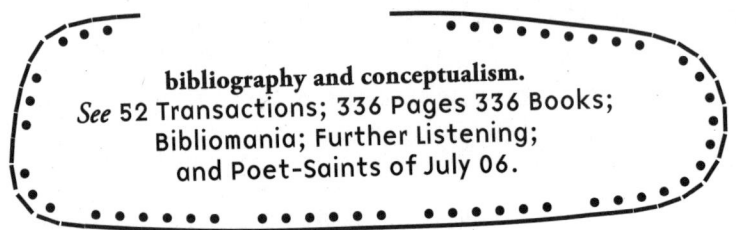

bibliography and conceptualism.
See 52 Transactions; 336 Pages 336 Books; Bibliomania; Further Listening; and Poet-Saints of July 06.

(B) We might also consider that books have long been depicted in art and one may readily visualize, say, Renaissance paintings of St. Jerome in his study or late eighteenth- and nineteenth-century Korean *chaekgeori* paintings of aristocratic bookshelves.[5] Books have been installed as objects to ponder in the art gallery at least since conceptualism. Such moves play on the readerly dimension of books, the frenzy of ideas that emanate from them, and their symbolic status as repositories of cultural heritage.

✳ 1967–2017: Joseph Kosuth's installation *Fifteen People Present Their Favorite Book* (1967) is a key example of an early visual bibliography, showing books selected by Carl Andre, Jo Baer, Mel Bochner, Dan Graham, Christine Kozlov, Sol LeWitt, Robert Mangold, Robert Morris, Ad Reinhardt, Michael Rinaldi, Ernest Rossi, Robert Ryman, Robert Smithson, Sinan Tanju, and Kosuth himself at Lannis Gallery in New York. The project is reimagined by Matthew Higgs in 2009 as *Fifteen People Present Their Favorite Book [After Kosuth]* with new contributors: Wade Guyton, Adam McEwen, T. J. Wilcox, Richard Prince, Nick Mauss, Anne Collier, Rob Pruitt, Joseph Logan, Galvin Brown, Ken Okiishi, Clarissa Dalrymple, Kelley Walker, Jonathan Horowitz, Elizabeth Peyton, and Pati Hertling. In 2017, a fiftieth anniversary commemoration is organized by Jo Melvin with the Mahler & LeWitt Studios in Spoleto, Italy, as *Fifteen People Select Their Favorite Book*.

✳ 2007–2011: Garret Stewart's *Bookwork: Medium to Object to Concept to Art* (2011) leans into the materiality of the book, locating examples of the book's intersection with contemporary sculpture and painting, the readymade, and the altered book.[6] One featured project, *Life Drawing Drawings* (2007–2011) by Fiona Banner, stands out as an example of visual bibliography. In it Banner hand-draws the covers of a variety of books about figure drawing, wraps the drawings around blank dummy books, and places these on a shelf in the gallery. The gallerygoer encounters a compilation of surrogates on a theme. The subject of this bibliography is an homage to drawing as a foundation of an artist's training, an art history lesson of stylistic changes within the history of art instruction and the representation of bodies, and a commentary on the female nude, gender, power, and the gaze.

✳ 2014: One sculptural project that functions both as an experimental subject bibliography and a visual bibliography is *The British Library* by Yinka Shonibare. It is a project of recovery, figuratively and literally. It collects 6,328 books written by first- and second-generation immigrants to Britain and re-covers the volumes in Dutch wax print fabrics. Such visual presentations draw attention to an expansive group of literature connected through author identity and immigration status, a cumulative history of achievements made by immigrant communities in Britain, as well as recognizes complex colonial histories and the effects of globalization. As part of an online component of the project, immigrant families to the UK can write and upload their own stories.

> books, symbolic status of.
> *See* Africanismus_12469; Bookcatalogtest; Hidden Histories; Juxtaposed; Lonely Books; Meanwhile, the Surrogate for the Presently Absent Gets a Proxy; and Someone Else—A Library of 100 Books Written Anonymously or Under Pseudonyms.

(C) Many contemporary artists have shown an interest in the library and the archive as a curatorial project. The lines between a subject bibliography and a library easily blur.

✳ 1993: Nina Katchadourian first begins her ongoing *Sorted Books* project working within the stacks of private and institutional libraries.[7] She creates poetic sculptures using the spines of books. Each grouping is in effect a playfully curated microbibliography.

* 1997–: Joseph Grigely initiates an open-ended unnamed bibliographic project (1997) with Hans Ulrich Obrist to archive materials connected to the curator's prolific career. In 2014, the project expands and is formalized with a team of research fellows at the School of the Art Institute of Chicago as *Nodes + Networks: The Publications and Publication Projects of Hans Ulrich Obrist*.[8] The project continues to evolve under Grigely's direction today with new teams of research fellows working on a digital bibliography, a printed compendium representing the archive, and a museum exhibition (first realized in 2022 at Serralves Foundation, Porto). The archive itself is a study in curatorial practice and art practices from the 1990s to the present. It uniquely navigates Grigely's vision as an artist and his bibliographic training as a literary scholar.

* 2001: The collaboration Temporary Services (Brett Bloom, Marc Fischer, and Salem Collo-Julin from 2001 to 2014) organizes *The Library Project*, a covert operation that interfiles one hundred independent publications with invented call numbers into the stacks of the Harold Washington Library Center, the main branch of the Chicago Public Library. One of their goals "was to bring obscure, subversive, self-published, hand-made, or limited edition works by underexposed artists to a wider audience."[9] It is an experimental bibliography, library intervention, and distributed time capsule with sixty-two contributors. Twenty-six titles have been located and archived by Chicago Public Library staff.[10]

* 2015–: Rebuild Foundation, the artist-driven place-making project founded and led by Theaster Gates,

opens Stony Island Arts Bank in a former bank building on the South Side of Chicago. The remodeled space is purpose-built to house and exhibit four key collections promoting Black experience and knowledge of the African diaspora: the Johnson Publishing Archive and Collections, the University of Chicago Glass Lantern Slides, Frankie Knuckles Vinyl Record Collection, and Edward J. Williams's "negrobilia" collection. It serves as a space for community arts interactions and in 2022 welcomed its first cohort of Mellon Archives Innovation Fellows. The aesthetic, theoretical, and community-minded dimensions of the endeavor fuse in harmony.

> libraries and archives, as curatorial space. *See* The Author of This Book Committed Suicide; The Bookshelf Project; The Mary Shelley Facsimile Library; and The Perverse Library.

(D) Community-forward initiatives have spurred opportunities to create reading rooms in gallery spaces. Galleries are inherently laden with associations and expectations about how to install and view an exhibition.[11] By bringing the reading room into the gallery, the familiar activities of an art viewer are transformed into that of a reader or researcher. The act of reading is also imbued with a new dimension, an aesthetic one, by dint of it occurring in a gallery.

✳ 2005–2009: Martha Rosler sends part of her library packing. *The Martha Rosler Library* project is installed at nine different storefronts, museums, and galleries in Europe and the United States. Visitors can peruse, read, and photocopy the books, magazines, posters, and ephemera from her growing collection. While not an experimental subject bibliography per se, it is a vulnerable artistic act to show one's bibliographic references and invite unknown publics to sift through them at leisure.

✳ 2016: Simon Morris curates the group exhibition *Reading as Art* at Bury Art Museum and Sculpture Centre and publishes a corresponding exhibition catalog with Information as Material. The show and catalog feature projects that "investigate the activity of reading: the forms it can take (silent reading, reading aloud, spontaneous reading, purposeful reading, and so on), the matter of reading (the book, the screen, the space of the page), the bodies that engage in it and the contexts in which it occurs."[12] A noteworthy chronological bibliography in the catalog presents "book related projects by artists and others" which coincidentally but not surprisingly overlaps with the interests of this present essay and catalogue.[13]

✳ 2017: Marshall Weber, Bridget Elmer, and myself, plus members of the Ringling College of Art and Design community, co-curate *Freedom of the Presses*, a multisite exhibition and event program focused on community-oriented art publishing practices. To loosen the strictures that typically surround artists' publishing, we turn part of the Richard and Barbara Basch Gallery into a reading room, create an immersive protest poster installation in the Brizdle-Schoenberg Special Collections Center, and host an event program in buildings and outdoor spaces across campus rather than in a typical gallery setting. The gallery becomes a pop-up library, the library becomes a gallery, and the programming is embedded within popular community gathering spaces.[14]

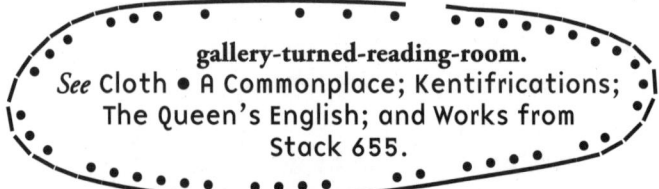

gallery-turned-reading-room.
See Cloth • A Commonplace; Kentifrications; The Queen's English; and Works from Stack 655.

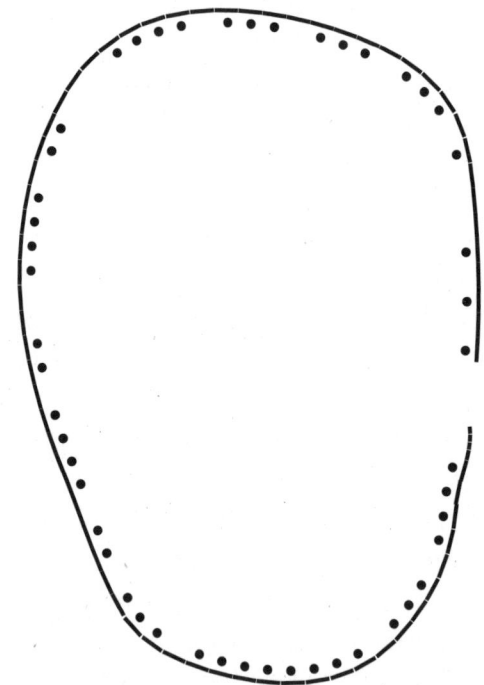

2. PUBLISHING AS A CREATIVE PRACTICE

(A) Let's turn now to look specifically at artist's books and artists' publication projects. Throughout generations of experimentation, artists' publications have pushed the boundaries of bookmaking and in turn expanded the visual, verbal, and tactile experience of reading. It makes sense that the pathfinders, subject bibliographies, and catalogs that spring up around these book works would encourage visual, verbal, and tactile discovery as well.

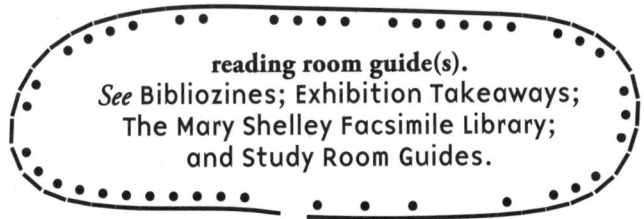

reading room guide(s).
See Bibliozines; Exhibition Takeaways; The Mary Shelley Facsimile Library; and Study Room Guides.

Both publishers' catalogs and booksellers' catalogs, for instance, are an opportunity for playful interactions with the reader.

✸ 1970–1980s: Hetty Huisman expands her ceramics practice by publishing her first artist's book *Livre de Terre* (1970). She subsequently issues limited edition catalogs for her publishing imprint VOID Distributors (active ca. late 1970s and 1980s). Catalogs like *Acte de présence* (1981) are designed, printed, and folded to feel like a piece of mail art while still functioning as a catalog of works by her and Ulises Carrión, John Liggins, Henryk Gajewski, and others.

Artist's book studios today take up similarly playful cues for their own publisher's catalogs.

✳ 2021, 2022: The publisher Small Editions gives away one-sheet-zine catalogs that feature bespoke artists' book cocktail recipes to advertise their latest batch of available books. The inspired recipes riff on the "drink preferences" of their featured artist-authors and "the formal and conceptual qualities of their books" while catalog descriptions about each book provide the basics to potential readers.[15]

In a similar vein, the dematerialization of art with its variety of sometimes ephemeral, performative, and event-based practices has incidentally placed emphasis upon the aesthetics of documentation and the importance of artists' archives.

✳ 1992–2019: Steven Leiber, an early purveyor of the editions, multiples, announcements, and other artist's materials associated with such movements, creates and distributes fifty-two inventive bookseller's catalogues between 1992 and 2010. Each issue is a visual bibliography, taking on a new format, and playfully designed to imitate the artists' publication projects and ephemera featured therein. For example, catalog 32 *Art by Tape: Not by Nam June Paik* from 1998 is issued as a cassette tape in a case. Leiber's dealer catalogs have become sought after as experimental artworks and are now collected and described in *Steven Leiber Catalogs* (2019) edited by David Senior and co-published by Inventory Press and RITE Editions.

artist's archive.
See 52 Transactions; All;
and Irma Boom.

(B) As creators engage in independent artists' publishing or publishing as a creative practice, they may wear multiple hats, merging various activities around publishing, collecting, documenting, exhibiting, and community-building. An artist's, designer's, or writer's practice, for instance, may entail an expansive bibliographic practice.

✷ 1980–: The growing book collection of Richard Prince is the raw material and subject for his own artworks and artists' publications. He publishes his first two artist's books in 1980 and his personal library starts appearing within his artist's books by 2003, for example, in *American English* (London: Sadie Coles HQ, 2003) and *Good Life* (New York: Glenn Horowitz, 2003). Three-dimensional bibliographic works follow suit like the series *Untitled (Originals)* (2007–2010) which pairs an original book cover illustration with the corresponding published paperback book, both from Prince's personal collection. Visual book arrangements and groupings are a part of his practice.

✷ 1998: Allan McCollum exhibits *THE EVENT: Petrified Lightning from Central Florida (with Supplemental Didactics)* at USF Contemporary Art Museum. He and co-compiler Kristen Welsh source, select, edit, and typeset sixty-six different texts on lightning and fulgerites (rootlike glass structures, also known as petrified lightning). Printed in a run of at least 10,000, these supplemental didactics are pamphlet-bound with colorful covers and exhibited alongside his sculptures.[16] Some are later distributed to local students. A parallel online pamphlet library of pdf downloads accompanies the project. The pdf library of scientific findings, news articles, and interviews functions as a tightly themed subject bibliography on lightning and extends the life of *THE EVENT* beyond any physical museum installation. Making the artist's research visible and available to readers is an important part of the project, so much so that *Bibliography: Selected Writings on Lightning and Fulgurites* compiled by McCollum and Welsh is included in the pamphlet library.

✳ 2010–: *The Self-Reliance Library* by Temporary Services is a socially engaged project that grants access to over eighty titles on DIY living. The project fluidly blurs the boundaries between an art installation, a site for educational activity, a print bibliography, and an exercise in pamphleteering. Featured titles are sourced from the group's working library plus publications from Half Letter Press, their publishing imprint. *The Self-Reliance Library* fashions a bibliography intertwining the group's influences with their own writings, all the while maintaining a non-competitive, community-first spirit.

publishing and book collecting.
See 336 Pages 336 Books; A Die with Twenty-Six Faces; Difficult Times; Hidden Histories; Human_3.0 Reading List; and The Perverse Library.

3. LITERARY INTERSECTIONS

(A) Alongside the history of writing and the history of libraries, parallels a history of creative practices in bibliographic enumeration within literature and experimental writing.

Subject bibliographies seemingly come on the scene in the sixteenth century . . .

✳ 1506–1549: Kevin Jackson notes that the "first rumblings of the coming information explosion, and beginnings of the specialized bibliography" appear with the likes of "Champier (1506) on medicine; Nevizzano (1522) on law; Erasmus (1523) on himself; and Gessner on everything."[17] Jackson's shorthand is referring here to Symphorien Champier's *De medicinae claris scriptoribus . . . tractatus* [Treatise on Famous Medical Writers] (1506); Giovanni Nevizzano's *Inventarium librorum in utroque iure hactenus impressorum* [An Inventory of the Books on Civil and Canon Law Printed to Date] (1522); Desiderius Erasmus's *Catalogus omnium Erasmi lucubrationum* [The Catalogue of All the Works of Erasmus of Rotterdam]; and Conrad Gessner's *Bibliotheca universalis* [literally Universal Library] (1545–1549).

and, bam, even in these early days of bibliographic practice, an instance of experimental bibliography appears:

✳ 1532: Right in the wake of such earnest endeavors comes book 1, chapter 7 of *Pantagruel*. In it François Rabelais pens a satirical, imaginary booklist for the library at the Abbey of Saint-Victor, a very real place with an intellectual heritage dating back to the twelfth century.[18] Rabelais takes a humanist jab at scholasticism inventing 140 titles for the pages of his novel, which as Jackson quips is "a copious list of patently bogus volumes."[19]

Following the example of Rabelais in France, sixteenth- and seventeenth-century writers across Europe spin up hundreds of fictional booklists, i.e., lists of imagined, unwritten books.[20]

✳ 1590: German Johann Fischart publishes a stand-alone farcical booklet that translates the booklist from *Pantagruel* as the *Catalogus Catalogorum perpetuo durabilis*. He expands the original bibliography to over 500 entries and includes fake books by real authors and real books by fake authors to further disorient the reader.[21]

✳ 1603–11, 1650: Around 1603–11 Englishman John Donne composes the *Catalogus Librorum Aulicorum incomparabilium et non vendibiliu* (known as *The Courtier's Library*) which is published posthumously in the 1650 *Poems*. As Piers Brown argues, this "catalogue of imaginary books" has a strong autobiographical bent, coinciding with "Donne's own attempts to reconcile the roles of secretary, scholar, and gentleman."[22]

✳ 1673, 1684: Also in England, Sir Thomas Brown's *Musaeum Clasum, or, Bibliotheca Abscondita: containing some remarkable Books, Antiquities, Pictures and Rarities of several kinds, scarce or never seen by any man now living* [possibly written c. 1673, published posthumously in 1684] falls into a genre of "mock catalogues" that mixes imagined, unpublished, and lost books with museum artifacts.[23]

Some writers are on record not to have written but to have proposed such fanciful lists.

✶ 20th c.: Alberto Manguel learns that, "Once, in the early years of his [Jorge Luis Borges's] friendship with Adolfo Bioy Casares [1914–1999], he had suggested to the younger writer that they compose together a history of the literature of an imaginary country, that would include the books of which they had dreamt but never written. Borges felt that to dream up plots was a profound intellectual pleasure, but to write a novel, he repeatedly said, was 'an exaggeration.' He preferred to review and compose introductions for non-existent books."[24]

Other creatives have boldly fabricated titles to intervene in the library stacks.

✶ 19th c.: In the account by Alberto Manguel, "Paul Masson [1849–1896], a friend of [Colette's] who worked at the Bibliothèque Nationale in Paris, noticed that the vast stacks of the library were defective in Latin and Italian books of the fifteenth century, and so began adding invented titles on the official index cards to save, he said, 'that catalogue's prestige.' When Colette naively asked him what was the use of books that didn't exist, Masson responded indignantly that he couldn't be expected 'to think of everything!'"[25]

imaginary or speculative books.
See A Final Companion to Books from "The Simpsons" in Alphabetical Order; Kentifrications; The Missing Pieces; A Stack of Books, A Book of Stacks; and Strike and Riot.

(B) Of course, less fantastical literary examples from the sixteenth to the twentieth century abound too. On occasion, writers use bibliographic enumeration within a work of literature to set a scene or build a character. The reader can quickly glean atmospheric insight from such detail, like a visitor glancing at someone else's bookshelves.

✳ 16th–20th c.: As Umberto Eco will tell you, "The taste for book lists has fascinated many writers from Cervantes [1547–1616] to Huysmans [1848–1907] and Calvino [1923–1985] . . ."[26]

✳ 1839–1979: Kevin Jackson registers the occurrence of book lists within "The Fall of the House of Usher" (1839) by Edgar Allan Poe, *The Unquiet Grave* (1944) by Cyril Connolly, and "The Estate of Maximilian Tod" [first published 1979] by Bruce Chatwin.[27]

(C) Taking this one step further, for authors like Raymond Queneau and Charles Olson the form of a subject bibliography is transformed into a stand-alone work of literature.

✳ 1956: In a quest to envision an ideal library, Raymond Queneau reaches out to French writers and critics to list their favorite one hundred books. In addition to reproducing these responses on the pages of *Pour une Bibliothèque Idéale* (1956), Queneau also forms a cumulative list, collating the top one hundred picks overall. Rabelais's *Gargantua and Pantagruel* (1532–1564) is fifth on this list.

✳ 1955, 1964: Charles Olson's *A Bibliography on America for Ed Dorn* [first presented in 1955, first published 1964] is a bibliographic essay on the West.

✳ 2022: Such present reverberations in this trajectory include *The Fern Rose Bibliography* by Tan Lin.[28] It delves into parental loss through books and scent memories. The first chapter of Lin's twenty-four-chapter bibliographic novel is issued as a pamphlet.

> bibliography, as literary narrative. *See* Atlas of Punctuation; The Best American Book of the 20th Century; Bib., Rev. Ed; A Die with Twenty-Six Faces; and Further Listening.

(D) Other inventive writers have drawn attention to the creative potential of bibliography as a paratext, as a book part, championing its marginal status in a written work. Bibliography is explored in the form of endnotes, footnotes, works cited, suggested reading, and the like.

✳ 1979: For example, the novel *Suburbia* by Paul Fournel is written entirely in paratexts and devoid of "body" copy. It foregrounds how the parts of a book, e.g. its dedications, footnotes, and indices shape our reading and subsequent understanding of a story. By focusing solely on paratextual framing devices, which may be rich in content or intentionally peripheral, the reader gains an impression of a narrative through suggestive fragments. Fournel's piece originally appears as number 46 in the Oulipian booklet series *Bibliothèque Oulipienne*.

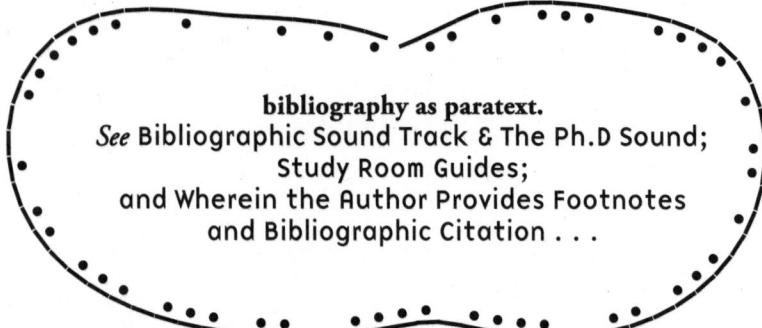

bibliography as paratext.
See Bibliographic Sound Track & The Ph.D Sound;
Study Room Guides;
and Wherein the Author Provides Footnotes
and Bibliographic Citation . . .

4. EXPERIMENTS IN ARRANGING THE LIBRARY

(A) While much library science literature has been devoted to the organization and classification of books, I am particularly interested in examples of visual categorization and unusual variants in the physical arrangement of books. For generations, bibliophiles have visually arranged their bookshelves. Terry Belanger opens *Lunacy and the Arrangement of Books* with his proposal "to discuss the lunatic arrangement of books according to principles of color, size, number, aesthetics, subject order, Grangerization, and kleptomania" and a promise to "detect madness among book dealers, book collectors, and librarians."[29]

> ✳ < 18th c.: Belanger's use of "lunacy" and "madness" is tongue-in-cheek, since he, like any respectable bibliographer, delights in the anomaly. He notes that library users form strong associations between written works and their book covers, bindings, and dust jackets. He infers that an aesthetic "organizing principle" was commonly used in private libraries for a time and that "not till the eighteenth century did book collectors generally bother to label the spines of their books, being confident that they could identify them by color and size alone."[30]

Since the rise of color lithography in the mid-nineteenth century, publishers have leaned into the use of color printing not only for book illustration but for marketing and categorizing their lists.

✱ 1930s and 1940s: Gerard Genette, taking stock of the color codes and visual symbols deployed on the covers of twentieth-century mass-market paperbacks writes, "We know that for a long time, the catalogues of pocket series have included genre specifications symbolized by the choice of color (as early as the Albatrosses, then the Penguins of the 1930s: orange = fiction, grey = politics, red = theatre, purple = essays, yellow = miscellaneous), by the choice of geometric form (Penguin after World War II: square = fiction, circle = poetry, triangle = mystery, diamond = miscellaneous; Idées-Gallimard: open book = literature, hourglass = philosophy, crystal = science, trio of cells = human sciences—a whole study, and an entertaining one at that, could be done of those broad symbolizations)..."[31]

In these two brief side-by-side examples, the visual markers that a reader might use to locate a book in a physical shelf arrangement are similar to those a reader might use to locate a new title of interest within a publisher's catalog.

bibliography and book cover design.
See Bibliozines; A Die with Twenty-Six Faces; Human_3.0 Reading List 2015–2016; Irma Boom; A People on the Cover; Pile of Books; and PM Tables, Visitor Tables, Your Tables; and Strike and Riot.

(B) Other thinkers have envisioned a whole host of organizational schemes for the physical arrangement of books. Many such variant schemes lend themselves to organizing a subject bibliography, whether in actuality or in theory.

✳ Early 20th c.: The library of image historian Aby Warburg (1866–1929) is famously organized by "the law of the good neighbor," a conceptual, conversational arrangement. Warburg's classification system of word, image, action, and orientation can still be found at the Warburg Institute Library today and is "designed not simply to make information rapidly accessible—as a search engine might—but to shape and channel scholarly investigations."[32]

✳ 1985: Georges Perec pens a thorough list called "Ways of arranging books." It reads:
  ordered alphabetically
  ordered by continent or country
  ordered by color
  ordered by date of acquisition
  ordered by date of publication
  ordered by format
  ordered by genre
  ordered by major periods of literary history
  ordered by language
  ordered by priority for future reading
  ordered by binding
  ordered by series[33]

✳ 1979, 1981: Doubling down on reader subjectivity, the reader/protagonist in Italo Calvino's *If On a Winter's Night a Traveler* (1979, first English edition 1981) drifts through the tables and shelves of a bookshop to encounter such relatable categories as:

the Books You've Been Planning
  To Read For Ages,
the Books You've Been Hunting
  for Years Without Success,
the Books Dealing With Something
  You're Working On At The Moment,
the Books You Want To Own So They'll
  Be Handy Just in Case,
the Books You Could Put Aside Maybe
  To Read This Summer,
the Books You Need To Go With Other
  Books On Your Shelves,
the Books That Fill You With Sudden,
  Inexplicable Curiosity, Not Easily Justified.[34]

✶ **1863**: Terry Belanger locates a seemingly quaint or "lunatic" arrangement mentioned in "an etiquette book of 1863, which decreed that 'the perfect hostess will see to it that the works of male and female authors be properly segregated on her book shelves. Their proximity, unless they happen to be married, should not be tolerated.'"[35]

5. DIVERSIFYING THE LIST & BLACK BIBLIOGRAPHY

(A) While siloing authors into gender binaries and marital relationships may sound strange, such biographic organizational methods nonetheless share a thin-thread connection with current feminist and anti-racist bibliographic projects. Honing in on author identities and affinity groups can uncover unsung heroes and piece together untold histories. Through the acts of sorting and arranging bibliographic resources or their surrogates, one can locate small or substantial collection gaps. It is a delicate dance for information professionals, scholars, and community members, however, to correctly assign author demographic information and tag bibliographic records. But bibliographies that tap into aspects of author identity—of gender, sexuality, race, ethnicity, religion, geographic region, etc.—can be tremendously useful to researchers and provide fertile ground for contemporary inquiries. Such projects make strides towards decolonizing and diversifying outdated canons. Building upon earlier foundations in gender studies, queer studies, African American studies, etc., some outstanding scholarly endeavors and projects in Black bibliography have cropped up in the last decade. Here are a few on my radar:

* 2011: The pilot project for Linked Jazz is organized by Pratt Institute School of Library Information Science and draws on oral histories of jazz musicians to visualize musical networks.

* ≈2012–: A Guide to Multicultural Resources at the Billy Ireland Cartoon Library & Museum at The Ohio State University identifies cartoonists, graphic novelists, and illustrators from their vast collection who are African American, Latin/x American, Asian American, and Indigenous Peoples of the Americas.

* 2012–: The database Umbra Search African American History, which covers African American theatre history, literature, art, and more, is first conceived in 2012 and spearheaded by the University of Minnesota and Penumbra Theatre Company.

* 2012–2020: The University of Delaware launches and cultivates digital exhibits for the Colored Conventions Project.

* 2017–: The first technical planning summit commences for the Black Bibliography Project (BBP), a web-based bibliography for African American literary studies with core teams at Rutgers University and Yale University.

* 2017–: The independent, subscription platform The Fashion and Race Database is established.

* 2018–: The foundational list for Black Self-Publishing: A Collaborative Research Project from the American Antiquarian Society is well under development by 2018.

✲ 2020–: The crowdsourced Google doc for design educators called Decentering Whiteness in Design History Resources formally takes shape in 2020, elevating the contributions of Black, Indigenous, Latin, Asian, and other non-White designers into the curriculum.

> **Black bibliography.**
> *See* Africanismus_12469; Barcode Cornel West & Barcode Oprah; The El Saturn Research Library; Hidden Histories; Human_3.0 Reading List 2015–2016; Kentifrications; A People on the Cover; The Queen's English; Reading Travon Martin; and Strike and Riot.

(B) Let's also not forget to mention sexy syllabi.[36] Some professors and instructors are devoted to crafting their required reading and optional reading lists and diversifying the weekly examples presented in their courses from year to year. A syllabus may unfold over time, out of sight from the rest of us. Its relevance and concepts are tested in classrooms and studios with students in real time, in concert with other faculty, and influenced by the currents of a particular field of study.

✲ 2016–: The Decentering Whiteness in Design History Resources project mentioned above, for example, is influenced by The Fashion and Race Syllabus that Rikki Byrd and Kimberly Jenkins launched in 2016. Their online syllabus encourages collaboration among educators and is open for public suggestion. It is organized into three sections for books, digital and media resources, and journal articles and papers.

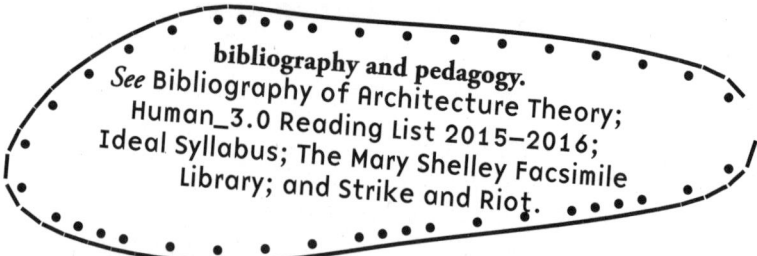

bibliography and pedagogy.
See Bibliography of Architecture Theory; Human_3.0 Reading List 2015–2016; Ideal Syllabus; The Mary Shelley Facsimile Library; and Strike and Riot.

(C) The formation of the literary anthology, particularly of themed compilations, is also a potential plot point in this wide-ranging discussion, though largely outside my present scope.[37] Like a subject bibliography, editors of anthologies attempt to define a territory and present a sample of writings by various authors for readers to dip into.

✷ 1836: One though-provoking arrangement cited by The Multigraph Collective is Theodore Echtermeyer's initial compilation for the 1836 anthology of German poetry, *Auswahl deutscher Gedichte*, "which had organized poetry according to ascending difficulty (in a kind of Faustian vector of elevatory reading)."[38] They note that "later editions placed the poems within more horizontally arranged conceptual rubrics."[39]

bibliography and literary anthology.
See The Artist's Novel & The Book Lovers; The Best American Book of the 20th Century; and Cyberfeminism Index.

Cross-institutional research projects online, individual course syllabi, literary anthologies, and other biblio-adjacent forms linked to diversity initiatives in education all present tremendous potential to radically reconstruct and decolonize the canon.

6. COMMONPLACING A CORPUS

(A) Looking at experimental subject bibliography and visual bibliography through the lens of creative reading, research, and writing practices, the form of the commonplace book and its history seems especially apropos.

I happened upon an archaic definition in Merriam-Webster's dictionary which notes that a "commonplace" is "a striking passage entered in a commonplace book."[40] The idea of "commonplacing" is at the root a practice of gathering and organizing striking passages. Scholars like Victoria E. Burke, Adam Smyth, and Earle Havens, plus artist-thinkers like Ann Hamilton and Matthew Goulish have variously been attracted to the history of commonplace books.[41]

According to Victoria E. Burke, "the term [commonplace book] refers to a book in which extracts were collected for reference, usually under topic headings."[42] She goes on to list examples in manuscript form (that is, handwritten works), and printed and published forms.

Earle Havens describes commonplace books as "treasure houses of ancient and modern knowledge [that] preserve quotations, anecdotes, maxims, jokes, verses, and magical spells, as well as astrological predictions, medicinal and culinary recipes, devotional texts, and mathematical tables—in short, subject matter of every stripe. As such, they have played an integral and abiding role in Western intellectual life throughout the ages."[43]

Adam Smyth suggests that its beginnings date "back to Aristotle, Cicero and Quintilian, and found expression in medieval Florilegia (collections of literary 'flowers')" although "it was in the early modern period that the commonplace book flourished as a crucial component in the humanist educational system, and as the principal technology for retaining, organizing and epitomizing a large body of information."[44]

✳ 1513: Smyth cites, "the most influential articulation of what we might call commonplace book method came in Erasmus' *De Copia Verborum* [*De duplici copia verborum ac rerum* sometimes translated as *On the Twofold Abundance of Expressions and Ideas*] (1513), which was not only directly influential in itself but was also the basis for many vernacular adaptations."[45]

Commonplaces can be compiled for an audience of one in the case of a private manuscript; co-compiled by multiple people and circulated among kin, including multi-generational commonplace books written in different hands by family members or salons of reader-writers; or typeset and printed for specific audiences for wider circulation. The compiler might directly quote or paraphrase their sources plus fluidly intermingle their own writing, notes, and sketches.

✳ 1574?–1636: Smyth names the components of an early modern commonplace manuscript by Anne Southwell [1574?–1636]. It "contains letters, poems (by Southwell, and by others including Walter Raleigh and Henry Kind), aphorisms, inventories (including lists of books), a mini-bestiary, psalm translations, scriptural commentary and financial receipts."[46]

(B) An author or orator may use the methods of commonplacing as a kind of prework as they prepare to tell a story or make an argument.

✳ 1851: The novel *Moby-Dick* (first published 1851) is a unique example where the commonplace becomes a literary device and appears boldly in the final outcome. The book kicks off with an etymology and eighty extracts. Matthew Goulish notes, "Herman Melville began *Moby-Dick* with a proto-chapter before chapter one, assembling an array of fragments relevant to his subject the whale. These handwritten archives communicate the richness of the ground out of which the writing grew, from books, journals, speeches, correspondences, dictionaries, song lyrics—even the range of sources is a resource and portrait of the time."[47]

Moby-Dick represents a slight twist from the bibliographic enumeration within literature that we discussed earlier, but similarly uses fragmented references to build a multidimensional intellectual world within the space of a novel. This is not a far cry from the artists, writers, and culture workers who engage in sample culture, writing with and through the texts of others.

✳ **1996**: Susan Hiller launches *Dream Screens*, an artist web project commissioned by Dia.[48] It is a commonplace performed, an interactive color-field painting and an audio dreamscape. Hiller abuts and overlays recollections of films with "dream" in their titles, plus summaries, adaptations, and direct quotes from dream-related texts. In the transcript on the site, the reader can experience these transitions visibly too, through changes to typeface, type size, type color, and paragraph indentations. The artist also provides an extensive list of books, articles, and websites on the topic that she co-compiled with David Coxhead.

✳ **2013**: My web project *As Soon As I Speak, I Speaks: A Project-Performance in Shorthand* goes live. It is named after a verse by Robert Creeley and samples excerpts I've collected in my journals by different writers in the realm of art performance, self-actualization, and epistemology. With the help of my mother, Mollie Cipriano, the passages are encoded into Gregg Shorthand, scanned, and uploaded. Visitors to the site can rouse the handwritten shorthand texts to speak using their choice of screen-reader and listen to each like tracks in a mixtape. The source of each passage or track is written in English (and displayed in the Latin alphabet) so visitors can read the bibliography even if they can't read the shorthand passages.

✳ **2007**: Jonathan Lethem pens a work of criticism called "The Ecstasy of Influence: A Plagiarism" for *Harper's Magazine*.[49] The distinction between different excerpts is detectable in projects like *Dream Screens* and *As Soon As I Speak, I Speaks*. Lethem's use of commonplacing by contrast, is a seamlessly integrated essay about authorial influence, appropriation, and postmodernism. Throughout it, he writes convincingly with the texts of others as if unravelling his own revelations. It isn't until the reader finds a color-coded key at the end of the article that they discover that each paragraph and delectable turn of phrase has been lifted verbatim from a whole score of writers.

commonplacing and the commonplace book. *See* Bib., Rev. Ed.; Cloth • A Commonplace; Common Threads; Cyberfeminism Index; and Saints & Guides.

Typographic commonplace books tap into the visual history of commonplace books as handwritten manuscripts. *How does the graphic textuality or patchwork quality of the form influence the reader?* In such cases, the fragmented texts in a typographic commonplace book are not meant for the compiler alone but for an audience. Such projects have a particular sequence and pace, and can be read as a continuous whole.

✳ **1969**: The fine press edition *A Commonplace Book with Something for Everybody* (Aptos, [CA: Grace Hoper Press], 1969) is graphically expressive, co-compiled and edited by Sherwood Grover and James D. Hammond with approvals from Blodwen Hammond and Katherine Grover. A wide selection of un-themed quotes capturing a late 1960s zeitgeist appears in a variety of letterpress fonts in red, black, and blue inks, allowing the editors to generate points of emphasis and to overlay their own typographic commentary onto the aphorisms of others. It is hand-typeset and manually printed on special papers, a labor-intensive production registered by the body and analogous in some ways to copying quotes out longhand. Grover and Hammond give the source of each quote at the back of the book and detail the typeface that each appears in. Their production is inspired by Monroe Wheeler's earlier *Typographical Commonplace Book* of 1932.

✳ 2018: *The God Within: Black Queerness Across the Diaspora, A Commonplace Book* is a commonplace zine published by Diasporan Savant Press out of Philadelphia. It quilts together memorable words from Black and queer writers, entertainers, and thinkers from around the globe. This commonplace is not organized into categories either. It is free flowing from page to page, mixing voices from the present and combining hand collage, digital production, and Risograph printing. The zine serves as a site for identity formation, affirmation, support, and community building. Its distribution model connects to histories of mutual-aid publishing and Black resistance.

Commonplace books can constitute new subjects and address new areas of inquiry. Of the commonplace book, Goulish observes, "the name identifies the book as ordinary, approachable, and accessible to all, a meeting place of reading and writing, research and creation. The *locus communis*, the 'communal place' is also the 'general theme' . . ."[50]

As such, it can be a casual form where readers encounter new topics by browsing or consuming standout bits of information that have been carefully selected by the compiler.

Throughout this essay I've outlined six theoretical and historical contellations of energy for further investigation: the dematerialization of art; the rise of publishing as a creative practice; the motif of bibliographic enumeration within literature and experimental writing; the visual categorization of books and unusual library arrangements; the uptick in feminist, antiracist, and critical scholarly practices in bibliography; and finally the influence of commonplacing and the commonplace book. As early as the sixteenth century we find evidence of traits related to the experimental subject bibliographies and visual bibliographies materialized by culture workers today.

(1) Kynaston L. McShine, ed., *Information* (New York: Museum of Modern Art, 1970). Exhibition catalog.

(2) Simon Morely, *Writing on the Wall: Word and Image in Modern Art* (Berkeley: University of California Press, 2003), 145.

(3) Morely, *Writing on the Wall*, 141.

(4) For a deeper dive, see Anne Dorothee Böhme and Kevin Henry, ed., *The Consistency of Shadows: Exhibition Catalogs as Autonomous Works of Art* (Chicago: Betty Rymer Gallery, School of the Art Institute of Chicago, 2003).

(5) The recent exhibition *Embodied Words: Reading in Medieval Christian Visual Culture* curated by Elizabeth Sandoval highlights early depictions of books and readers in the art collection at William College Museum of Art (March 18, 2022—ongoing). For a brief introduction to *chaekgeori* screens, see "Books and Scholars Accoutrements," Cleveland Museum of Art, accessed July 5, 2023, https://www.clevelandart.org/art/2011.37#.

(6) It lays some historical groundwork of this niche area, albeit with a roll call of artworks by mostly male practitioners and a few artworks by Ann Hamilton, Heather Weston, Rachel Whiteread, and Christine Borland.

(7) See catalogue entry for "Sorted Books" for more details.

(8) I was on this first team of research fellows as a bleary-eyed grad student and set up the bibliographic style guide outlining the level of description, types of materials described, and more.

(9) Temporary Services, "The Library Project," accessed July 29, 2023, http://www.temporaryservices.org/Library_Project_TS_2007.pdf

(10) See Temporary Services: The Library Project 2000–2001, Chicago Public Library, catalog record, https://chipublib.bibliocommons.com/v2/record/S126C1162466.

(11) Not long ago, a community visitor to *Jay Youngdahl: The Mangroves of Masters Bayou* (2023), pointedly asked me why we had mounted the artist's vinyl photographs to the table tops in our reading room instead of to the walls. Was she expected to view the photos on a ladder and look down? The exchange was unpleasant, but the jab that was meant as an insult isn't an altogether bad idea for another show: images mounted to table tops or floors with a ladder or ramped platforms for gazing down upon them, a sort of reversal of the viewing ladder installed with Yoko Ono's 1966 *Ceiling Painting* in which one had to ascend to see the art mounted on the ceiling. All that to say, gallery visitors arrive with their own set of expectations.

(12) Information as Material, "Reading As Art," accessed July 7, 2023, http://www.informationasmaterial.org/portfolio/reading-as-art/.

(13) Simon Morris, *Reading as Art* (York [England]: Information as Material, 2016), 102–4. I started my research into experimental bibliographies in earnest by 2014. Morris and I individually seem to have landed on several of the same references from the zeitgeist: projects by Joseph Kosuth, Kynaston McShine, Jerry Saltz, Temporary Services, Martha Rosler, Craig Dworkin, and of course Morris's own *Bibliomania* project.

(14) See Bridget Elmer, Janelle Rebel, Marshall Weber, "Freedom of the Presses: Activating Library Resources Through Collaborative Curating" in *Freedom of the Presses: Artists' Books in the 21st Century*, ed. Marshall Weber (Brooklyn: Booklyn, 2018), 125–35.

(15) Small Editions, *Summer Sippers* (2021); Small Editions, [*Artists' Book Cocktails*] (2022).

(16) The artist's website states that there were 13,000 pamphlets, while the museum's website says 10,000.

(17) Kevin Jackson, *Invisible Forms: A Guide to Literary Curiosities* (New York: Thomas Dunne Books, 2000), 276. For an extremely short and helpful history of bibliography through the centuries, please see Jackson, *Invisible Forms*, 274–77.

(18) See Brett Bodemer, "Rabelais and the Abbey of Saint-Victor Revisited," *Information & Culture* 47, no. 1 (2012): 4–17, http://www.jstor.org/stable/43737416.

(19) Jackson, *Invisible Forms*, 226.

(20) See Anne-Pascale Pouey-Mounou and Paul J. Smith, "Imaginary Booklists—History and Typology: An Introduction," in *Early Modern Catalogues of Imaginary Books: A Scholarly Anthology*, ed. Anne-Pascale Pouey-Mounou and Paul J. Smith (Leiden: Brill, 2020), 1–2.

(21) See Pouey-Mounou and Smith, "Imaginary Booklists," 18–19 for details on Fischart's work plus other translations of Rabelais by Thomas Urquhart and Nicolaas Jarichides Wieringa.

(22) Piers Brown, "'Hac Ex Consilio Meo via Progredieris': Courtly Reading and Secretarial Mediation in Donne's The Courtier's Library," *Renaissance Quarterly* 61, no. 3 (2008): 833, https://doi.org/10.1353/ren.0.0178.

(23) Jackson, *Invisible Forms*, 227. See also Pouey-Mounou and Smith, "Imaginary Booklists," 4.

(24) Alberto Manguel, *The Universal Dream Library* (Berkeley: Codex Foundation, 2016), 16.

(25) Manguel, *Universal Dream Library*, 15.

(26) Umberto Eco, *The Infinity of Lists*, trans. Alastair McEwen (New York: Rizzoli, 2009), 377.

(27) See Jackson, *Invisible Forms*, 277–78.

(28) *The Fern Rose Bibliography* is mentioned briefly in a footnote in the catalogue entry for "Bibliographic Sound Track & The Ph.D. Sound."

(29) Terry Belanger, *Lunacy and the Arrangement of Books* (New Castle, DE: Oak Knoll Press), 1.

(30) Belanger, *Lunacy and the Arrangement of Books*, 3.

(31) Gerard Genette, *Paratexts: Thresholds of Interpretation*, trans. Jane E. Lewin (Cambridge: Cambridge University Press, 1987), 22–23.

(32) Anthony Grafton and Jeffrey F. Hamburger, "Introduction: Warburg's Library and Its Legacy," in "The Warburg Institute: A Special Issue on the Library and Its Readers," special issue, *Common Knowledge* 18, no. 1 (Winter 2012), 3. For an excellent rumination on the Warburg Institute Library and "the law of the good neighbor," see the full issue of "The Warburg Institute: A Special Issue on the Library and Its Readers."

(33) Georges Perec, *Brief Notes on the Art and Manner of Arranging One's Books*, trans. John Sturrock ([London]: Penguin, 2020), 66. Essay first published 1985 by Hachette in *Penser/Classer*. Most of the listed ideas could function today as

a filter or sort preference in an online library catalog or digital bibliography, except for the individually subjective "ordered by priority for future reading" which would require some additional user input and programming magic.

(34) Italo Calvino, *If On a Winter's Night a Traveler*, trans. William Weaver (Orlando: Harcourt, 1981), 5.

(35) Belanger, *Lunacy and the Arrangement of Books*, 24.

(36) While I won't be exploring the history of the syllabus for this discussion, the *Oxford English Dictionary* locates the first English usage of the word "syllabus" to 1653.

(37) The first English usage for this definition of "anthology" is also traced to the seventeenth century, dating back to 1624 according to the *Oxford English Dictionary*.

(38) The Multigraph Collective, "Anthologies," in *Interacting with Print* (Chicago: University of Chicago Press, 2018), 36.

(39) The Multigraph Collective, "Anthologies," 36.

(40) *Merriam-Webster*, s.v. "commonplace (n.)," accessed July 1, 2023, https://www.merriam-webster.com/dictionary/commonplace.

(41) For the latter, see the catalogue entry for "Coth • A Commonplace."

(42) Victoria E. Burke, "Recent Studies in Commonplace Books," *English Literary Renaissance* 43, no. 1 (2013): 153, http://www.jstor.org/stable/43607607.

(43) [Earle Havens], "Commonplace Books: Manuscripts and Printed Books from Antiquity to the Twentieth Century," Yale University Library, accessed October 8, 2022, https://beinecke.library.yale.edu/exhibitions-visiting/special-exhibitions/commonplace-books-manuscripts-and-printed-books-antiquity.

(44) Adam Smyth, "Commonplace Book Culture" in *Women and Writing c.1340–c.1650: The Domestication of Print Culture*, ed. Anne Lawrence-Mathers and Phillipa Hardman (Woodbridge: York Medieval Press, 2010), 92.

(45) Smyth, "Commonplace Book Culture," 92.

(46) Smyth, "Commonplace Book Culture," 98.

(47) Matthew Goulish, "The Spaces of Reading," in *The Spaces of Reading: Object, Image, Word, Event*, ed. Ann Hamilton, Matthew Goulish, and Lin Hixson (Chicago, IL: School of the Art Institute of Chicago, 2018), [49].

(48) The site was originally in Flash and reprogrammed in HTML5 in 2020 and can be accessed here: https://awp.diaart.org/hiller/dreamscreens.html. The catalogue entry for "Bibliomania" includes mention of Dream Screens.

(49) The catalogue entry for "The Best American Book of the 20th Century" includes mention of Lethem's piece.

(50) Goulish, "The Spaces of Reading," [49].

Scope of the Catalogue

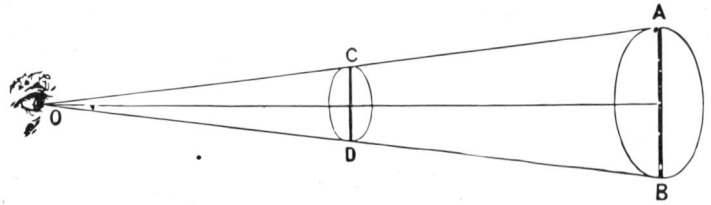

What follows is a visual catalogue of contemporary subject bibliographies and bibliographic projects from the last twenty years that perform in different ways. They gather unconventional collections and/or activate resources unconventionally. In part, the project's aim is to acknowledge bibliography as a site of knowledge production as well as to draw attention to the visual and phenomenal forms that influence such production.[1] Johanna Drucker has noted that "description IS interpretation," and yet subject bibliographies, particularly in the realm of library and information science, are generally cautious about claiming such interpretation.[2] Why project a false objectivity? Why not expose or even embrace these subjectivities? The examples that I've selected for this survey have been created or influenced by a variety of cultural workers including artists, writers, designers, curators, and some bibliographers proper. The projects span from artists' books and digital media to stack interventions and reading room installations. They operate somewhere on a continuum of bibliographies, artworks, and literature.

The survey is of course a partial picture, reflecting projects that I've come across in the last eight years. There are bibliographies that I've passed on if they didn't meet my selection criteria (stated below), had a lack of documentation, or if they'd already been copiously written about. No doubt many terrific projects presently unknown to me will cross my path in the future.

To shape the content in this bibliography of bibliographies, I set up a few loose guidelines. One of my criteria for selection was that the projects be public and open for use, whether that is as a formally published work, an online release, an exhibition, or a product for sale. I did not include personal bibliographies or working bibliographies that are not intended to circulate to an audience.[3] Another was that I wanted to gather a group of projects by international creators that would represent different strengths. I wanted to design an inclusive catalogue, committed to finding diverse bibliographers and representing a range of emerging and established voices.[4] I tried to consider what makes this or that bibliography unique, considering for instance its theoretical development, its addressee, its design, its language, its functionality. A third guideline was to consider selective, evaluative, or experimental (i.e. uncategorizable) bibliographies first. A fourth consideration was to evaluate the bibliography from a position of hospitality. *When is a bibliography inviting or compelling? How are the multifaceted dimensions of resources in a bibliography conveyed? What information is captured and how much? What about its overall tone? Can a bibliography speak with something other than an overtly pedagogical tenor or quasi-scientific jargon?* The last parameter for selection was that the projects be contemporary in some way, not just recent.[5] Or perhaps, what I was (and am) looking for is actually akin to what Jan Verwoert has referred to as "uncontemporary"— something "slightly ahead of the world" that "sets the stage for future codes and operates in a place that precedes our ability to apply language to these codes."[6]

To this end, a series of questions arises, particularly around the hybrid realities of print and screen that the bibliographic world exists in. *How do offline bibliographies communicate with a computationally networked world? And vice versa, how do online bibliographies and database projects communicate with rarefied or unique offline objects? How does a bibliography accommodate and document electronic works and alternative formats? What other kinds of graphic expressions can be utilized to reflect the visual, material, and linguistic complexity of books and publications beyond the default list or the linked listicle?*[7]

Bibliographies are mobile hubs that promote the existence of a set of resources-in-motion. When tracking down project details for the examples in this study, I found that many of the bibliographic projects *themselves* were shape-shifters, morphing from form to form. For example, *Bib., Rev. Ed.* slid from a blog to an online book to an artist's book. *The Author of This Book Committed Suicide* transformed from an installation and publication to a durational stack intervention to framed wall prints. I often came into contact with only one iteration of an expandable project firsthand, and could not personally examine every publication or attend exhibitions or events already past. I therefore relied heavily on the documentation that exists and/or contacted the creators directly to verify information and answer any lingering questions.

The survey is organized alphabetically using the project titles as entry points. The alphabetical order haphazardly shuffles the juxtapositions of entries, but gives the reader the opportunity to dip in and out of this work using the table of contents, entry headings, index, and images as guides. To document any related forms a project may have taken, I have included multiple project citations ordered chronologically under each main entry. The citation style is an adaptation from the Chicago Manual of Style and OCLC cataloging standards with a dash of descriptive bibliography. While consistency is the goal of any bibliographer, this set of projects is not always easily classifiable as a book, an exhibition catalog, an artwork, a website, an exhibition, etc., which all warrant slightly different citation structures.

As the catalogue aims to bring a series of exemplars together, I tried to keep an open mind about selection. I evaluated the projects as someone who is invested in making and thinking about the future possibilities of bibliographies, and subject bibliographies in particular. The librarian-designer mind is like that of a curator-critic. You are constantly negotiating two different, though not wholly incompatible selves. My bias is therefore present throughout, especially within the annotations. But what is storytelling without character?

(1) At least one book in the survey is intentionally "undesigned," however. See catalogue entry for "Bibliomania."
(2) Johanna Drucker, "Excerpts and Entanglements," keynote, Danish Institute for Document Design and University of California, Berkeley, August 13, 2003.
(3) I have included some private and working bibliographies that do circulate in public. See, for example, catalogue entries for "Difficult Times" and "Poet-Saints of July 06."
(4) My curatorial MO is to blur the value lines between well-known creators and projects and lesser-known creators and projects. For more insight into my psyche, please see the "Preface" in this work.
(5) Essay not written, "A strange new 'hell:' let's define the contemporary!" which will feature the perspectives of Claire Bishop, Bruno Latour, Boris Groys, Marc Augé, and others.
(6) The quote is actually a paraphrase of Verwoert's ideas: "Artists, [Jan Verwoert] writes, should be slightly ahead of the world, slightly uncontemporary, setting the stage for future codes and operating in a place that precedes our ability to apply language to these codes. The relevance of making art today, he argues, does not lie in reproducing existing values, nor in rejecting them . . . but in performing them differently, speaking in a new key, using a different mode of address." Anthony Huberman and Will Holder, *For the Blind Man in the Dark Room Looking for the Black Cat That Isn't There* (Saint Louis, MO: Contemporary Art Museum St. Louis, 2009), 147.
(7) The work of design and development studio Astrom / Zimmer has intentionally shied away from "the alluringly efficient but dangerously simplified lists [that are] popping up everywhere." "Studio," Astrom / Zimmer's website, accessed April 26, 2016, https://astromzimmer.com/studio. For an example of their projects see the catalogue entry for "Bibliozines."

Catalogue of Bibliographies

52 Transactions

Slade, Kathy. *Fifty-Two Weeks of Transactions at the Lending Library*. Performance. Curated by Lorna Brown for Group Search: Art in the Library. Vancouver: Vancouver Public Library, September 2006–September 2007.

Slade, Kathy. *Fifty-Two Weeks of Transactions at the Lending Library*. One of a kind artist's book + box. 2007.

Slade, Kathy. *52 Transactions*. Vancouver: Trapp Editions, 2007. [64 leaves]: ill.; 16 × 11.5 × 2 cm.

A performance utterly ordinary. Every week, on Thursdays, usually but not always in the evenings, artist Kathy Slade visits the Vancouver Public Library and checks out one item. Week after week over the course of a year.

The documentation of the performance is rather unremarkable yet perfectly emblematic: No carefully composed photography or video, no diaristic ramblings of the events that evening, no audio of ambient sounds—simply a thermal-printed library checkout receipt in monospaced lettering from the Central Branch. "Please Keep Slip With Book," it entreats. The scraps of ephemera build and Slade's visits stack up in the handmade publication *Fifty-Two Weeks of Transactions at the Lending Library*. Set against white pages, the mounted receipts have already begun to yellow and fade in their white cloth binding. In the offset edition, *52 Transactions*, reproductions of the receipts, ordered by date and time of checkout, are bound in a petite red cloth binding with a white book jacket. Like the art of the conceptualists "using unassuming letterforms, [and] non-expressive surfaces," Slade's work has an "anti-aesthetic" look.[1]

At the heart of this performance project is a solitary game between the reader and her library. The events constitute a durational and cumulative bibliography driven by the impulses of a library consumer who fastidiously mines her public library for unlikely gems and notable finds. What is she searching for? What does she gravitate towards? The bibliographic detail on Slade's receipts is limited to title and subtitle—truncated to 42 characters including spaces—a library-issued barcode, and a Dewey Decimal Classification Number. With a little investigation, the fragmented information attests to a fascinating array of artist biographies, French symbolist poetry, music criticism, modernist writing, sci-fi, American independent cinema, avant-garde architecture, short stories, and fiction. Disparate figures in close proximity take up sympathies with one another or give the reader pause: Dusty Springfield, Neil Young, Bob Dylan, Baudelaire, Freud, Jean-Luc Godard, Ed Ruscha, Artemisia Gentileschi, Yoko Ono, Gertrude Stein, John Lennon, Lester Bangs, Dan Graham, James Elkins, Sonic Youth, Ant Farm, Philip K. Dick, Ursula K. Le Guin, Alfred Jarry, Djuna Barnes, Elsa von Freytag-Loringhoven, Virginia Woolf.

Throughout *52 Transactions* the reader glimpses Slade's interests, habits, and unforeseen circumstances. Following the steady march of checkout receipts is a visual pause of six blank entries with asterisked endnotes. For the last weeks of the project, the public library was closed due to a civic strike. Transactions 47–52 never occurred. In an appendix of payment receipts, the reader can further track Slade's movements: She checks out the same item twice and pays eight nominal fines for items not returned on time.

As an artist's book, *52 Transactions* functions on multiple levels—as the proof of existence of a library borrower visiting a particular municipal building to make repeated transactions, and as the intimate portrait of a media consumer willing to self-disclose perhaps the most personal data there is: one's reading history.

52 Transactions, 2007, cover.

52 Transactions, 2007, interior spread.

(1) Simon Morely, *Writing on the Wall*
(Berkeley: University of California Press, 2003), 145.

336 Pages 336 Books

Prill, Tania, Alberto Vieceli, and Sebastian Cremers.
336 Pages 336 Books.
Zürich: everyedition, 2013.
336 p.: ill.; 16 × 11.5 cm + 1 insert (index of books).

One might recall a book by its cover, but why not by the design of its page number? *336 Pages 336 Books* by designers Tania Prill, Alberto Vieceli, and Sebastian Cremers is an extended ode to the page number, that essential and underappreciated element of bibliographic navigation. The page number often takes up the least amount of space on the page, yet can be tricky to place properly in relation to the body copy, illustrations, running heads, gutters, and other elements of a book. Too close to the action and it runs interference. Too far away and it's lonely and adrift. As the authors note about their collab, "For this 336-page book we have sighted thousands of books of all different periods, on different topics and focuses, in search of 336 headstrong, incorruptible and humoristic page numbers."[1] This is a visual bibliography of typographic multiplicity for the design-iest among us. High resolution black-and-white scans of these "headstrong, incorruptible and humoristic page numbers" have been scaled up to take center stage and printed on glossy paper.

On each page Prill, Vieceli, and Cremers offer an arty crop of an enlarged page number. The first page of *336 Pages 336 Books* shows numeral 1; page two, a 2; page three, a 3; and so forth, with each numeral reproduced from a different source book. The sources are all identifiable in a loose inserted, folded index included with the book. The page number's original surroundings of text, image, white space, and the physical page edge have become abstract graphic forms in the photographic crop. Halftone dot patterns and paper fibers are visible. Some printed impressions are faint like "142," ink splotched like "170," frenetically fuzzed out like "248," reversed out of black like "62," or spelled out longhand like "thirty-four." Exploring the visual dimensions of text, the authors disrupt the historically observed divisions between word and image.

The project accumulates an expressive variety of letterforms and subtle detail. At such magnification, readers can tell if the numbers were first printed or handwritten. Other symbols or graphic devices that may help define the location of a page number within a layout become more apparent, and this compilation is an apt study. One finds here broken or continuous ruled lines in close proximity; brackets, tildes, or guillemets (aka French quotes) surrounding the number; a pipe, forward slash, greater than sign, or bullet preceding the number; and a period, arrow, or solo right parenthesis succeeding the number. Non-typographic anomalies make appearances, too, like the pencil drawing of a foot that encircles "169" from Nanne Meyer's *Luftblick* (2003) and the ink drawing of gridded Xs behind "219" from Metahaven's *Uncorporate Identity* (2010).

In the colophon, an intriguing clue, a reader's key to the work appears: "The idea to this book emerged from Bram Stoker's 'Dracula'—see page 243."[2] When the reader jumps

336 Pages 336 Books, 2013, cover.

to page 243 in *336 Pages 336 Books*, the visual is "»243«" with the "4" and "3" dramatically extending below the baseline. A closing guillemet leads and an opening guillemet follows the page number, posing as arrows rather than quotes. For this self-initiated project, the authors add that it was Vieceli who was reading *Dracula* when the idea first struck.[3] Including a page number from *Dracula* at an exaggerated size gives insight into the kinds of numeric details the authors were inspired by. They also indicate that "the structure refers to *book* by George Brecht" where the parts of a book are defined by verbal description, and "the title is inspired by the artist books by Ed Ruscha" where the title precisely demonstrates what's inside.[4]

The accompanying two-sided index-as-poster is an easy-to-follow numbered list 1–336. Each entry notes the title, author, publisher, and date, in that order. The list contains books in English, French, and German sourced from the authors' home libraries. Most titles are from the mid-twentieth century to the present with a few earlier outliers like Jacque de La-Font's *Les Principes de la Theologie Morale* (1701) and *Interprétation des psaumes de David et des cantiques* (1743). Many titles are related to art and design topics and cultural criticism, although there is a broad mix of literature, philosophy, travel guides, cookbooks, and at least one toy brochure represented.

The project intertwines the reading and personal publication collections of three designers through an unusual but rigorous search-and-evaluation process for the best page numbers. As an experimental bibliography, *336 Pages 336 Books* gathers an uncommon selection of titles and provides a view inside each that stresses the notability of their page numbers through extra-large print.

336 Pages 336 Books, 2013, interior spread.

(1) everyedition studio, "336 pages 336 books by Prill Vieceli Cremers," accessed October 5, 2022, https://everyedition.ch/336-pages-336-books/. At the time of this collaboration, the authors worked together under the studio name Prill Vieceli Cremers.
(2) Tania Prill, Alberto Vieceli, and Sebastian Cremers, *336 Pages 336 Books* (Zürich: everyedition, 2013), colophon.
(3) Tania Prill, email message to author, October 6, 2022.
(4) Tania Prill, "Works: 336 Pages 336 Books," accessed October 5, 2022, http://taniaprill.com/.

Africanismus_12469

Cyrus, Jamal.
Africanismus_12469. 2006.
Found padded vest,
paperback books,
cotton shirt.
Collection of the artist.

Created by Jamal Cyrus in 2006, *Africanismus_12469* is a wearable bibliography, a shield, and an artwork that taps into the histories of fashion and dress as a political statement. Cyrus has affixed nine books by Black liberationists to a vintage baseball catcher's chest protector which is slung over a turtleneck. The books cannot be read at present—they are held shut by transparent poly straps—but clearly they have led active lives and are well-worn, creased, and even missing bits of a cover or spine here and there.

The books are symbolic of a Pan-Africanist movement of the 1960s and 70s, and are recognizable by their front cover designs and the information supported therein—their titles and subtitles, author names, illustrations and photographs, and other marketing copy. Looking a bit closer, one realizes a connection to the prison system with the incarcerated writings of several authors including Angela Y. Davis in

If They Come in the Morning, George Jackson in *Blood in My Eye*, and Eldridge Cleaver in *Soul on Ice*. According to an exhibition guide by The Institute of Contemporary Art in L.A., *Africanismus_12469* is allied to "a common practice by incarcerated people in which protective vests are fashioned from phone books to lessen the impact of punches, knives, and other assaults."[1] Utilizing books as padded armor is a makeshift solution in a dangerous situation. Cyrus's selection of volumes are emblematic on both an intellectual plane and a physical one. Adhered to the tail pad, the book *Negroes with Guns* by Robert F. Williams defends the groin. The book first came out in 1962, detailing Williams's account of racialized violence and advocacy of self-defence.

The garment's color—black vest, black shirt—acknowledges the Black Power movement and the heyday of the Black Panther Party (BPP) with its members' penchant for wearing black attire. This gathering of books suggests the party's community focus on Black solidarity, mutual-aid publishing, and self-determination. The title of the artwork is also a memorial, commemorating December 4, 1969, the date that Fred Hampton (1948–1969), an activist and rising BPP leader in Illinois, was brutally assassinated in his home by a coordinated effort between the FBI and the Chicago Police.

The imagined wearer of Cyrus's repurposed catcher's gear is readied by the knowledge of their foregoers—literally covered with the writings of Civil Rights activists and Black Nationalists—and is signaling their worldview through sculptural fashion. The chest protector, however, only covers so much. The supposed wearer, while perhaps emboldened, could still be vulnerable to today's injustices of racial profiling, police brutality, and systemic racism. The idiom "tools of ignorance," which Herold "Muddy" Ruel used to describe catcher's equipment when he played for the major leagues in the early twentieth century, is an apt correlation here.² The *MLB Glossary* says "the term is meant to point out the irony that a player with the intelligence needed to be effective behind the plate would be foolish enough to play a position that required so much safety equipment."³ Cyrus seems to tap into this sardonic humor while flipping "tools of ignorance" on its head.

Africanismus_12469, 2006.

(1)
Exhibition Guide: Jamal Cyrus: The End of My Beginning
(Los Angeles: Institute of Contemporary Art, 2022),
https://cdn.filepicker.io/api/file/HeFcxPgARuyUy3oszIRs?.
(2)
MLB Glossary, s.v. "Tools of Ignorance,"
accessed October 2, 2022, https://www.mlb.com/glossary/idioms/tools-of-ignorance. Herold "Muddy" Ruel's Major League career as a catcher lasted nineteen seasons from 1915–1934.
(3)
"Tools of Ignorance."

All: The Books I Never Wrote or Wrote and Never Published

> Drucker, Johanna.
> *All: The Books I Never Wrote or Wrote and Never Published.*
> Forthcoming.
>   (In progress database memoir.
>   Online version and print version anticipated.)

While Johanna Drucker was packing up her house in the summer of 2008, she started scanning the pages of her unpublished writing in preparation for an auto-bibliography. She's kept all of her manuscripts from childhood to the present and envisioned a memoir that was "about and through writing," a project that would fittingly show a life and love of writing in writing.[1]

All: The Books I Never Wrote or Wrote and Never Published is currently in progress, with an online database version and a book-based version planned for the future. The website will contain over 200 distinct pieces of Drucker's unpublished writing including completed manuscripts as well as proposals, sketches, and ideas for books. Handwritten, typescript, and digital writings are each assigned a structured filename and will be available to view or download as PDFs. Each book never written or never published will be accompanied by the author's critical recollections about when and where the writing was produced, what technological means she used, what kind of work it is, the themes present in the work,

all

the books I never wrote or wrote and never published

PDFs · About · Index · Contact

The young writer, notebook in hand. Philadelphia, PA, 1964

Introduction: *Note: This landing page is a placeholder; active site to come Spring 2016.*

I am eleven years old in this picture, sitting in the dining room of my family house in Philadelphia. Writing is the focus in my existence; it defines my identity. Since I was small, I have carried a notebook and pen with me everywhere, hoping that the books will flow onto the pages in some unstaunchable spontaneous expression manifesting itself in prose and poetry. I write by hand, and yet, I think in terms of the book format, because that is the way literature has made itself familiar to me. My desire, drive, is not to *be* a writer, but *to write*. The activity and its absorptions are addictive. My ideas of how writing is created, what it expresses, and what its forms and sources might be are gleaned largely from the exposure to the canonical works of English authors. That changes in the decades ahead as I move through different communities — of school, friends, poets, artists, scholars, book artists, and printers, designers, and finally, writers working in the digital modes.

This is a memoire about and through writing. The texts in these pages are all unpublished, and there are many of them. I wrote prolifically, regularly, and in each instance of writing, with a specific script in mind about what the possibilities were for writing. This project is about what I thought I was doing in writing, the constructs that produced and constrained these works. It is an autobiography as gloss, the detailed annotation of manuscripts. In some cases they are transcribed, in others, they are attached as full PDFs. They are the evidence of a life lived in writing, now refracted through critical self-reflection. They do not tell story of their making, so that is added, provided as the narrative frame.

Each of these artifacts speaks of a moment, place, mood, attitude, passion, drive, emotion and aspiration through its physical, documentary materiality and its textual specificity. Whether they are of literary value is not an issue, they are of evidentiary value, a testimony to their own production and my history.

All materials on this site were written, drawn, and commented upon by **Johanna Drucker** and are subject to copyright. To enter, select from the columns below or click **here** to enter and move through chronologically. *N.B. At present none of the links below will work.*

Titles by Dates:	Period:	Writing category:	Creation Place:
1960-63 Poems	Family life	Personal	Philadelphia 1969
1963 Kennedy Assassination	Puberty	Fictions	Rochester 1969-70
1964 The Letter	Amy	Experimental	Philadelphia 1970
1964-65 Dear James Diary	After Amy	Procedural	Channing Way, CA 1970
1965 Cat the Herman and	Freshman year	Commercial	Hillegass 1970-72
1965 Reddy	Art School	News	Philadelphia 1971
1965 The Arbor	Drugs	Essayistic	Ocean View Fall 1972
1965 Felice	John / Isolation and Work	Project List	Candlewood Island 1973
1965-6 Mirror Mirror	Art life	Associational	North Berkeley 1973
1964-5 Mss titled 1964	Maude/John/Sandra/Charles	Language Writing	Philadelphia Winter 1973
1967-8 Poems	Jeryl	Women's Narrative	Santa Cruz 1974-1975
1967-8 Minnie Malouse	John and Mountains	Theoretical	Ross Avenue, CA 1975-76
1965 Prose manuscript	Books and printers	Accounts	John St., Oakland, 1976-77
1968 Nameless I	Betsy and Jim	Diaristic	Philadelphia 1977

All home page, screenshot.

and what individuals were influential in her life at the time. As an auto-bibliography, it will combine candor with great depth of access, allowing readers to view most of Drucker's unpublished work in full.

All will be formally unique as a database memoir that readers decide how to navigate. The online landing page shows the general direction of the project and Drucker's underlying metadata structure. Readers will be able to access works and entries through four main avenues: Titles by Dates, Period, Writing Category, and Creation Place. These metadata schemes will allow readers to group and to find connections between entries. The subsets beneath the main headings are hyper-specific and tailored for this personal bibliography. Period is an especially noteworthy category that describes a life in intervals. In this system, periodization is connoted by such labels as "Betsy and Jim," "Art life," "Puberty," and "Paris interlude."

Where Foucault has addressed the relationship between the author and the text as a place "where the writing subject endlessly disappears," *All* is a project that dutifully brings the subject back.[2] Drucker arrests the networked bibliography to surround the texts in authored biographical detail.

(1)
"Introduction," *All: The Books I Never Wrote or Wrote and Never Published*, accessed March 13, 2016, http://www.johannadrucker.net/All2_Home_index.html. The direct link is, at the time of writing, currently active. In 2016, it had been available from the home page of Johanna Drucker's website.

(2)
Michel Foucault, "What Is an Author?," in *Language, Counter-Memory, Practice: Selected Essays and Interviews* (Ithaca, NY: Cornell University Press, 1977), 116.

The Artist's Novel & The Book Lovers

Maroto, David, and Joanna Zielińska, curators. *The Book Lovers*. Project. 2011—.

Maroto, David, and Joanna Zielińska, curators. *The Book Lovers*. Online database. 2011—. http://ensembles.mhka.be/ensembles/the-book-lovers?locale=en.

Maroto, David, and Joanna Zielińska, eds. *Artist Novels: The Book Lovers Publication*. Designed by Jakub de Barbaro. Berlin: Sternberg Press, 2014. 256, [16] p.: col. ill.; 21 × 17 × 1.5 cm.

Maroto, David. *The Artist's Novel: The Novel as a Medium in the Visual Arts*. 2 vols. Designed by Jakub de Barbaro. Milan: Mousse Publishing, 2019. Vol. 1, *A New Medium*: 284 p.: ill.; 21 × 15.5 × 2.5 cm. Vol. 2, *The Fantasy of the Novel*: 292 p.: ill.; 21 × 15.5 × 2.5 cm.

Artist Novels, 2014, cover.

Curators David Maroto and Joanna Zielińska didn't set out to define a new genre — at first. Maroto was working on *Illusion*, an art project "in the form of a novel" and began assembling a list of narrative fiction written by other artists.[1] What began as a modest working bibliography turned into a much larger research project when Zielińska began asking questions. The two discovered that there were many past precedents of artists who write novels and who "create different strategies to integrate their novels into their artistic practice."[2] But there was little information about it as a subject, that is, as an *artist's novel*. Maroto and Zielińska started the *The Book Lovers* project to promote novels as a recognized medium within the visual arts, and since 2011 have organized a series of international exhibitions, programs, and performances.[3] They launched an online database with M HKA that catalogs the prose and novellas of such artists as Fiona Banner, Liam Gillick, Alasdair Gray, Will Holder, Brion Gysin, and Yayoi Kusama. It is illustrated with cover images and author photos, and has the advantage of being updated on a rolling basis.

Artist Novels: The Book Lovers Publication (2014) is the first collected print component to this ongoing research. It includes essays from guest contributors, transcripts from event interviews, an overview of *The Book Lovers* curatorial projects, two sections that present excerpts from novels, a bibliography of artists' novels, and biographies of the book's contributors. Taken as a whole, the publication is an expanded bibliography whose sampled fiction effectively *shows* a genre and whose list of citations *tells* descriptive information about the books.

Maroto and Zielińska are interested in demonstrating the creative strategies at work in artists' novels—for example, what forms of authorship are utilized and what genres influence the works—and the relationship between the novel and the artist's practice—for example, how a novel might be integrated with other media. The chapter "The Exhibition Space: Redefining Art Practice" presents excerpts from novels that were part of recent installations by Lindsay Seers, Cheng Ran, and Jill Magid. Each is set off within the book by a bright blue cover page and typeset in large, blue serif letters—a departure from the small, black sans serif typesetting used elsewhere. The reader can transition from essayistic writing to narrative forms with these visual cues. "Artist Novels: First Published" reveals the innards of novels that were until recently "not available to a wider public."[4] Two such cases are photographs of the manuscripts *Espahor Ledet Ko Uluner!*, Guy de Cointet's 1973 story in a made-up language, and *The Story of the Vivian Girls…*, Henry J. Darger's illustrated thirteen-volume epic. The book-as-bibliography is designed to give you a taste of the subject matter and exhibit the research, letting the reader ponder *is there something recognizably different about an artist's novel?*

In 2019, David Maroto released the two-volume work *The Artist's Novel: The Novel as a Medium in the Visual Arts* based on his PhD research and creative practice at Edinburgh College of Art. The experimental subject bibliography that tracks, "narrative fiction written in prose, 20,000–60,000-word long (novellas) or 60,000 words onwards (novels), created by visual artists" has now been digested into several embodied pieces of writing.[5] Part 1 (volume 1) opens with some historical and theoretical context about the artist's novel, followed by illustrated chapters analyzing projects by Benjamin Seror, Cally Spooner, Mai-Thu Perret, and Goldin+Sennedby. The last half is made up of appendices of interviews with artists, curators, and editors plus a Chi-

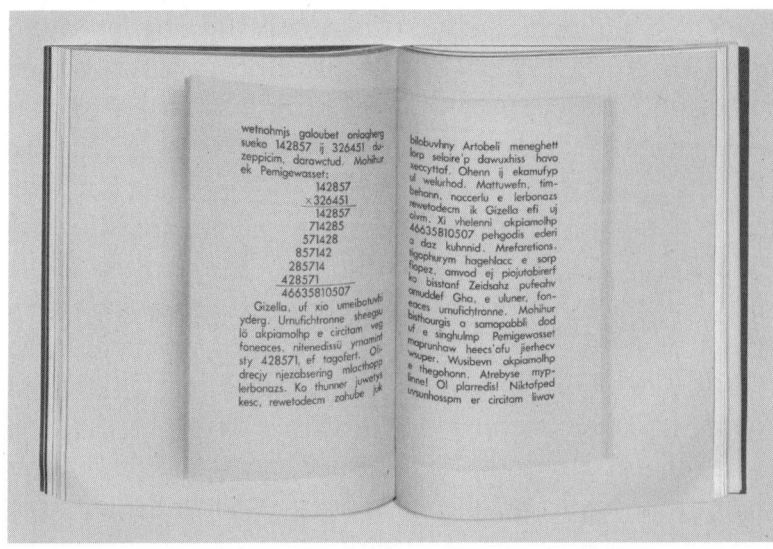

Interior spreads of *Artist Novels*, 2014,
showing *Espahor Ledet Ko Uluner!*, and *The Story of the Vivian Girls....*

cago-style bibliography of artists' novels and novels written by visual artists. Instead of using excerpts as bibliographic surrogates, the 2019 edition relies on book cover images and performance and installation photography to visualize the artists' novels being discussed. The appendix with the full bibliography is unfortunately not illustrated like the online database. In part 2 (volume 2) Maroto traces the real development of a co-commissioned artist's novel by Alex Cecchetti through a fictional retelling of the process.

With *The Artist's Novel* we gain insight into Maroto as bibliographer. He continues to gather examples through word-of-mouth recommendations, reads and compares the novels "whilst paying special attention to the traces of the artistic process in the narrative text," and speaks to the creators whenever possible.[6]

(1) David Maroto and Joanna Zielińska, eds., *Artist Novels: The Book Lovers Publication* (Berlin: Sternberg Press, 2014), 8.
(2) Maroto and Zielińska, *Artist Novels*, 7.
(3) Maroto and Zielińska, *Artist Novels*, 7.
(4) David Maroto, *The Artist's Novel: The Novel as a Medium in the Visual Arts* (Milan: Mousse Publishing, 2019), 1:16–17.
(5) Maroto, *The Artist's Novel*, 1:17.

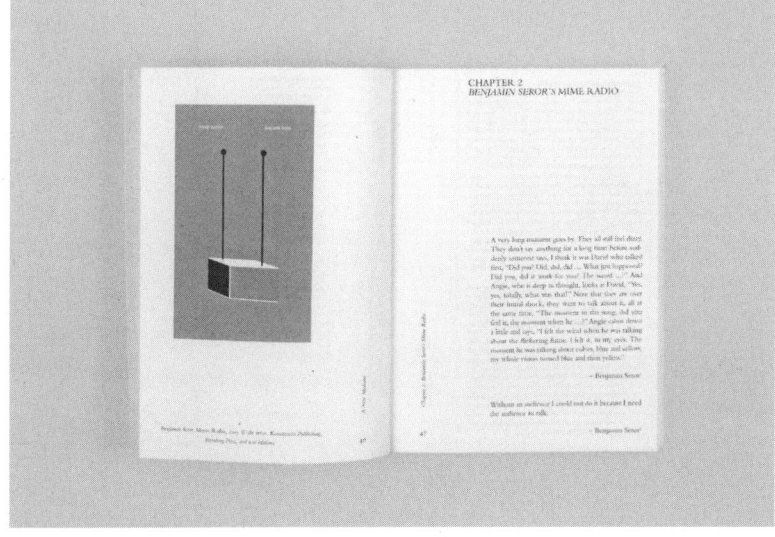

The Artist's Novel, 2019,
covers of both volumes and interior spread from part 1 (volume 1).

Atlas of Punctuation

Neilson, Heidi.
Atlas of Punctuation.
Design by the author.
Rosendale, NY:
Women's Studio Workshop,
2004.
[32] p.;
25 × 22 × 1.5 cm.

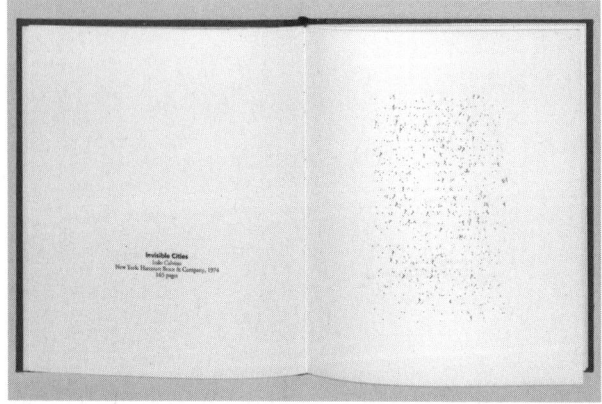

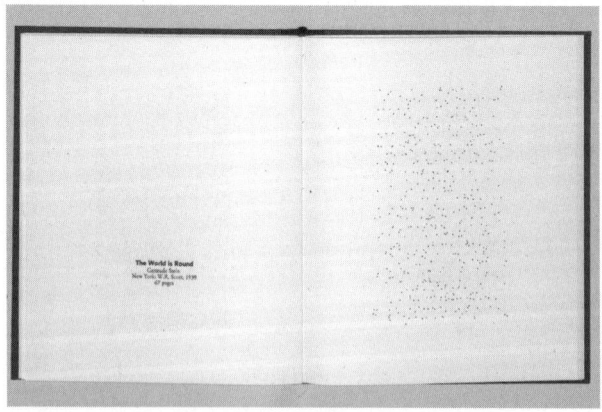

Interior spreads of *Atlas of Punctuation*, 2004.

One of Heidi Neilson's earliest bookworks, *Atlas of Punctuation*, was conceptualized around fourteen literary classics "that convey qualities of space and scale" and letterpress printed in an edition of one hundred during an artist's residency at Women's Studio Workshop.[1] The slim case-bound volume is tactile and unassuming with brown handmade paper-over-boards and a recessed title plate.

Within, Neilson's bibliographic selections are ordered alphabetically by title, beginning with *Alice's Adventures in Wonderland*, *Ficciones*, and *Flatland*, and concluding with *A Wrinkle in Time*.

Each entry functions as a map and key. The title, author, publication info, and page count for each literary work are recorded on the verso, while the complete end-of-sentence punctuation for each source book is mapped onto a single plane on the recto wherein typographic marks stochastically dance in the text block. These literary maps adhere to a particular set of margins, according to the dimensions and page ratios of their referents.

As a subtle visual, the reader may notice that some of the punctuation marks are mirrored in the maps. In the act of plotting typographic data from her source books, the artist has collapsed the dimensions of the codex, flipping any marks that would have originally appeared on the verso of a typeset page. Neilsen thus presents the reader with an unseen visuality, a typographic x-ray view of the pages in a closed volume.

In her hands, *Twenty Thousand Leagues Under the Sea* by Jules Verne becomes a densely layered image map of questions and exclamations. As visualized, other authors sprinkle a little inflection across the story, questioning and exclaiming sparely, like in Italo Calvino's *Invisible Cities*. Gertrude Stein's illustrated classic for children, *The World is*

Round, is notable for only employing the full stop and for doing so with such economy that hardly any punctuation collisions occur.

    The time and labor spent analyzing the occurrence of punctuation in these literary works in turn opens the texts up to instantaneous meta-readings. *Atlas of Punctuation* invites a new kind of reading or re-reading of the original texts that draws closer attention to the writer's craft, the granular construction of each sentence, and the territory that these occupy on the topographic page.

(1) "Atlas of Punctuation," Women's Studio Workshop, accessed January 5, 2022, https://wsworkshop.org/collection/atlas-of-punctuation/.

The Author of This Book Committed Suicide

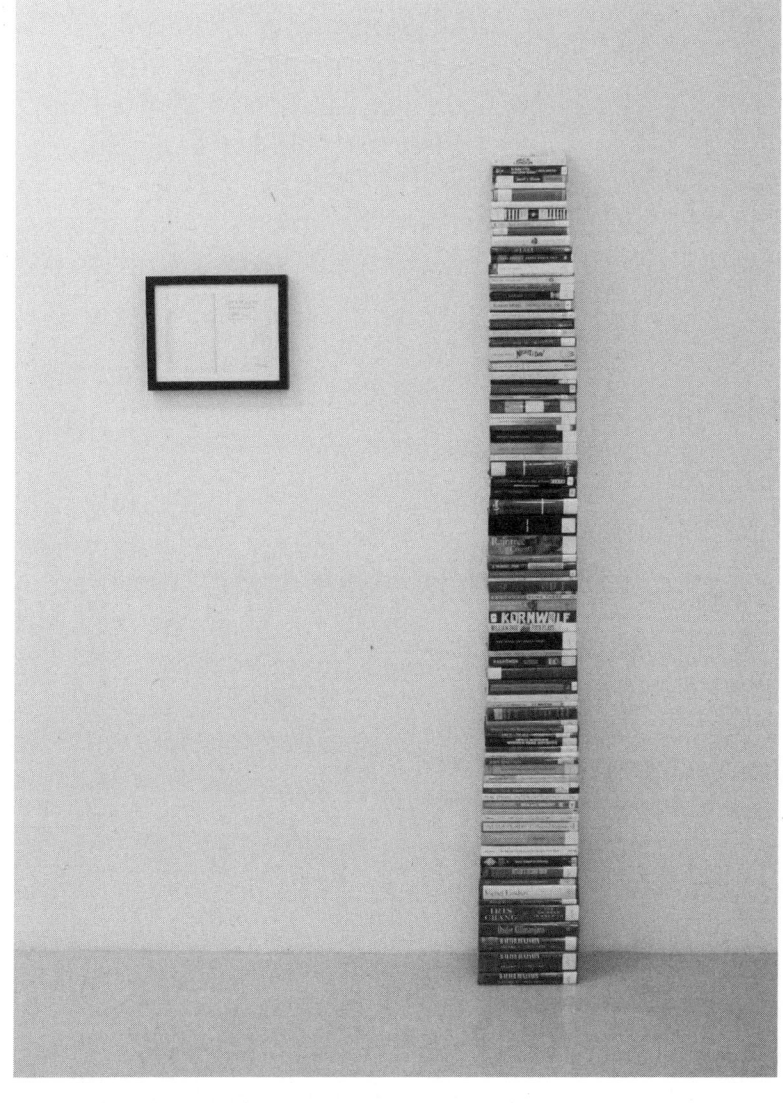

The Author of This Book Committed Suicide,
2012, installation view at Field Projects.

Krach, Aaron. *The Author of This Book Committed Suicide*, 2012. Installation. On the occasion of the group exhibition *How to Write a Novel* at Field Projects, New York.

Krach, Aaron. *The Author of This Book Committed Suicide*. New York: printed by the author, 2012. 160 p.: ill.; 20.5 × 26.5 × 1 cm.

Krach, Aaron. *The Author of This Book Committed Suicide (NYPL in SF)*, 2014. Three framed prints. On the occasion of the group exhibition *Codex* at CCA Wattis Institute for Contemporary Arts, San Francisco.

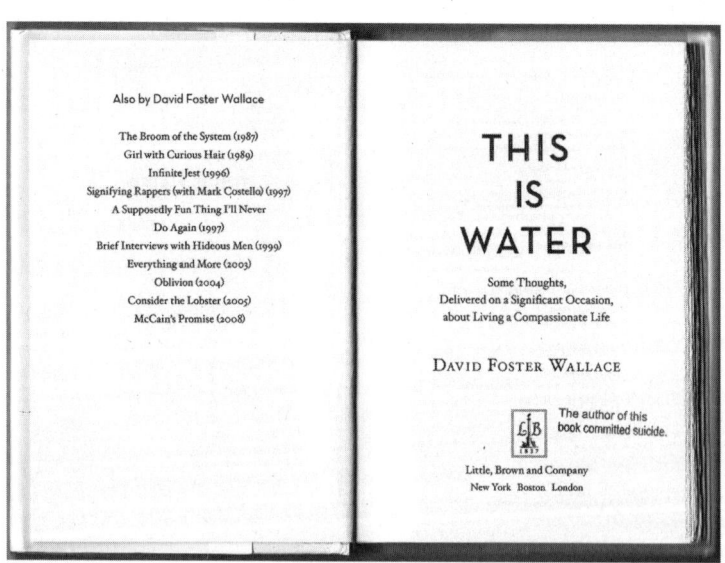

A stamped intervention into an NYPL book.

In July of 2012 artist Aaron Krach began checking out all of the available titles from the New York Public Library (NYPL) by Virginia Woolf. And David Foster Wallace. And Jack London. And Gilles Deleuze. And Walter Benjamin. . . He amassed eighty-six library books of poetry, fiction, and non-fiction by forty-nine authors for an installation at Field Projects, New York. From ancient philosophers (e.g., Seneca), to modern dictators (e.g., Adolf Hitler), to confessional poets (e.g., Sylvia Plath), Krach stacked the books up by size along a gallery wall in a spine-out tower.

This disparate collection of books is thematically linked by a common macabre thread: the authors all have the same cause of death.[1] The title page of each volume bears a blue sans serif stamp created by Krach that starkly reads: "The author of this book committed suicide." The unexpected matter-of-factness of the language, told through the nearly invisible mode of ordinary library processing technology, makes for a cocktail of deliberate unease. For the duration of the two-week show, the closed books formed a silent totem pole in the gallery. A framed reproduction of one of the "enhanced" title page spreads—John Berryman's *Love & Fame* (1970)—hung nearby to show an example of the artist's interventions into public property.

Before returning the books back to the NYPL, Krach scanned all of the freshly stamped title pages and assembled the images for publication. The resulting book, designed by Justin Yockel, reproduces the title page spreads in black and white at slightly smaller than full scale. The visual information captured in the scans, namely the title page typography and ornament, give a subtle indication of the time period that each book was typeset but not necessarily when it was written. That Krach chose to focus on this particular book part for his interventions, fortuitously ties into standardized library description practices. The title page, as well as the copyright page, are considered key sources of information for writing bibliographic descriptions and library catalog records. As such, Krach's gesture insinuates that the author's cause of death is bibliographically significant and paratextually important.

The third part of this project involves the public patron at the NYPL. Krach's conceptual collection of books are now embedded and dispersed within the daily life of a metropolitan library system. The books are not in a special display case but on the shelves. They do not have any outward markings, only an interior stamp.[2] The stamp forever links the physical items to Krach's bibliographic project. On any given day, a patron might encounter a book bearing his soft vandalism. When the wording on the stamp, "the author of this book committed suicide," is read, it implicates the person holding the book. Suddenly aware of the author's final move, *how will the patron react? How will this biographical information affect their understanding of the book in their hands?*

Interior spread of *The Author of This Book Committed Suicide*, 2012.

(1)
For other projects related to author deaths,
see the catalogue entries for "The Missing Pieces"
and "Poets-Saints of July 06."

(2)
For a project that artistically intervenes on the exterior
of the book, see catalogue entry for "Hidden Histories."

Barcode Cornel West & Barcode Oprah

Blake, Scott. *Barcode Cornel West*. Omaha: printed by the author, 2013. 50 p.: ill.; 6.5 × 13.5 × .5 cm.

Blake, Scott. *Barcode Oprah*. Omaha: printed by the author, [2005]. 50 p.: ill.; 6.5 × 13.5 × .5 cm.

In the commercial book trade, an International Standard Book Number or ISBN is assigned to every edition and every variation in format or binding of that edition. The system was introduced in the 1970s. If one wanted to assemble a bibliography for a prolific author publishing from 1970 forward, say Cornel West, one way to track the many revised editions, translations, etc. would be to use the ISBN system.

To create a digitally networked portrait-as-flipbook, artist Scott Blake collected forty-two ISBN barcodes of the books written by Cornel West in *Barcode Cornel West*. If you flip the pages from the front cover to the back, a black-and-white headshot of West gradually morphs, zooming in closer and closer to his right eye. As the portrait becomes more abstract, the construction of the image is revealed to be made up of strategically placed ISBN barcodes.[1] If you flip the pages from the back cover to the front, a selection of West's books are visible—one per page—and show the title information and the ISBN barcode for each. Any of the barcodes can be scanned with a smart phone to automatically generate an online search to get more details about the book. The artist has also included a few Easter egg UPC codes for the scan-curious that play funny clips of West from Saturday Night Live and the *Matrix*.[2]

Blake has a whole series of different barcode flipbooks featuring portraits of cultural icons which are an offshoot of his wall-sized portraits. One of his earlier projects corresponds to the titles promoted by Oprah's Book Club. Blake used a total of 1,824 ISBN barcodes to create a mosaic of a smiling, youthful Oprah.[3] The flipbook is similar to *Barcode Cornel West* in form and layout. *Barcode Oprah* features a selection of books on the verso pages, this time delineating the author, title, and ISBN barcode information of Oprah-branded recommendations.

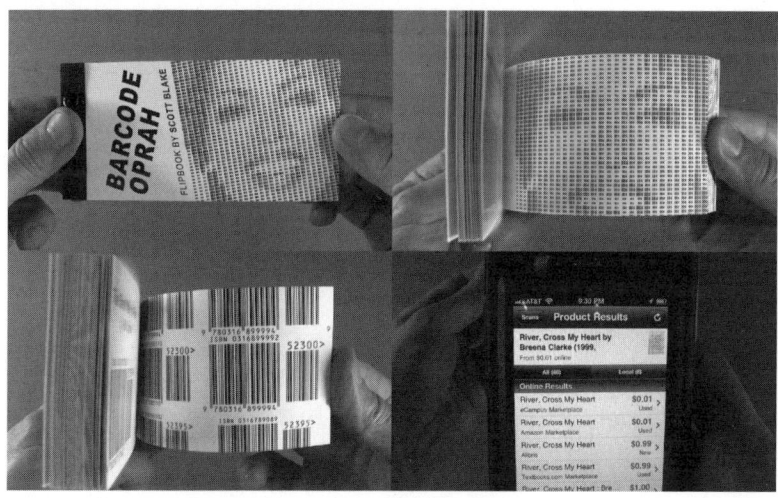

Barcode Oprah, [2005], in action.

These flipbooks may seem like novelty items. However, a lot of information is packed into a small book object and it's incidentally an example of a hybrid bibliography that tries to straddle the space between page and screen. The written works included in each bibliography are represented by their ISBN barcodes which are then brought together to form a portrait of their subject. There is no question about who or what is the organizing principle of these visual bibliographies. Blake may have seen the potential for ISBN barcodes to act as building blocks for an interactive artwork, but the portraits themselves make for a friendly bibliographic interface. Seeing the face of the icon creates a welcoming and personal invitation. It's like bibliographic devotional ephemera.

(1) And apparently if you were to count these, they'd number 2,521 ISBN barcodes. "Barcode Cornel West Flipbook," Scott Blake, accessed November 5, 2022, http://www.barcodeart.com/store/collectible/barcode_flipbooks/Cornel.html.
(2) Scott Blake, email message to author, December 6, 2022.
(3) "ISBN/Oprah/Book Club/Scaled," Scott Blake, accessed November 5, 2022, https://www.barcodeart.com/artwork/portraits/barcodes/isbn_oprah_scale_01.html. In 2000, Blake created three versions of Oprah's portrait with barcodes and one version with book cover images.

Barcode Cornel West, 2013, in action.

The Best American Book of the 20th Century

The Best American Book of the 20th Century*

A NOVEL

Société Réaliste

designed by Project Projects

"A novel of stunning power... unmatched by any American writer in this century—perhaps in any century"
—Richard Toney, *San Francisco Review of Books*†

ONOMATOPEE 100

The Best American Book of the 20th Century, 2014, cover.

Société Réaliste. *The Best American Book of the 20th Century: A Novel*. Designed by Projects Projects. Eindhoven, Netherlands: Onomatopee, 2014. 112 p.; 21 × 13 × 1 cm.

Société Réaliste. *The Best American Book of the 20th Century–Société Réaliste*. Exhibition at the Onomatopee project space, Eindhoven, Netherlands, August 21–October 26, 2014. Curated and edited by Niels van Tomme, Freek Lomme, Prem Krishnamurthy and Société Réaliste. Exhibition design by Niels Van Tomme (concept development and advice), Project Projects (graphic design), and Freek Lomme & Tineke Polak (production).

Société Réaliste. *The Best American Book of the 20th Century*. Special exhibition. New York: New York Art Book Fair PS1, September 26–29, 2014.

As someone wise once wrote, "any text is woven entirely with citations, references, echoes, cultural languages, which cut across it through and through in a vast stereophony. . . For substantially all ideas are secondhand, consciously and unconsciously drawn from a million outside sources. . ."[1] *The Best American Book of the 20th Century: A Novel* is indeed chock-full of the echoes of a bygone era but by design rather than by circumstance or coincidence.

Ferenc Gróf and Jean-Baptiste Naudy, the artists behind the Paris-based cooperative Société Réaliste (2004–2014), have assembled what at first blush looks like an ordinary paperback novel. *The Best American Book of the 20th Century* has the hallmarks of a work of fiction with descriptive passages and character dialogue. It has the trim size and heft of a slim, readable volume. However the narrative, set in a generous 14-point type with a gentle serif, was written using the cut-up technique. It excavates the world of mass-market literature. The selection and arrangement of its sentences is governed by a clearly defined set of rules:

> the first sentence of the first best-selling book of 1900, as listed;
> the second sentence of the second best-selling book of 1900, as listed;
> the third sentence of the third best-selling book of 1900, as listed;
> . . . and so on up to the end of the century, to the thousandth sentence of the tenth best-selling book of 1999.[2]

It is both an experiment in writing and a conceptual dare, carried out to the nth degree by Société Réaliste, the design studio Projects Projects, and the publisher Onomatopee.[3]

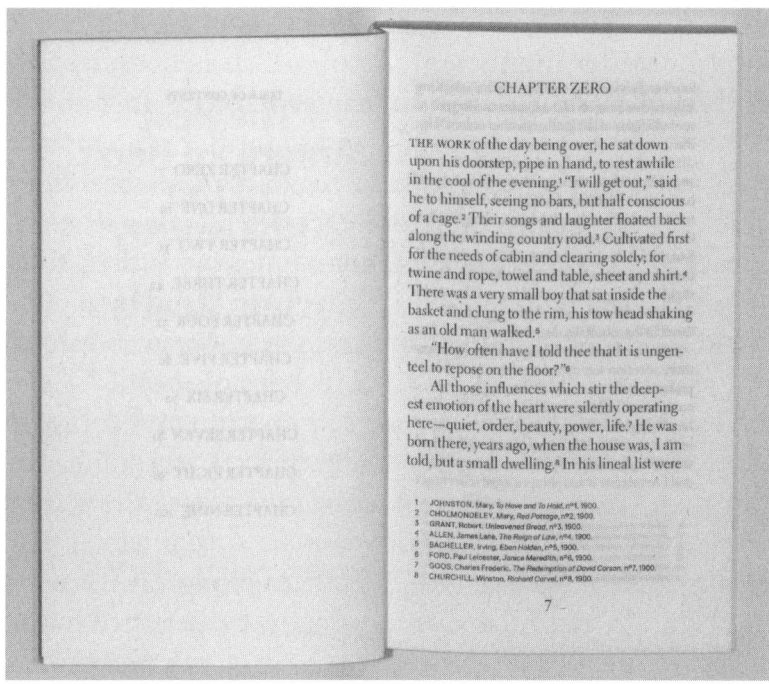

The Best American Book of the 20th Century,
2014, beginning of chapter 0.

Their historic title list is culled from the 20th-Century American Bestsellers Database which is compiled "by undergraduate and graduate students at the University of Virginia, the University of Illinois, Catholic University, and Brandeis University, from 1998 to the present, using the rankings from *Bowker's Annual/Publisher's Weekly*."[4] The database, while an incredible resource for bibliographic descriptions, publication and performance history, author bios, reception history, and critical analysis, contains very few full-text versions of the novels as the vast majority are still under copyright. So using the database as a starting point, Société Réaliste has had to locate every novel listed individually and dig into their texts.

The Best American Book of the 20th Century cleverly opens with a chapter numbered "Zero" which is dedicated to the bestsellers of the 1900s. Chapter 1 corresponds to the 1910s, chapter 2 to the 1920s, and so forth. Each sentence reads as an odd yet enjoyable surrogate for the novel from which it was plucked. Every reference behind every sentence is tracked with a tidy citation containing the author, title, bestseller ranking (e.g. n°1, n°2, n°3, etc.), and date published. One thousand continuously numbered footnotes run along the bottom margins in 8.5-point type.[5] Since the citations are brief, they are easy to skim and compare across pages. The reader can easily see what was popular in any given year. *Can one get a sense of the zeitgeist from these brief encounters?* There are many familiar author names (e.g. in the 1920s, Sinclair Lewis, Frances Hodgson Burnett, and Edith Wharton) and titles which have persisted in the public eye (e.g. in the 1960s, J. D. Salinger's *Franny and Zooey*, Harper Lee's *To Kill a Mockingbird*, and Mario Puzo's *The Godfather*). Certainly there are plenty of lesser-known references scattered throughout the century, too, despite their popularity at the time.

In terms of editorial decision-making, the artist collective has replaced any proper nouns with pronouns to facilitate some narrative cohesion. They've also leaned in to the use of paragraphing for sense-making. The reader attempting to peruse the novel may come up with their own bizarre connections to parse out the wild intertextual relationships therein. Occasionally, and surprisingly, flickers of recognition do transpire when characters or environments or bits of conversation recur, as some novels have appeared on more than one year's list of best-selling books. Still, some passages are totally oblique while others do persuasively hold together. One such lucky example of the latter can be found on page 35:

"Lord!" Well, you may go to heaven now if you really desire it, and if you know what heaven means. Scarcely were the words spoken when she was gone with the quickness of a bird, her long hair streaming about her like a veil as she ran.[6]

The project is at the outset serious fun, well-designed and approachable. It is an exciting experiment executed with skill, the best of the best American fiction in 112 pages. *The Best American Book of the 20th Century* gives us a new lens through which to reflect on the last century and its well-loved and forgotten literary hits.

---

(1) Jonathan Letham, "The Ecstasy of Influence: A Plagiarism," *Harper's Magazine*, February 2007, 68, "plagiarizing" Roland Barthes and then Mark Twain here.

(2) Société Réaliste, *The Best American Book of the 20th Century* (Eindhoven, Netherlands: Onomatopee, 2014), back cover.

(3) The novel was released and exhibited in the Onomatopee project space and then at the New York Art Book Fair. The exhibition at Onomatopee took the form of a tradeshow-style display of boxes of books artfully stacked into a twisting tower flanked by a few loose copies.

(4) Société Réaliste, *The Best American Book*, back cover. The 20th-Century American Bestsellers Database can be found at http://bestsellers.lib.virginia.edu/.

(5) For projects that heavily utilize the possibilities of the footnote, see the catalogue entries for "Study Room Guides" and "Wherein the Author. . ."

(6) Société Réaliste, *The Best American Book*, 35, referencing three books from 1924—*The Little French Girl* by Anne Douglas Sedwick, *The Heirs Apparent* by Philip Gibbs, and *A Gentleman of Courage* by James Oliver Curwood.

Bib., Rev. Ed.

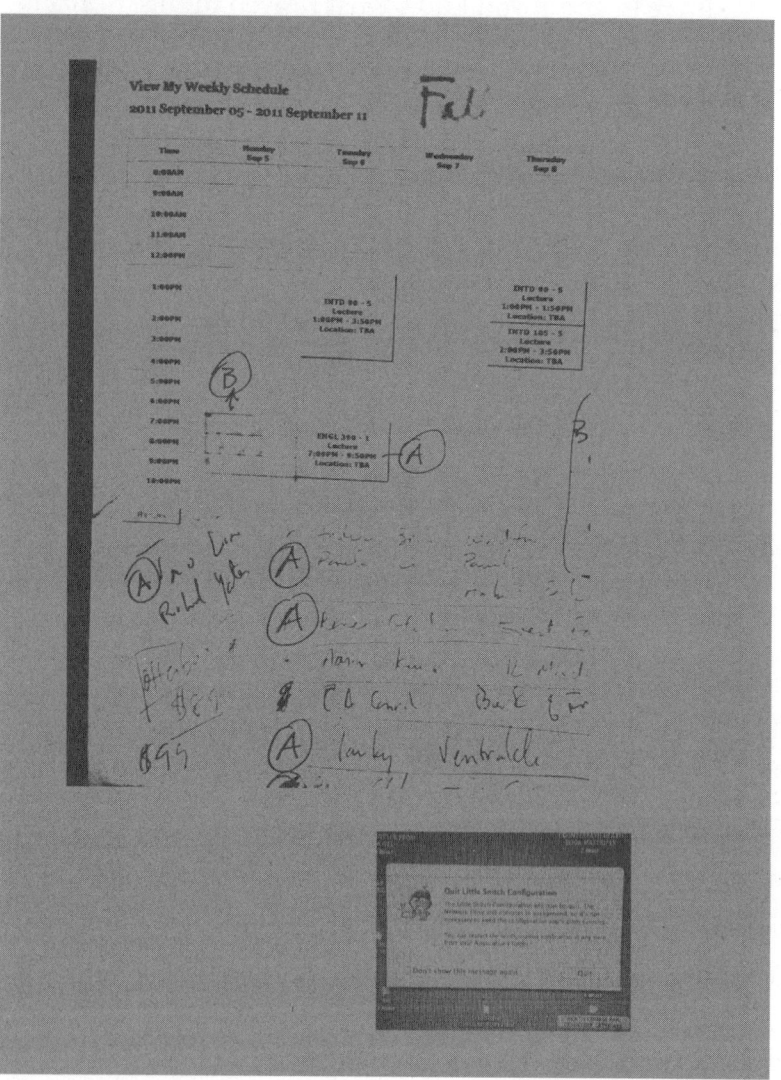

Bib., Rev. Ed., 2011, cover design.

Lin, Tan.
Ambient Fiction Reading System 01 (blog).
2006–2007.
http://ambientreading.blogspot.com/.
    Lin, Tan.
    Bib.
    Ubu Editions, 2007.
    http://www.ubu.com/ubu/unpub
    /Unpub_018_Lin_BIB.pdf.
        Lin, Tan.
        Bib., Rev. Ed.
        Vienna: Westphalie, 2011.
        152 p.: ill.;
        21.5 × 28 × 2 cm.
            Lin, Tan.
            Bib., Rev. Ed.
            Vienna: Westphalie,2011.
            https://issuu.com/westphalie
            /docs/bib._rev.ed.
            152 p.: ill.

This is me reading... This is reading.

On January 10, 2006, poet and author Tan Lin started cataloging everything he read, every day. He dutifully recorded the date, time, and location, as well as what was being read, and how much of it was read.

Thursday, April 13, 2006

5:59–6:05 NY WATERWAY Librarians Win As US Relents on Secrecy Law
6:05–7 Tycoon of Chinese Real Estate Is Leasing at Trade Center Site
6:18–24 LIGHT RAIL Run Windows and Mac OS Both at Once
6:27–31 Excuses from the Jury Pool: He's Heard it All
8:55–9:20 PATH Alain Badiou The Inaesthetic 5 pages[1]

Over a year's worth of this data was published to *Ambient Fiction Reading System 01*, Lin's asynchronous blog project; then it was reformatted as *Bib.*, a digital book in Ubu's Publishing the Unpublishable series.[2] *Bib., Rev. Ed.* is an artist's book published by Westphalie Verlag that collects all the dated entries from 2006 through July 21, 2008.[3] Within any given log entry Lin encounters written language in the form of mail, email, newspapers, magazines, scholarly journals, all kinds of books, and a plethora of information online. He keeps a careful account too, delineating the number of emails or student papers he reads within a time frame. When he is particularly interested in remembering a piece of writing, he pastes the entire article into the accumulating bibliography. Some days are filled with notations, other days only have a few references, and occasionally a day goes by where nothing is read (or read and recorded). The locations in Lin's reading universe are primarily on public transit, e.g. Bus #10; at the school where he teaches, e.g. NJCU faculty dining room; and in his house, e.g. Couch L/R. Amidst all of these bits of information, one can flesh out the different scenarios in which Lin is reading. He is sitting or standing; he is likely surrounded by people or possibly alone; he is browsing the Internet or deep reading.

As a language project, Lin's self-produced report is in the vein of an expanded Google Analytics, tracing every act of his personal reading online *and* offline. Abbreviated daily entries cross back and forth between low brow and high brow texts. His extreme transparency washes over you, until something catches your eye:

February 27, 2006

9:27-34 HOME OFFICE Ratemyprofessors.com 'Tan Lin Ethan Bumas Hilary Englert Chris Cunningham Mary Blanchard'[4]

As a bibliography, it functions as a time capsule of news stories, popular culture, and trends in academia, but also as an archive of platforms and formats. In the short time since *Bib., Rev. Ed.* was written, some of the references have already begun to show their age. For instance, 2007-Lin reads CD liner notes, peruses Yahoo Finance pages, and checks his Ebay account.

Bib., Rev. Ed. is yes, about the act of reading, but it's also about our active immersion in the bibliographic web of daily life. The sheer number of occurrences in Lin's catalog shows the reader a new contemporary reality and ushers in a self-awareness regarding how it is we touch information every day. Lin considers this enmeshment—all of these engaged and flitting acts of reading—ambient reading. *This is reading* according to *Bib., Rev. Ed.*

(1) Tan Lin, *Bib., Rev. Ed.* (Vienna: Westphalie, 2011), 24.
(2) The blog's all caps tagline says it well: "A LIST OF THINGS I READ DIDN'T READ AND HARDLY READ FOR EXACTLY ONE YEAR."
(3) In *Bib., Rev. Ed.* Lin extends the project into 2011 adding an introduction, a link history for September 8–12, 2011, and several photos taken "before the project was sent to the press (September 17–18, 2011)." "BIB., REV. ED.," Art Metropole, accessed March 20, https://artmetropole.com/shop/5228. Also of note, David Jourdan the publisher of Westphalie has published two experimental bibliographies as well: *Untitled (Ritournelle)* (Vienna: Westphalie, 2016) and *The Promise of Total Automation* (Berlin: Sternberg Press, 2018) coedited with Anne Faucheret.
(4) Lin, *Bib., Rev. Ed.*, 17.

11:02 HOME OFFICE 2 emails
11:03-6 NYPost.com Slain Co-Ed

Wednesday, March 1, 2006

2:45 LIVING ROOM New York Mag "Scarlett's Ex Carries a Torch Song"
2:46 "A Bioterrorist at the Biennial"
2:47 Party Lines "What was your worst NY apartment" Amanda Peet
2:48-50 Books "Keeping Up with the Dead" The Dead Beat by Marilyn Johnson
11:35-7 HOME OFFICE 3 emails
11:37-9 Google.com "Sebastian Junger" "Glue" "Jessica Rankin" "Roland Barthes and Photography"

12:02 LIVING ROOM Comments Push Down Google 7%
12:03 Jet Blue to Try New Route to Profitability: Higher Prices

Thursday, March 2, 2006

4:31 HOME OFFICE Yahoofinance.com Your Porfolios "Speculate"
4:32 The Street.com "DRAM diversity refreshes"
4:33 NY Mag "Best Bets Epson Movie Mate DVD Projetor" "Preventing those Toe Chiller Moments" "A No Brainer Thermometer"
4:44 The Look Book "Kate Chapman Gallery Assistant"
4:45 "A Lamp for Every Room" Biagio Table Light" "Fold Light"
4:46-7 Market Driven The Goods Essex Street Market DiPialo's
4:49 Real Estate Out with the New, In with the Newer
4:49 Triple Assessment 120 Riverside Drive
5:21 NYTimes About New York Filling all the Pockets Except his Own
5:25-8 Public Library Buys a Trove of Burroughs Papers (organized by date, subject matter or whim)
5:30-4 London Journal They Stole $92 Million, but What Can They have Done with It (game show/lottery)
5:36-7 Calm Suspect Shocks France in TV Talk about Killing
5:38 Cheaspeake Oystermen, in Decline, Place Hopes in an Asian Import
5:41 Yahoofinance.com OmniVision's Future Looking Cleaner The Motley Fool

7:24 DINING ROOM TABLE NY Times Richard Meier Condos Dressed Accordingly
7:25 From China to Chairs
7:38-40 When the TV Picture Runs to Trip Digits
7:40-1 From Blogger to Published Author, for $30 and Up

7:45-6 MacWorms Crash the OS X Party
7:46-51 Apple Laptop Has Looks and Brains
7:56-8:03 Stretched to Limit, Women Stall March to Work
8:18-24 Who Killed Student? 17 Hour Gap Holds Answer
8:24-6 US Is Reducing Safety Penalties for Mine Flaws
8:27 In Paris Splashes of Black
8:28-30 Booted Off an Island Called Manhattan

11:32-53 Kasia Houlihan "Roland Barthes' Camera Lucida"
11:53-9 Summary: Camera Lucida
11:59-1:18 Roland Barthess Camera Lucida 25 pages

Friday, March 3, 2006

8:29-36 HOME OFFICE NYTimes Biennial 2006: Short on Pretty, Long on Collaboration
8:46-48 NYTimes Archive "Murder for the Millions"
8:49-9:02 NYTimes.com Questions For Mike Leigh Connie Mack Herbie Hancock

9:07 LIVING ROOM A Heroine in a Hurry, Via Ibsen

6:34-6 Tradingmarkets.com 7 Stocks You Need to Know For Monday
6:26 - dot-cum.com
6:26- Lev Manovich The Language of New Media
10:16-23 In Baby Boomlet, Preschool Derby is the Fiercest Yet
10:34-5 NYTimes.com Between High and Low

Saturday, March 4, 2006

11:55-7 DINING ROOM TABLE NY TIMES Art Military Maneuvers with Computer and Color
12:07-9 NYTimes Mag Questions for Bruce Katz Battle for the 'Burbs'
12:14-16 It is What it Is

7:51-2 HOME OFFICE Women is the Story of Man (Hong)
8:10-51 Manovich Language of New Media 57 pages
10:40-11:30 John Cayley The Code is Not The Text

Sunday, March 5, 2006
2:05-10 SUBWAY NYTimes "The Art of Building a Robot to Love"
2:10-14 The Ads Discriminate But Does the Web
3:24-29 PS1 Peter Burger Theory of the Avant Garde 2 pages
5:24-45 Burger 8 pages

Monday, March 6, 2006

2:12-22 LIVING ROOM SOFA Carl Rakosi Droles de Journal

2:54- HOME OFFICE Peter Burger Theory of the A-G 11 pages
3:45 -4:20 Mitchell London Foods NY Mag Best of NY skimmed
5:45-6:55 HOME OFFICE Wikipedia.com interface header file modular C++, Manovich New Media 4 pages
11:10 LIVING ROOM OFFICE NY Mag Best of NY

Tuesday, March 7, 2006

12:57-1:07 LIVING ROOM NY Times Los Angeles Retains Custody of Oscar
1:10-13 Making Sure that the Gone are Never Really Forgotten"
1:14-20 Bouncer's Home Searched in Student's Killing
1:21-23 Landmark Ferry Building May Become Food Market
1:25-27 Whites to Be Minority in New York Area Soon, Data Show
1:29 Urban Riddles, Best Pondered in aa Long Line
1:29 Questions Rise from the Dust of an Old Synagogue
1:30 Path Track at Trade Center is Scrapped
1:33-40 Many Coupeles Must Negotiate Terms of Brokeback Marriages

1:57-2:04 HOME OFFICE 4 emails ebay listings
2:08 Cnn.com Cybercrime on the Rise
2:16-6:17 Matthew Gold The Expert Hand and the Obedient Hand: Dr. Vittoz, T.S. Eliot, and the Therapeutic Possibilities of The Waste Land. Lambert Zuidwevaart, The Social Significance of Autonomous Art: Adorno and Burger 3 pages. John Cayley, Literal Art 8 pages. Juan Suarez T.S. Eliot's The Waste Land, the Gamophone, and the Modernist Discourse Network.

6:50-7:03 willtoexchange.blogspot.com/2005/06/interview-with-k-silem-mohammad.html
9:05- 45 John Cayley Inner Workings code and representations of interiority in new media poetics 4 pages
11:03-12:07 Cayley 8 pages

Wednesday, March 8, 2006

9:52-7 LIVING ROOM NY Times For Trader Joe's, a New York Taste Test
9:57-9 A Dining Circle Dresse up and Savors a Bygone Era
10:03-5 Edelweiss, With A Dash of Oompah
10:08-10 Time for Some Irish, but why the Wait
10:10 The Last Flight of the Torilla Chip
10:10-12 Federal Grants of $27 Million are set to Aid Cultural Activity Downtown
10:15-20 Reality TV For Those Infatuated with Passing
10:21-2 Greenspan Book Deal is Said to be Among the Richest

Thursday, March 9, 2006
2:21-36 HOME OFFICE Charles Bernstein The Sophist 12 pages
2:36-48 John Cayley Inner Workings 5 pages
2:48-3:07 Katherine Hayles Print is Flat, Code is Deep 8 pages
3:07-56 Lev Manovich The Language of New Media The Interface Transcoding
3:56-58 K. Silem Mohammed Deer Head Nation 3 poems
3:58-403 Noah Gordon review of The Sound of the Subtone

Friday, March 10, 2006

11:19-21 LIVING ROOM NY Times The World Tour Rolls into Town, Sprawing but Tidy
11:21 Diner's Guide The Orchard Blaue Gans Del Posto
11:28-30 Where Buy Low and Sell High are a Co-Op's Fighting Words
11:30 Company Erros on SAT Scores Raise new Qualms About Testing
11:30-2 Jerry Saltz Biennial in Babylon
11:42 HOME OFFICE Tradingmarkets.com 7 Stocks you need to know for Friday
11:43 CBOE.com calls vs. puts
11:53 The Motley Fool The Latest Losers
1:02-3:45 Geoffrey Winthrop-Young Silicon Sociology, or, Two Kings on Hegel's Throne? Kittler, Luhmann, and the Posthuman Merger of German Media Theory.10 pages
Nicholas Gane Radical Post-Humanism Friedrich Kittler and the Primacy of Technology 16 pages
3:45-4:05 Marjorie Perloff Radical Artifice 12 pages
4:05-45 Yahoofinance.com MOGN analyst opionions. Etrade.com research MOGN LU THOR ANN
8:10-9:21 Silcon Sociology 4 pages

Saturday, March 11, 2006

12:06-8 DINING ROOM NYTimes Symbol of Abu Ghraaib Seeks to Spare Others His Nightmare
12:08 Profumo Scanda Focus Dies
Sunday, March 12, 2006

4:16-18 LIVING ROOM NY Times Alive and Well in Silicon Alley
4:19-21 Buttoned up bouncers on Defensive
4:21 Peasant Chic, No Permafrost
4:22 The Actress What I'm Wearing Now

5:59-6:04 DINING ROOM TABLE Police Say DNA Links Bounce to Body of Slain Student
6:04-8 Two Killings that Didn't Make News

7:43-9 HOME OFFICE L. Suidervaart The Social Significance of Autonomous Art: Adorno and Burger 5 pages

8:22-5 LIVING ROOM NY Times Book Review The Postmodern Novelist

Interior pages of *Bib., Rev. Ed.*, 2011.

Bibliographic Sound Track & The Ph.D Sound

Lin, Tan.
Bibliographic Sound Track, 2012. PowerPoint performance.
A video projection of the work premiered at Ludlow 38/MINI Goethe-Institut on March 31, 2012, and at Artists Space on July 24, 2012.

Lin, Tan.
The Ph.D Sound, 2012. PowerPoint performance.
A video projection of the work premiered at the MINI/Goethe-Institut Curatorial Residencies at Ludlow 38 on March 31, 2012, and at Artists Space on July 24, 2012. With a soundtrack by DJ Mösco.

Lin, Tan.
Bibliographic Sound Track, 2012. PowerPoint recording, 39 min., 56 sec. https://www.youtube.com/watch?v=-RQwXlbSRuE.

Lin, Tan.
The Ph.D Sound, 2012. PowerPoint recording, 15 min., 28 sec. With a soundtrack by DJ Mösco. https://www.youtube.com/watch?v=-wsNf8VtvBs.

The "I Designed It Myself" Effect in Mass Customization
Nikolaus Franke Institute for Entrepreneurship and Innovation, Vienna User Innovation Research Initiative, WU Vienna

University of Economics and Business, A-1090 Vienna, Austria, nikolaus.franke@wu.ac.at **Martin Schreier** Marketing Institute, Department of Management and Center for Research on Organization and Management, Bocconi University, I-20136 Milan, Italy,

martin.schreier@unibocconi.it **Ulrike Kaiser** Institute for Entrepreneurship and Innovation, Vienna User Innovation Research

Initiative, WU Vienna Universi of Econor ar Bu: A

Nov 21, 2011
846 notes http://fuckyeahmenswear.tumblr.com/
Accessed 2012-01-05 5:51PM EST

The Ph.D Sound
PowerPoint recording,
2012,
screenshot.

Bibliography can be the description of all kinds of things, of everything really. It's a way of mapping and understanding the material world. A good cataloger will tell you that they can catalog anything, no matter how challenging it may seem at the outset. In 2012 Tan Lin screened two PowerPoint recordings at Ludlow 38/MINI Goethe-Institut and Artists Space respectively that tap into the universe of a confident cataloger, poetically processing the kinds of uncloaked metadata that zip through our minds, environments, and computational devices. *Bibliographic Sound Track* was accompanied by a live perfume soundtrack that scented the air and *The Ph.D Sound* had a live DJ set by Mösco.[1] Both were projected with the lights out for silent reading and later made available on YouTube.

Bibliographic Sound Track is a soundless mixtape, a raw visio-verbal performance, and an unhurried PPT experiment.[2] Publications, objects, and communication platforms are scraped and fragmented in a steady stream of animated texts for forty minutes and seven seconds. Dates, times, names, titles, temperatures, page numbers, file types, URLs, color codes, and model numbers all stroll across a black background interspersed with occasional, excitable color blocks. Poetic interludes—passages found in Tumblrs, role-playing video games, and maybe even composed by Lin himself—address "you" and "I" and appear and disappear on screen. Lines are segmented to arrive in timed fragments, unordering the beginnings, middles, and ends of passages. Bulleted lists are not parallel. Word maps are fields of unrelated topics. This is writing staged to disorient. A language of vertigo for the reader to cycle round.

Lin has referred to *Bibliographic Sound Track* as a "mood-based system" and that "these mood-based systems, which are common to Zen meditative states, are bottom-up, non-directed, allotropic modes of general receptiveness."[3] A viewer's sense-making skills may want to kick into high gear though it may be best to relax and wait for something to resonate: "BOUNCE | BOUNCE | SNUGGLE."[4] A beat quickly shifts to a sequence about laundry brands when the last word is revealed. Lin examines the death and resurrection of the piano on another slide. In a series of deft moves he links the *Vertigo* score to Erik Satie's *Vexations* to jazz musician Ornette Coleman to John Cage's *4'33"* to the destruction of the piano in a work by George Maciunas which "brought the piano back to life."[5] The theory behind the work is embedded in the work.

In *The Ph.D Sound*, textual citations of scholarly books, articles, and online links about branding, selfhood in relation to goods, behavioral science, and the psychology of consumerism play out to danceable, upbeat music. Resources like D. W. Dahl and C. P. Moreau's "Thinking Inside the Box: Why Consumers Enjoy Constrained Creative Experiences," M. Csikszentmihalyi and E. Rochberg-Halton's *The Meaning of Things: Domestic Symbols of Self*, and http://fuckyeahmenswear.tumblr.com/ are revealed inside bright RGB-colored boxes, once again set on a black backdrop. Paragraph- and slide-transition features built into PowerPoint are tweaked to allow bibliographic citations to appear letter-by-letter as if live-typed or to glide in from the left or right as a solid block. There is no strict order of the elements in any given citation—e.g., does the author come before or after the article title? does the citation begin or end with a stable URL? Serif and sans serif texts of various sizes interact to emphasize or minimize each element. URLs are underlined, random elements shift in color or appear in bold, and italic only rarely exists.

Bibliographic Sound Track and *The Ph.D Sound* are time-based bibliographies. They are multimedia literary works that collect and propel surrogate readings. They are not selective but exhaustive. Through a method of unveiling waves of information, the reader comes into contact with the boredom and exuberance of bibliographic networks, the Internet of Things, and mediated communications swirling around in bits and bytes.

(1) Tan Lin's latest and ongoing biblio-literary endeavor *The Fern Rose Bibliography* delves into the olfactory and sense memories as well. See the first chapter of an anticipated 24-chapter novel, Tan Lin, *The Fern Rose Bibliography*, Cookie Jar (Andy Warhol Foundation Arts Writers Grant, 2022), https://cookiejar.artswriters.org/#cookiejar. Tan Lin, email message to author, February 6, 2023.
(2) Lin has said that his original idea was to make a 24-hour piece for "drift-like distracted reading." Tan Lin, "'Bibliographic Sound Track' and 'The Ph.D. Sound': Tan Lin" (screening and lecture, Woodberry Poetry Room, Harvard University, Cambridge, MA, March 4, 2014, 32:03–33:30).
(3) Tan Lin, "A Book is Technology: An Interview with Tan Lin," interview by Angela Genusa, *Rhizome*, Oct 24, 2012, https://rhizome.org/editorial/2012/oct/24/interview-tan-lin/.
(4) Tan Lin, *Bibliographic Sound Track*, 2012, PowerPoint recording, 17:00, https://www.youtube.com/watch?v=-RQwXIbSRuE.
(5) Lin, *Bibliographic Sound Track*, 12:28.

Bibliography of Architecture Theory

Emilio Rodríguez Almeida. *Forma Urbis Marmorea: Aggiornamento Generale 1980*, 2 vols. Roma: Quasar, 1981.	Giovanni Battista Piranesi. *Opere*. Multiple vols. Roma, 1750–1807. [Prints of Antichità Romane.]	Piranesi. *Opere*. [Prints of Campo Marzio.]	Piranesi. *Opere*. [Prints of Carceri d'Invenzione.]	Daniel Libeskind. *Daniel Libeskind: Cecil Balmond, Unfolding*. Rotterdam: NAi, 1998.
city plan	splendid	memory	toil	unfolding
shards	ruins	drawn	stacks	infinity
missing	mystery	reenactments	fractures	journey
pieces	overgrowth	imaginary	disorienting	segmented
assembly	decay	constructions	fictions	space
maps				spirals
Filarete. *Treatise on Architecture*, 2 vols. Translation and facsimile. New Haven, CT: Yale University Press, 1965.	Vitruvius Pollio. *I Dieci Libri dell'Architettura Di M. Vitruvio*. Venetia: Francesco de Franceschi, 1584.	Leon Battista Alberti. *L'Architecture et Art de Bien Bastir*. Paris: J. Kerver, 1553.	William C. Gannett. *House Beautiful*. Boston: James H. West, 1895.	William C. Gannett and Frank Lloyd Wright. *House Beautiful*. River Forest, IL: Auvergne Press, 1897.
Adam	technique	theoretic	lily	prairie
centering	know-how	art	furnishings	dresses
geometry	precise	makings	stamp	tangle
humanist	situation	ornamented	thanksgiving	word
Sforzinda	etchings	disciplines	praise	settings
El Lissitzky. *Lissitzky's 1st Kestner Portfolio*, 1923. Reprint, Rotterdam, Holland: Van Hezik-Fonds, 1992.	Zaha Hadid. *Zaha Hadid: Planetary Architecture Two*. London: Architectural Association, 1983.	Le Corbusier. *Vers Une Architecture*. Paris: G. Crès et cie., 1924.	Le Corbusier. *Aircraft*. New York: The Studio, 1935.	Alison Smithson. *AS in DS: An Eye on the Road*, 1983. Reprint, Baden: Lars Müller, 2001.
axonometric	hover	aerial	flight	windshield
projections	tilt	X	formations	atmospheres
determine	sway	marks	jump	capture
new	landforms	upward	shadow	shifting
publics	revolution	plan	landscapes	horizons
Uriel Birnbaum. *Der Kaiser Und Der Architekt*. Leipzig: Thyrsos, 1924.	Paolo Soleri. *Arcology: The City in the Image of Man*. Cambridge, MA: MIT Press, 1969.	John Ruskin. *The Seven Lamps of Architecture*. 4th ed. Sunnyside, England: G. Allen, 1889.	Ben Nicholson. *Appliance House*. Chicago: Chicago Institute for Architecture and Urbanism, 1990.	
dream-state	eco-astro	aging	cupboard	
questions	desert	time	action	
glow	hippie	preserves	consumer	
iterative	vision	craft	collage	
cities	system	production	dwelling	

Bibliography of Architecture Theory

Bibliography of Architecture Theory, 2016, poster.

Rebel, Janelle.
Bibliography of Architecture Theory.
Selection by Ben Nicholson.
Chicago: printed by the artist, 2015.
1 folded leaf: col. ill.;
42 × 60 cm.

Rebel, Janelle.
Bibliography of Architecture Theory.
Selection by Ben Nicholson.
Chicago: printed by the artist, 2016.
1 folded leaf: ill.;
43.5 × 28 cm.

Architecture theory can be philosophical, fantastical, satirical, or rooted in practice. It can reflect on the past; it can meditate on the future. *Bibliography of Architecture Theory* brings a set of diverse primary resources and key writings together from the Western traditions, held by the Ryerson & Burnham Libraries at the Art Institute of Chicago, and chosen by Ben Nicholson for a class visit. The one-sided foldout poster written and designed by Janelle Rebel uses citations and experimental annotations to describe works that span from the 1750s to the 1990s. The annotations are visually larger than the citations and consist of five to six word stacks that use natural language with all its "ambiguities and contradictions."[1] For example, Uriel Birnbaum's *Der Kaiser Und Der Architeckt* (1924) is "dream-state | questions | glow | iterative | cities" and Alison Smithson's *AS in DS: An Eye on the Road* (1983) is "windshield | atmospheres | capture | shifting | horizons."[2] Each bibliographic word poem is based on examining, handling, and skimming an extant physical copy. In an attempt to open up a work and loose the bound ideas à la Karl W. Bührer, the descriptions seek to give a work of theory new mobility.[3] By circumventing the world of subject headings, controlled vocabularies, and artificial languages, these annotations are human-scale but not reductive, aiming to animate rather than drill down the material.

The bibliography invites reading and the reader can jump in at any entry. Visually there is no "correct" place to start. Conceptually, one could begin in the upper left corner with the documentation of the lost map of ancient Rome (the famed Forma Urbis Romae or Severan Marble Plan) whose material shards have fascinated artists and intellectuals for centuries. For instance, in the eighteenth century Giovanni Battista Piranesi tried to *image* Rome, incorporating several of the marble fragments into the picture plane of his *Antichità Romane* etchings: "splendid | ruins | mystery | overgrowth | decay."[4]

Although the potential to see and compare works between rows and columns is accommodated, the grid layout of *Bibliography of Architecture Theory* may be too strict for the jumble of ideas it represents. A set of cards or an interactive media project would allow sets of relationships to be grouped and regrouped, and additional entries to be added to this limited list.

(1) For a brief discussion of Gottfried Wilhelm Leibniz's investigations into natural and artificial languages, see Susanne Bieri, "Art: Introduction," in *The Dynamic Library*, ed. Ariane Roth and Marina Schütz, trans. Alta L. Price (Chicago: Soberscove Press, 2015), 62.

(2) Janelle Rebel, *Bibliography of Architecture Theory*, selection by Ben Nicholson (Chicago: Janelle Rebel, 2016).

(3) Although not well known in library science, Bührer in the 1890s–1910s saw a future for knowledge in unbound books, "the ideal mobility of written sets of thoughts." His writings "called for the library as a whole to be converted into a kind of card file." Anthon Astrom, Fabian Wegmüller, and Lukas Zimmer, "New Orders of Knowledge," in *The Dynamic Library*, 55.

(4) Rebel, *Bibliography of Architecture Theory*.

Bibliomania

* Morris, Simon, ed. *Bibliomania*. York, England: information as material, [1998–2004]. Online database. Constructed by Christine Morris. http://www.bibliomania.org.uk/. Archived at https://web.archive.org/web/20040101125938/http://www.bibliomania.org.uk/.

* Morris, Simon, and Helen Sacoor, curators. *Bibliomania*. Designed by Peter McGrath of Goundwork Design Ltd. York and London: printed by the curators, 1999. 120 p.: ill.; 22.5 × 17 × 1 cm.

* Morris, Simon, curator. *Bibliomania 2000/2001*. Undesigned by Pavel Büchler. York, England: information as material, 2002. 619 p.: ill.; 29.5 × 21 × 4.5 cm.

Susan Hiller's entry in *Bibliomania 2000/2001*, 2002.

Bibliomania is a sprawling, expansive endeavor that began in 1998 as a meta-artwork and curatorial project by Simon Morris and Helen Sacoor. They solicited fifteen international artists and curators to submit a list of book recommendations based on their respective interests and working practices, with an emphasis on identifying in-print titles. Morris writes: "The project hypothesizes that the 'reading list' is a formal structure through which meaning is made. It visually represents a cognitive map of each artist's conceptual or intellectual concerns."[1] Like endeavors to study the artist's studio with the hopes of better understanding the influences, techniques, and aims of that artist, *Bibliomania* seeks to investigate the artist's library—thinking through what materials have been selected and "how they are ordered / arranged / collated / shelved."[2]

The conceptual underpinnings of *Bibliomania* are inspired by the work of those first contributors: Julie Ault, Victor Burgin, Ben Crane, Neil Cummings, Mark Dion, Andrea Fraser, Matthew Higgs, Daniel Jackson, Joseph Kosuth, Marysia Lewandowska, Jeremy Millar, Hans Ulrich Obrist, Cindy Smith, Haim Steinbach, and Greville Worthington.[3] In 1999, participants' book selections were used to create rotating interventions at two locations of Waterstones, a popular British bookstore chain, that offered

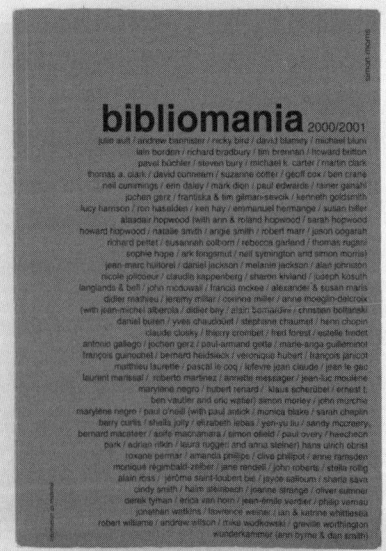

Bibliomania 2000/2001, 2002, cover.

the books for sale. In these performances, *Bibliomania* was a three-dimensional bibliography perched on the bookstore shelf and ready to circulate through conventional channels of bookseller and book buyer. The bookshop "exhibitions" were nearly invisible, utilizing the retailer's bookshelves and signage, and injecting art experiences into the everyday. The full list of titles by contributor was compiled and presented as an exhibition catalog, also called *Bibliomania* (1999).

The *Bibliomania* project rapidly branched out as an initiative and extension of Morris's collaborative art practice. The original fifteen participants were asked to invite an array of "new and existing voices" to contribute booklists; the online database www.bibliomania.org.uk launched to offer the lists as openly accessible HTML texts; and exhibitions were staged in bookstores, libraries, and galleries in Leeds, London, and New York.[4] Soon the project ballooned from thirty contributors to a global network of over 150 artists, curators, art historians, filmmakers, psychoanalysts, theorists, and writers. From Morris's view, "it is always better to operate on a policy of inclusion as opposed to exclusion."[5]

By 2002, Morris published the book *Bibliomania 2000/2001*, a hefty telephone-book directory of entries arranged alphabetically by contributor. The entries are written in French or English, range in length from one to twenty-eight pages, and contain a mix of sincere and nonsensical recommendations. The publication project, like the website and exhibition program, intends to operate as an artwork that contains other artworks, that shows the thought processes of different cultural workers through a bibliographic lens. While a theoretically thought-provoking assemblage publication and work of experimental writing, *Bibliomania 2000/2001* does not provide enough editorial context for the reader. Because of the collaborative nature

Joseph Kosuth's bibliographical selection in Waterstone's, Albion Street, Leeds, 1999.

of the participant selection, many names are unfamiliar (e.g., lesser-known but established artists, students, etc.); and unless a contributor folded a few personal details into their written submission, the entries are not supplemented by biographical information. *Why would the reader feel compelled to sift through these personal bibliographies?* The project assumes that the reader is already familiar with participants' work and thus curious about their bibliographic choices, or, that this or that bibliographic submission can stand alone on its own merits. The artistic and intellectual networks that have formed as a result of *Bibliomania* could have also been teased out, offering readers nodes of familiarity and hospitality. *Who invited who? Who is connected and how?*

The reader needs some way to meet the thinkers and makers driving this project to immerse themselves in the mania.[6]

One of the many challenges of working on a compendium of this scale is figuring out how much design is the right amount of design as well as respecting individual authorial intention. For *Bibliomania 2000/2001*, Morris worked with Czech artist Pavel Büchler to "undesign" the edition and was careful not to alter the presentation of contributors' submissions, considering each entry to constitute an artist's work and a visual representation of their interiority.[7] Morris notes: "If contributors wanted to handwrite their submission, it was represented in that form. If they submitted their selection word-processed in Arial, I reproduced it in Arial."[8] By and large participants focused on the work of conceptualizing, selecting, compiling, and ordering a list of resources, and gathering author, title, facts of publication, and/or ISBN information for their submissions. There is less variation in form and style than one might expect from a compilation of text-based artworks.[9] The display variants

Simon Morris' book selection next to Auguste Rodin's *Age of Bronze* (1876), *Bibliomania in the museum* (15 contributors), curated by Simon Morris and Helen Sacoor at Leeds City Art Gallery, July—August 1999.

are subtle, for example, in the number of columns, the use of indents or tabs, the margin settings, and the size of the type. The system defaults of word processing and email programs current at the time are prevalent throughout the anthology, and the inclusion of images is rare. Many contributors have not utilized the space of the page in the way that say a copy artist might. The only designed elements structuring the experience are small vertical running heads, page numbers, and participant names. Undesigning, while perhaps a democratic impulse, marks a refusal to contextualize someone else's work. In doing so here, the resulting book is not visually inviting and keeps the reader at a safe distance.

Nevertheless, several distinct contributions flit in and out of *Bibliomania 2000/2001*. For Mark Dion's entry, a duration of time is represented via fax. On different occasions he sent in images of his notebook pages, a scanned bibliography from a book he authored, and an addendum to these lists in a handwritten note to Morris.[10] Susan Hiller points readers off the page, opting to list a single website typeset across the gutter of a two-page spread: "http://www.diacenter.org/hiller/dreamresource.html."[11] "Summer shelf 2000" and "Winter list 2000/2001" are the brainchild of Claudia Kappenberg who regularly compiles her home reading-shelf by season.[12] Jane Rendell similarly provides two lists, though hers are labeled "books taken from me" and "books taken by me." Stephen Bury uses a homegrown classification system to organize his list, based on a boyhood misunderstanding of how the Dewey Decimal Classification System works. A few submissions show images of books including those of Melanie Jackson, Marylène Negro, John McDowall, Greville Worthington, and Joanne Strange. Michael K. Carter's entry, on the other hand, is textually inventive. His submission "Notes to Illustrations" begins

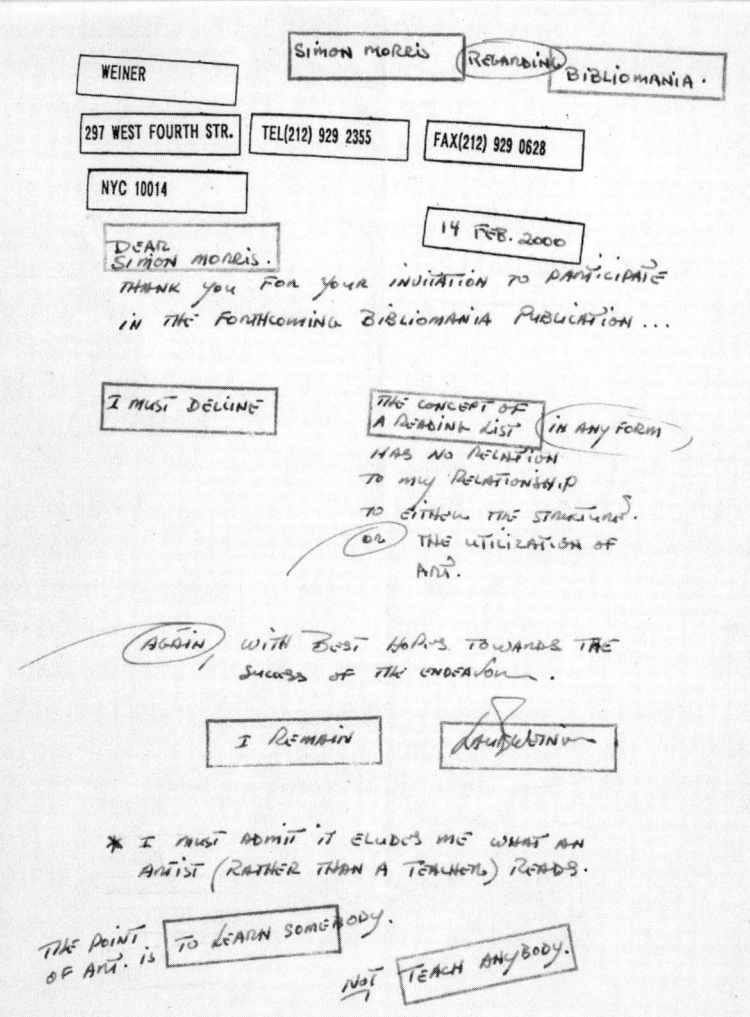

Lawrence Weiner's submission for *Bibliomania 2000/2001*, 2002.

with a section of twenty illustration notes without their images, followed by a list of sources documenting where these notes and illustrations first appeared. The reader has to use their imagination to construct the illustrations from these obscure clues. This is one of the most successful "artworks" in the book. Lawrence Weiner's contribution—a polite, professional refusal to participate—is equally successful. On a piece of handwritten and handstamped correspondence Weiner writes, "*I MUST ADMIT IT ALLUDES ME WHAT AN ARTIST (RATHER THAN A TEACHER) READS. THE POINT OF ART IS TO LEARN SOMEBODY <u>NOT</u> TEACH ANYBODY."[13]

In its early iterations, *Bibliomania* imagined and embraced the opportunity to create a collaborative space of exchange outside the walls of an art museum. It seemed at its most playful (and thoughtful) when only a few lists were used to make exhibition-like interventions in mainstream bookstores and university libraries. As the scale of the project became less intimate and more complex for the viewer, inventive responses got lost in the web of contributions.

(1) [Simon Morris], "Bibliomania: A Shared Space of Encounter" (unpublished manuscript, [2006]), [18], Microsoft Word file.

(2) [Morris], "Bibliomania," [4]. Although plentiful, a few works on the artist's studio come to mind, see for instance, Mary Jane Jacob and Michelle Grabner, eds., *The Studio Reader: On the Space of Artists* (Chicago: School of the Art Institute of Chicago, University of Chicago Press, 2010); Jens Hoffmann, ed., *The Studio* (London: Whitechapel Gallery, 2012); Hossein Amirsadeghi, ed., *Art Studio America: Contemporary Artist Spaces* (London: Thames & Hudson, 2013); Joe Fig, *Inside the Artist's Studio* (New York: Princeton Architectural Press, 2015).

(3) One connection, for example, is the curatorial model of continuous growth exemplified in Hans Ulrich Obrist's *do it* exhibition project (1993/1997–).

(4) Simon Morris, ed., *Bibliomania 2000/2001* (York, England: information as material, 2002), 4.

(5) [Morris], "Bibliomania," [22].

(6) For instance, a directory with very brief bios in the end matter, or, perhaps a single "Invited by __" line after the name of the contributor in each entry would be helpful and not distracting.

(7) Morris, *Bibliomania 2000/2001*, 619.

(8) [Morris], "Bibliomania," [6]. For more on Arial, see catalogue entry for "Cyberfeminism Index."

(9) I have to wonder if some participants thought their words would be typeset and designed for them.

(10) Morris was so taken, in fact, by the materiality of Dion's faxes that he drove from York to London to make high res scans of the artist's notebook. Simon Morris, email message to author, December 23, 2022.

(11) Morris, *Bibliomania 2000/2001*, 240–41. The URL linked readers to Hiller's Dia-commissioned web project *Dream Screens* (1996). In 2020, Dia reprogrammed the site which can now be found here: https://awp.diaart.org/hiller/dreamscreens.html.

(12) Morris, *Bibliomania 2000/2001*, 307–8.

(13) Morris, *Bibliomania 2000/2001*, [unnumbered page].

Bibliozines

Sitterwerk.
Bibliozines.
Community-generated publication project.
 Designed by
 Christian Kern (InfoMedis AG),
 Anthon Astrom,
 Lukas Zimmer (Astrom/Zimmer GmbH),
 and Fabian Wegmüller.
 2015–.

The Sitterwerk in St. Gallen, Switzerland is host to a publicly accessible art reference library called the Kunstbibliothek with "around 30,000 volumes on sculpture, architecture, photography, material and casting technology, and material science and restoration" and a collection of material samples in the Werkstoffarchiv.[1] To foreground the idea of the library as a laboratory and the importance of serendipitous discovery, the Sitterwerk developed a dynamic system of organization based on RFID (radio-frequency identification) technology. A transponder chip is attached to each book in the library. RFID reading devices (i.e. library robots) continually inventory the shelves, detecting the location of titles by their unique radio detection signals. The online catalog is updated with shelf location information on a regular basis. The books are then free to roam around the library,

View of the Sitterwerk's Werkbank.

allowing researchers to organically shape the organization of the collection through use. The design of the flexible shelf arrangement is largely influenced by the associative working methods of the library's major benefactor, Daniel Rohner.[2] Additionally, with the RFID system in place, no call numbers, special labels, or library barcodes are needed on the books. The spines and covers are relatively unencumbered, enabling researchers to easily browse the spine titles in the stacks, among other advantages.

To further explore the idea of dynamic order and to utilize the knowledge-base of Sitterwerk's researchers, the library installed an interactive table in 2010 that could trace what books and material samples were being grouped together on the table. Researchers could create interactive lists from their compilations that would then get linked back to the library catalog for other patrons to utilize. In cooperation with Christian Kern (InfoMedis AG), Anthon Astrom, Lukas Zimmer (Astrom/Zimmer), and Fabian Wegmüller, the Sitterwerk expanded this initiative and launched the Werkbank project in 2015. The new workstation consists of a sensory table with RFID and image-recognition technology and a digital platform that automatically creates a color visualization of the items placed on the table. The Werkbank is more sophisticated than the previous iteration, allowing users to stack books as well as set them flat on the table. It maps how the books are placed on the table rather than just saving the title selections and allows the bibliographer to add notes to items.[3]

The Werkbank's zine module has a drag and drop interface that lets researchers organize objects, add notes, and generate full citations to create booklets.[4] The table displays are first materialized as a digital network of cross-references that are then rendered into new analog forms. The inscribed notebooks or "bibliozines" can be printed, folded, and assembled on site, with special papers for the covers and interiors. Each title is assigned a consecutive number, displayed on the cover, to lend some uniformity to the ongoing community publication project. The booklets can be given an RFID tag, cataloged, and added to the shelf for future researchers or read in the online catalog as a digital publication.

Examples of *Bibliozines*.

(1) "Kunstbibliothek," Sitterwerk Foundation, accessed November 5, 2022, https://www.sitterwerk.ch/En/Kunstbibliothek; and "Werkstoffarchiv," Sitterwerk Foundation, accessed November 5, 2022, https://www.sitterwerk.ch/En/Werkstoffarchiv.
(2) Notably Rohner would arrange, regroup, and devise subject constellations from his 25,000 volume library for visiting artists and researchers. See Felix Lehner, "The Backstory of the Art Library," in *The Dynamic Library*, 17–21; "Collection Daniel Rohner," Sitterwerk Foundation, accessed March 24, 2016, http://www.sitterwerk.ch/kunstbibliothek/sammlung-daniel-rohner.html.
(3) Related to the idea of mapping books on a table, see the catalogue entry for "PM Tables, Visitor Tables, Your Tables."
(4) It appears that an early version of the Bibliozine project launched in 2014. See "bibliozine," November 23, 2014, http://www.sitterwerk.ch/kunstbibliothek/ereignisse/ereignisdetail/article/bibliozine-digitale-notizhefte.html. Archived at https://web.archive.org/web/20160409112057/http://www.sitterwerk.ch/kunstbibliothek/ereignisse/ereignisdetail/article/bibliozine-digitale-notizhefte.html.

Bookcatalogtest

Bookcatalogtest

Bookcatalogtest, 2012, cover.

English Edition

Tamm, Triin.
Bookcatalogtest.
Zürich: Rollo Press, 2012.
144 p.; 30 × 21.5 × 2 cm
+ 1 booklet (8 p.: ill.; 21 × 15 cm).

Riffing off psychiatrist Moritz Tramer's *Bücherkatalogtest* (1953), Triin Tamm overhauled the "characterological test tool" for a new work in 2012.[1] Her aptly named *Bookcatalogtest* was published as part of an ongoing artist's book series initiated by David Senior, then bibliographer at the MoMA Library, for the Contemporary Artists' Books Conference in New York. Her bibliography-cum-personality test is a spiral bound directory of 432 numbered entries containing book titles and author information. Urs Lehni, the designer and founder of Rollo Press, typeset all of the entries in the same font and blue color. The entries each correspond to one of twenty-four personality sectors, and Tamm maps these to a range of current and classic works of literature, theory, popular fiction, self-help, and more.[2]

To use the *Bookcatalogtest*, the test taker flips through the pages and selects ten titles in an allotted amount of time. The test subject, who is given title and author references and nothing more, has to decide which titles are the most appealing. The tester, referring to Tamm's guide "Notes and Instructions on How to Use the Bookcatalogtest," can then perform a personality reading to unveil the test subjects hidden interests. The pamphlet accompanying the book includes a key, legend, and circle graph to mark the test takers book choices. The real art, Tamm stresses, is in

September 9, 2012   Tallinn

           NOTES AND INSTRUCTIONS ON HOW TO USE
                      THE BOOKCATALOGTEST

                              * * *

        Dear Reader,

            You must be wondering about
            this "Bookcatalogtest" that you
            just flipped through and in-
            deed, it is an oddity at first
            glance. But let me explain
            to you a couple of things about
            the background of this book,
and I'm sure it will become
clearer immediately.

   In 1953, Swiss psychiatrist Moritz Tramer
(1882-1963), a pioneer on the field of "child
psychiatry", published a slim volume entitled "Der
Bücherkatalogtest als charakterologisches Prüf-
mittel" (The Bookcatalogtest as a Characterological Test Tool), in which he outlines the concept
for a personality test that tries to evoke different interests that lie buried deep down in each of
us. He found that book titles are the right means
to transport these interests, and so he elaborated
a library catalog consisting of 430 titles, from
which testees were to choose 10 in about 10-20
minutes. What they didn't know was, that all the
titles in the list were connected to a certain
category, or "interest vector", how Tramer calls
them. Which means that if you choose e.g. the book
"Otto, der Ausreisser" (Otto, the Runaway), it

                                1

Interior spreads of *Bookcatalogtest*.

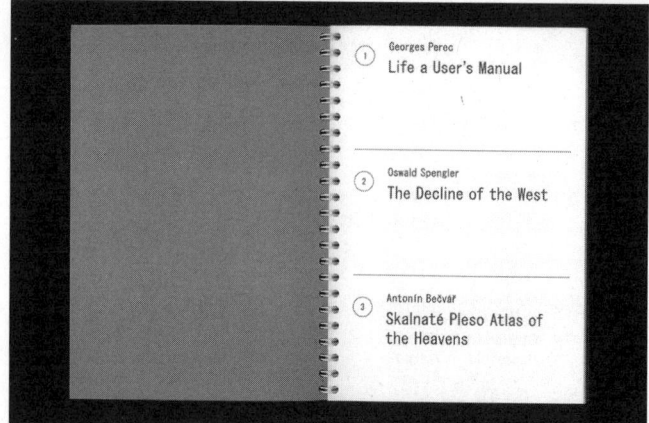

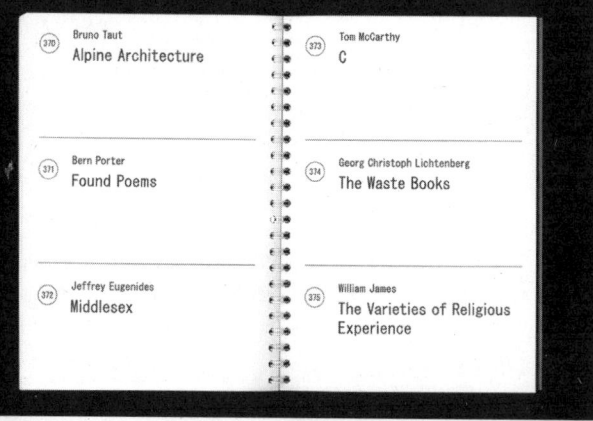

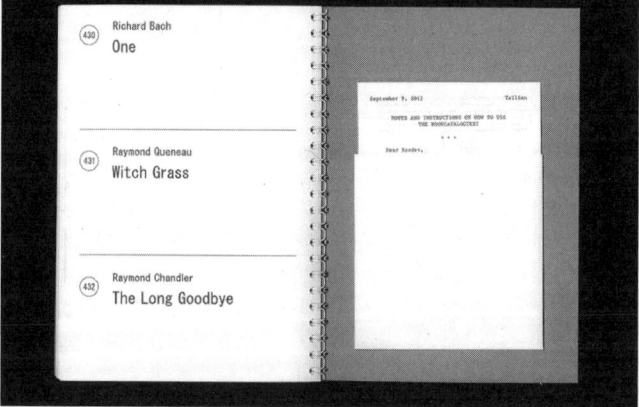

interpreting the filled-in diagram, an act of bibliopsychology which Tamm cannot script. She prompts the tester to have fun with the mood and style of the session. She encourages that the consultation and evaluation is akin to reading and reacting to the works on someone's bookshelves.

As a bibliography, the *Bookcatalogtest* could be used for alternative purposes, for example to locate additional reading recommendations within one's personality sector(s). Tamm's terrific directory classes works by: Adventure, Work, The Universe, Fate, Research, Nature, Stories, Family, Facts, Money, Health, The Arts, Entertainment, Humor, War, Love, Folklore, Ethics, Education, Spirituality, Human Condition, The Future, Animals, and Food & Drinks.

(1)
Triin Tamm, *Bookcatalogtest*
(Zürich: Rollo Press, 2012), pamphlet, 1.
(2)
Some of the titles in the *Bookcatalogtest*
appear in another of Tamm's works,
A Stack of Books, A Book of Stacks, e.g. the unattributed
History of the Origin of All Things.
See catalogue entry for
"A Stack of Books, A Book of Stacks."

The Bookshelf Project

Davidson,
Laura.
The Bookshelf Project.
Ongoing series of
eight unique artist's
books, to date.
Clamshell boxes
by Erin Fletcher of
Herringbone Bindery.
Boston: 2015–.
Box size: 19 ×
14 × 4 cm.

Artist Laura Davidson is a keen observer fascinated by collections and propelled by a love of books. *The Bookshelf Project* pays homage to the placement and arrangement of one's books on the shelf. She has found inspiration in collections at the Boston Athenaeum, the Morgan Library, and the Gardner Museum as well as the private libraries of those in and around her Boston circle.

Davidson's output is a series of one-of-a-kind, hand-drawn artist's books. She hones in on one bookshelf with a unifying theme — not a whole bookcase or a vast library — and renders a row of books in situ, spine out. She spends a few hours looking through and photographing a collection before deciding if it will become part of *The Bookshelf Project*.[1] Then back in her studio, using pigmented ink on paper, she paints groupings of anywhere between twelve to fifty-two books. *Books Checked Out by Louisa May Alcott in 1871* from 2015 revolves around a set of books at the Boston Athenaeum that the famous writer borrowed and is the first in Davidson's series. *Math at the Ath* soon followed when the artist's imagination took to a section of nineteenth- and twentieth-century math books also at the Boston Athenaeum. *Modern Magic* (2016), on the other hand, takes stock of her neighbor Steve Hollinger's personal collection of early magic books and *L. Frank Baum & Oz* (2016) mines Jamie Guggina's growing collection. The horizontal orientation of each sequence of books is pleated into an accordion-fold book structure and together with additional hand-drawn ephemera is packaged in a custom clamshell box. To further connect the series, each book's box is a uniform 19 by 14 centimeters and is equipped with the artist's own call-number labeling system.

Despite the name *The Bookshelf Project*, the surface of the shelf is never actually drawn in the picture plane. No matter. The focus is entirely on the materiality of the books. Cumulatively, the artworks record different eras of book production—from leather bindings with gilt embellishments and decorated papers over boards to publisher's bindings in colorful book cloth and illustrated paper book jackets. Rubbing, stains, bleaching from light-exposure, tears and cracks, exposed sewn bindings, and other hallmarks of age and use are all emulated in ink. The trace of the borrower or owner can be felt in such wear. These are the books that have charmed the artist. These are the books that the artist has chosen to spend time with, carefully rendering each set in permanent acrylic ink.

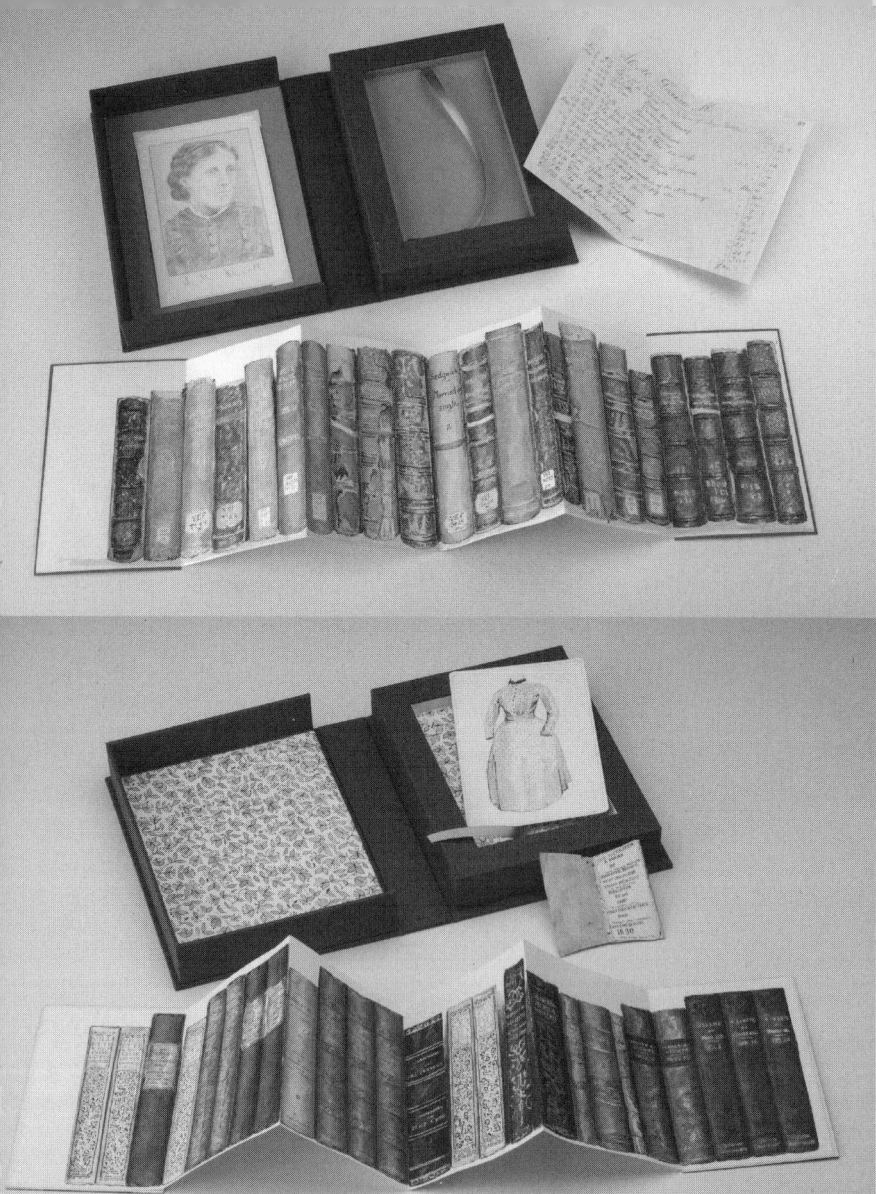

Books Checked Out by Louisa May Alcott in 1871, 2015.
Brontë Books at the Morgan, 2016.

Several shelves have female protagonists. *She Cooks* from 2016 renders twenty-six contemporary cookbooks from the working library of Davidson's wife, Gabrielle Schaffner. In 2016's *Brontë Books at the Morgan*, Davidson had special access to peruse the works of Charlotte Brontë at an exhibition at the Morgan Library curated by Christine Nelson. Her latest iteration from 2020, *Travel Books and the Company They Keep* inventories twenty-four books from Isabella Stewart Gardner's shelf.

By documenting personal or institutional bookshelves, Davidson gives us access to readers and book collectors from the past and present. The drawings of the books are not life-size but at a slightly smaller scale, allowing the viewer to take in a reader's shelf all at once—their selection decisions, the order of their arrangements, and subjects of reading interest. The varying heights of the books allow for quick comparison between different volumes. The drawings are near facsimiles of the spines, however legible or illegible in their present state of decay, that display information of bibliographic interest (e.g., a title, author, publisher's name or logo, or call number/accession number). There are other particularities that one can glean from this project too. *What is the spacing like between the books? Are they huddled together, condensed upright on the shelf? Or are there large gaps where a book may have been removed? As in* Travel Books and the Company They Keep, *are any titles anomalies amongst their shelf companions?*

When the *The Bookshelf Project* leans into the provenance of a collection, emphasizing the owner or borrower(s) in some way, the project is at its best. The artist's books as a package try to transfer the wonder that the artist felt in the environment of a particular library and their protocols around handling the books as well as the tactility and smell and allure of individual volumes. *The Bookshelf Project* is a series of artworks that give access to resources one might not otherwise see in person through attentive surrogate objects that hold their own allure. These experimental bibliographies conjure a feeling more than anything. A mood of books.

(1) Laura Davidson, Zoom conversation with author, October 8, 2022.

Bulletins of the Serving Library—*Test*

Bertolotti-Bailey, Stuart, Angie Keefer, and David Reinfurt, eds. *Bulletins of the Serving Library—*Test**, no. 10 (Winter 2015). 240 p.: col. ill.; 16.5 × 12 × 1 cm.

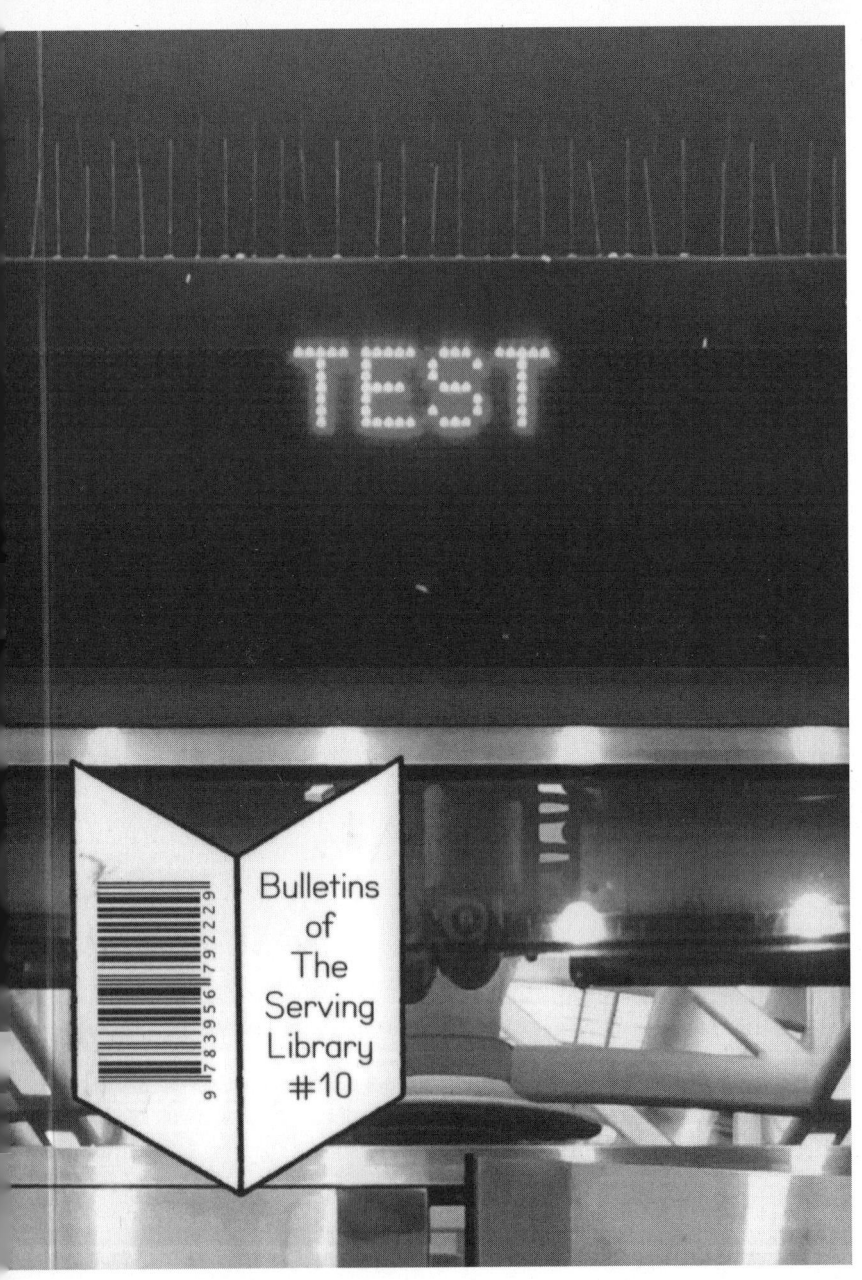

*Bulletins of the Serving Library—*Test*,*
no. 10 (Winter 2015), cover.

Referred to by its editors as a "sampler," issue number ten of the *Bulletins of the Serving Library* is an archival snapshot of the previous nine, plucking "one choice bulletin from each" issue for reprint.[1] The Serving Library uses a hybrid method of publishing that privileges digital distribution—first releasing individual articles or "bulletins" as downloadable PDFs online, then assembling them into printed issues. To date, there are 176 bulletins which snake through topics in design, literature, science, mathematics, sports, and philosophy.[2] The print issues are formally akin to magazines or journals. But without being squarely popular *or* academic, they have proven challenging for bookstores to shelve. Issue number ten, the **Test** issue, is certainly more bookish, printed at half the scale of the previous issues and released in full color. The entire work functions as a visual bibliography, miniaturizing a library in process and acting as an exercise in compression.

The front matter opens with the front covers of all nine issues as a sequence of recto pages. A summary of the issue's theme, cover art description, and artist or photo credits is printed on the verso. Similarly **Test** concludes with a sequence of all the back-cover images cleverly laid out on the verso pages with any information regarding publication, production, or acknowledgments appearing on the recto. In other words, the front covers appear as front covers normally do—on the right-hand side of a central spine as the back covers do on the left.

The interplay of online and print cultures is ever present. In the directory online at www.servinglibrary.org each bulletin is represented by an image, with the author and title information appearing directly below it. In the twelve-page

Interior spread of "Bulls Redux" section in
Bulletins of the Serving Library—*Test*.

section "Bulls Redux" in the **Test** issue, the editors expand this visual directory, adding a 140-character description to each bulletin. Appropriating the then-current 140-character Twitter limit for this printed use may seem like an arbitrary restriction.[3] However, it works seamlessly without being obvious or gimmicky. Plus, designing a page in terms of characters per line rather than words per line is a boon. The editors can create a visual density of image and text that rhymes with the multi-column arrangement used on the website. In **Test**, the reader can easily browse the library, seeing over twenty bulletins at a glance.

By using the restrictions of a social networking site, the editors have playfully adopted online structures of writing and reading for print. The writing of these mini abstracts is part summary, part advertising hook—delightfully shirking the responsibilities of keyword-driven writing. For example:

The Serving Library's vertical scroll directory, screenshot.

David Reinfurt:
A Million Random Digits . . .
Pure noise not at all how it sounds.

David Senior:
Access to Tools. In the way that children play at
being grown-ups, we played at being self-sufficient.

Lars Bang Larsen:
Giraffe and Anti-Giraffe. The glorious political f-youto-
pia of proto-hippie Charles Fourier.

Angie Keefer:
Where Were We. Following Mallarmé's Latest Fashion,
what's the meaning of a dress?

Perri MacKenzie:
A Running Composition. Dandyism from the
vantage of a middle-distance jogger.[4]

In combination with intriguing thumbnail images, the bibliography fluidly draws readers into its own microcosm of interdisciplinary inquiries.

---

(1) The Serving Library, accessed December 18, 2022, https://www.servinglibrary.org; Stuart Bertolotti-Bailey, Angie Keefer, and David Reinfurt, eds. *Bulletins of the Serving Library—*Test**, no. 10 (Winter 2015), 20.
(2) Bertolotti-Bailey, Keefer, and Reinfurt, **Test**, 20.
(3) Twitter upped its character limit to 280 in 2017.
(4) Bertolotti-Bailey, Keefer, and Reinfurt, **Test**, 22–26.

Cloth • A Commonplace

Hamilton, Ann. *cloth • a commonplace*. Tumblr site. The Fabric Workshop and Museum, published 2015. https://cloth-a-commonplace.tumblr.com/.

> Hamilton, Ann. *(habitus • cloth • a commonplace)*, 2016. Commonplace project pages with binder, 29.5 × 22 cm. Edition of 67. In collaboration with The Fabric Workshop and Museum, Philadelphia.

Ann Hamilton is part of the unique, time-unlimited Artist-in-Residence Program at the Fabric Workshop and Museum (FWM) in Philadelphia which invites contemporary artists to explore new ideas and experiment with the support of FWM Studio staff. In Hamilton's most recent FWM project, *habitus*, she taps into the nature of cloth, its role in our lives, and its enmeshment in our language and verbal expression. She writes:

> Held by cloth's hand, we are swaddled at birth, covered in sleep, and shrouded in death. A single thread spins a myth of origin and a tale of adventure and interweaves people and webs of communication. Coat and tent are the first portable architecture for the body; a flag carries the symbol of nationality; a folded blanket is a

cloth · a commonplace

a collection of texts · a project by Ann Hamilton with The Fabric Workshop and Museum · habitus

on cloth   on commonplacing   on searching text   on habitus   on FWM   submit

She abruptly took off her dress and, standing in her chemise, reached under it and unfastened her corset, dropping it to the floor. Opening the package and shaking out the filmy fabric, she began to drape it from her shoulders, checking the fall of the cloth in the mirror.
Then she laid out the fabric on the bed.
The next evening, Tom, dressed in a smart new blazer, was seated with Alice and Hubert. Keziah entered in a corsetless, eggshell colored dress modeled after the French designer Paul Poiret. It fell in one unbroken line, skimming her hips loosely and ending just above the ankles.
Alice paled. "You're going out? In... in those... undergarments?"

— Lynn Blackwell Denton, *The Milliner* (Philadelphia, Lynn Blackwell Denton, 2016), 28. Submitted by Lynn Blackwell Denton

...moon-beams

the sight of the cover of a book one has previously read retains, woven into the letters of its title, the moon-beams of a far-off summer night

— Marcel Proust, "The Past Recaptured," trans. Frederick A. Blossom, in *Remembrance of Things Past*, Vol. 2 (New York: Random House, 1932), p. 1008

#habitus #2 #woven #submission

3 notes

...soul or body

Thinking thought to be a body wearing language as clothing or language of a body of thought which is a soul or body the clothing of a soul, she is veiled in silence. A veiled unavailable body makes an available space.

— Harryette Mullen, *Trimmings* (Minneapolis, MN: Graywolf Press, 1991)

Submitted by Vanessa Baish

#habitus #2 #veil #veiled #clothing #wear #worn #Mullen #Harryette #trimmings #submission

2 notes

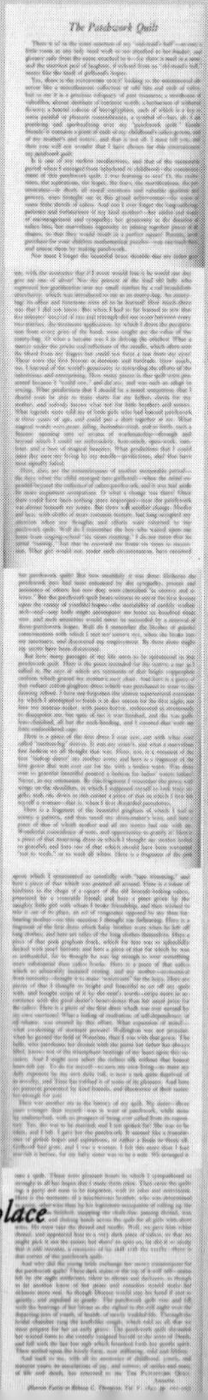
The Patchwork Quilt

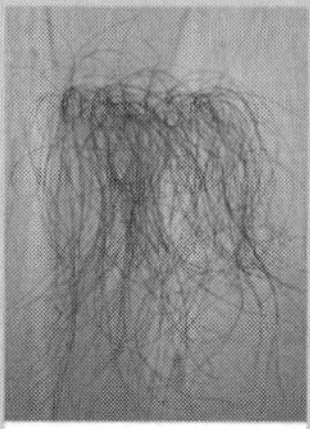

Kindness

Naomi Shihab Nye

Before you know what
kindness really is
you must lose things,
feel the future dissolve
in a moment
like salt in a weakened
broth.
What you held in your
hand,
what you counted and
carefully saved,
all this must go so you
know
how desolate the landscape
can be
between the regions of
kindness.
How you ride and ride
thinking the bus will
never stop,
the passengers eating
maize and chicken
will stare out the window
forever.

Before you learn the
tender gravity of kindness
you must travel where the
Indian in a white poncho
lies dead by the side of
the road.
You must see how this
could be you,
how he too was someone
who journeyed through the
night with plans
and the simple breath that
kept him alive.

Before you know kindness
as the deepest thing
inside,
you must know sorrow as
the other deepest thing.
You must wake up with
sorrow.
You must speak to it till
your voice
catches the thread of all
sorrows
and you see the size of
the cloth.
Then it is only kindness
that makes sense anymore,
only kindness that ties
your shoes
and sends you out into the

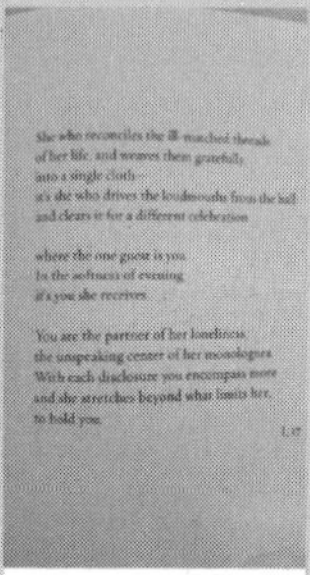
She who reconciles the ill-matched threads
of her life, and weaves them gratefully
into a single cloth—
it's she who drives the loudmouths from the hall
and clears it for a different celebration

where the one guest is you.
In the softness of evening
it's you she receives.

You are the partner of her loneliness,
the unspeaking center of her monologues.
With each disclosure you encompass more
and she stretches beyond what limits her,
to hold you.

Pg.77

Rilke, Rainer Maria. *Rilke's book of hours: Love poems to God*. Penguin, 2005.

7 notes

...lace gazed

Undine's white and gold bedroom, with sea-green panels and old rose carpet, looked along Seventy-second Street toward the leafless tree-tops of the Central Park. She went to the window, and drawing back its many layers of lace gazed eastward down the long brownstone perspective. Beyond the Park lay Fifth Avenue—and Fifth Avenue was where she wanted to be!

— Edith Wharton, *The Custom of the Country* (New York, NY: C. Scribner's Sons, 1913) p. 18

#habitus #2 #carpet #lace #curtains #curtain #submission

"America is not a blanket woven from one thread, one color, one cloth." -Jesse Jackson.

3 notes

Colonna, Francesco. *Hypnerotomachia Poliphili*. Translated by Joscelyn Godwin. New York: Thames and Hudson Inc, 1999.

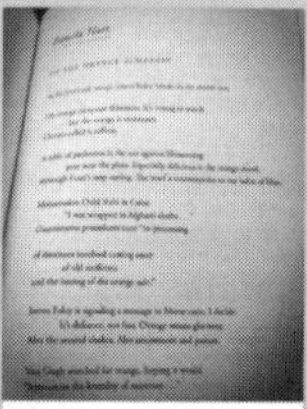

Pamela Hart, "On the Orange Jumpsuit." *Southern Humanities Review* 49 no. 4 (Summer 2016) p. 89

#habitus #2 #jumpsuit #pashmina #shawl #scarf #garment #drape #suit #uniform

3 notes

cloth • a commonplace on Tumblr.

story of trade. Like weather, however changeable, cloth envelops experience.[1]

The artist's fascination with our shared experiences of cloth and the language that binds us together led her to unravel commonplace books and the history of commonplacing—that is, the practice of collecting and copying "striking passages" from one's various readings into hand-assembled manuscripts.[2] Hamilton notes, "Traditionally a commonplace book reflects the idiosyncratic interests, organization and practices of an individual reader."[3] In the past, commonplace books have indeed gathered disparate sources for an audience of one in the case of a personal manuscript, but they've also been, for example, co-compiled and intended for a limited group of readers in the case of a family commonplace book written in different hands across decades, as well as typeset, printed, and distributed commonplaces for audiences of like-minded folx. Something that centuries of commonplace books share is a graphic textuality and a visual patchwork of the juxtaposed quotes within.

Expanding the boundaries of what one might expect from a commonplace book, Hamilton decided to make a crowd-sourced work with FWM and launched the public Tumblr site *cloth • a commonplace* in 2015 to solicit and collect excerpts that reference cloth and clothing. The public sage-green website ties into her larger *habitus* project and is headed by a blurry photo of a hand touching a set of curtains—in the act of either opening or closing them—to set the tone. On the Tumblr site Hamilton guides readers into her open prompt, quoting fabric-centric selections from the likes of William Faulkner, Virginia Woolf, Beatrix Potter, and Walter Benjamin, and providing a long list of keywords sympathetic to the theme such as "Drape," "Dyed," "Gauzy," "Skein."[4]

Installation view of commonplace book pages. *(habitus • cloth • a commonplace)*, 2016, at The Fabric Workshop and Museum.

Submitters could send texts and images through a simple online submission form, deliver their "striking passages" by mail or email, or participate in an open-call workshop at FWM. Contributors were welcome to sign their entries or submit anonymously, although every entry needed to cite its bibliographic sources in Chicago style.

The resulting Tumblr swells with photographs of printed texts sometimes with hand annotations, typewritten passages keyed directly into the Tumblr form, scans of handwritten entries on note cards or ruled journals, and screenshots of scholarly articles seen through a moiré pattern.[5] It is a bibliographic collage in pixels. All manner of published writing takes up residence here: books on the textile trade, scientific works, poetry, classics and popular fiction, song lyrics, etc. It is a multigenerational project, too, with the artist and FWM organizers giving a thank you shout out on

April 19, 2016, to Donna Romero's ninth-grade class whose students sent in excerpts from J. D. Salinger, Maya Angelou, Pharrell Williams, and this passage from Geoffry Chaucer's *Canterbury Tales*: "He wore a homely parti-coloured coat, / Girt with a silken belt of pin-stripe stuff; / Of his appearence I have said enough." Each excerpt and its citation lets the reader dip into and perhaps later seek out various texts on their own.

The project compiles a seemingly inexhaustible set of references on cloth from the bibliographic universe and participating public readers. *cloth • a commonplace* does well to keep the citations and their sources together in a web-based display. However, it is a sea of texts. Without the guideposts one might find in a commonplace book like a table of contents, headings, or index, it is a daunting read. The snippets appear in reverse chronological order in a multi-column format, with the newest entries from 2018 listed first and the oldest, from 2015, last. Assessing the work through the lens of experimental subject bibliography, the never-ending lazy-loading Tumblr scroll is a navigational challenge. It's hard to know where it ends (or rather begins) and just what to click on with so many entries. There is no search function on the site to see if the same books or authors have been quoted by different contributors, just scrolling and more scrolling. The user-generated tagging system attempts to gather entries with some thematic similarity. Unfortunately, the tags are ineffective in action because they were inconsistently applied. There was one suggested tag of #submission in the online entry form which is too broad and not descriptive as every entry is a #submission. Tagging could have been better integrated if submitters were prompted to create tags based on the same or similar specialized terms that were in the suggested list of key search words or if the artist and FWS staff had applied tags when approving the posts.[6] Such is the wily nature of crowd-sourcing, trying to anticipate how content will grow, and discerning how to shape it without imposing unnecessary restrictions.

However experienced by the reader, the Tumblr aptly serves as generative source material for Hamilton and her 2016 installation *(habitus • cloth • a commonplace)*. As Adam Smyth notes of commonplace book history, "the compiler could develop 'the habit of *using* the riches supplied by your reading' to produce his or her own persuasive discourse."[7] Using this pool of publicly obtained excerpts, Hamilton shows the social life of texts, and from it, creates an edition of sixty-seven commonplace books. These are installed on a single long shelf in FWM, running the length of a room that's been designed to print continuous pattern on fabric bolts. Hamilton's commonplace books are taken out of their binders and displayed unbound in stacks of loose sheets. To keep the stacks orderly, two holes punched in the top margin are fitted over evenly spaced vertical hooks or rods. Each stack is a different thickness and features a different page from the book. The pages have been layed out with the content from the Tumblr site and feature a small but thorough citation at the bottom of each page. For instance, a photo containing a scrap of text or cloth, or an excerpt that has been re-typeset and resized to flow on the page are centered above the citation with a generous margin. Reprinting photographed book pages results in a colorway of whites and creams and tawny yellows down the length of the long shelf. Photographed textiles pepper-in an array of muted colors as well. The work has been shaped by Hamilton into a poetic and cohesive whole. You can no longer tell what community member has contributed what text. Each page is inviting to skim or study or sift through.

(1)

Ann Hamilton, *Ann Hamilton: Habitus*, poems Natalie Shapero, Susan Stewart, contributors Patricia C. Phillips, Susan Lubowsky Talbott (Philadelphia, PA: The Fabric Workshop and Museum, 2017). Published on occasion of an exhibition of the same title, organized by The Fabric Workshop and Museum (Municipal Pier 9: September 6–October 10, 2016; The Fabric Workshop and Museum: September 17, 2016–January 8, 2017).

(2)

Merriam-Webster, s.v. "commonplace," accessed October 8, 2022, https://www.merriam-webster.com/dictionary/commonplace.

(3)

Ann Hamilton, "on commonplacing," *cloth • a commonplace*, The Fabric Workshop and Museum, published 2015, https://cloth-a-commonplace.tumblr.com/on-commonplacing.

(4)

Ann Hamilton, "on searching text," *cloth • a commonplace*, The Fabric Workshop and Museum, published 2015, https://cloth-a-commonplace.tumblr.com/on-searching-texts.

(5)

Hamilton, "on commonplacing."

(6)

For a project with public submissions that utilizes tagging suggestions, see catalogue entry for "PM Tables, Visitor Tables, Your Tables."

(7)

Adam Smyth, "Commonplace Book Culture" in *Women and Writing c.1340-c.1650: The Domestication of Print Culture*, ed. Anne Lawrence-Mathers and Phillipa Hardman (Woodbridge: York Medieval Press, 2010), 92-93.

Common Threads

Hicks, Candace.
Common Threads.
Ongoing numbered series of 143 unique artist's books, to date.
TX: produced by the artist, 2004–. [8] p.; dimensions variable.

Candace Hicks, avid reader and artist interested in "speculative areas of science," has been gathering coincidences from daily life-events and the media she consumes—films, television shows, podcasts, print books, audiobooks, etc.—for the past eleven years.[1] Her long-running project *Common Threads,* a series of variable sewn-canvas notebooks, is a bibliography of reading synchronicities.[2] It demonstrates connections between media resources that would otherwise not be apparent in something like a universal cataloging system. In the tradition of a diary, logbook, or commonplace book, Hicks uses a first-person narrative to bridge quoted, paraphrased, and summarized passages together from books and media she is reading and watching. For example, in volume 122, the references go fluidly and somewhat miraculously back and forth between *Underland: A Deep Time Journey* (nonfiction), *The Line Becomes a River* (nonfiction), the HBO series *The Watchmen* (action fiction), and *Red at the Bone* (novel) covering cave exploration, border patrols, race and the Tulsa Massacre, African American families, hermit crabs, and plastic pollution.

Each individually numbered volume in *Common Threads* has "COMPOSITION" embroidered on the cover along with a customized cover pattern that reflects one of the details or topics discussed within. The cover pattern on volume 122, for one, is of hermit crab shells. The interior page structure throughout the series is constant, imitating the look of inexpensive notebooks with light blue machine-stitched ruled lines and vertical margin lines hand-stitched in a bold red. Following the intentionally imperfect ruled lines, texts are embroidered in the style of the artist's handwriting with the titles of books underlined like one might do if writing in a diary longhand. Occasionally Hicks adds doodles, illustrations, and text corrections to her fabric pages to make the laborious work of embroidery seem as provisional as a quick pen stroke. Two pieces of canvas are sewn back-to-back to create a single page with writing-in-thread on both sides. The under side of the needlework is thus not seen but hidden. The aim of the artist is "to make the text, image, and substance of the book inseparable."[3] Though the scale is roughly the size of a commercial (paper) composition book, its familiarity is made strange through the floppiness and hypertactility of its materials.

The well of coincidences that Hicks draws from is not to be underestimated. The more observant she is, the more occurrences she seems to uncover year after year. Collectively the volumes in *Common Threads* share a quality of "ongoingness" with commonplace books.[4] New discoveries will continue to be added. In his research on historic commonplaces, Adam Smyth observes that "to read a commonplace book today is to encounter a text which is not only unfinished but which possesses a quality of existing, very vividly, in the present tense."[5] Similarly, the tension of provisionality keeps the notebook writings by Hicks in the present tense.

Common Threads
volume 122,
2020,
cover.

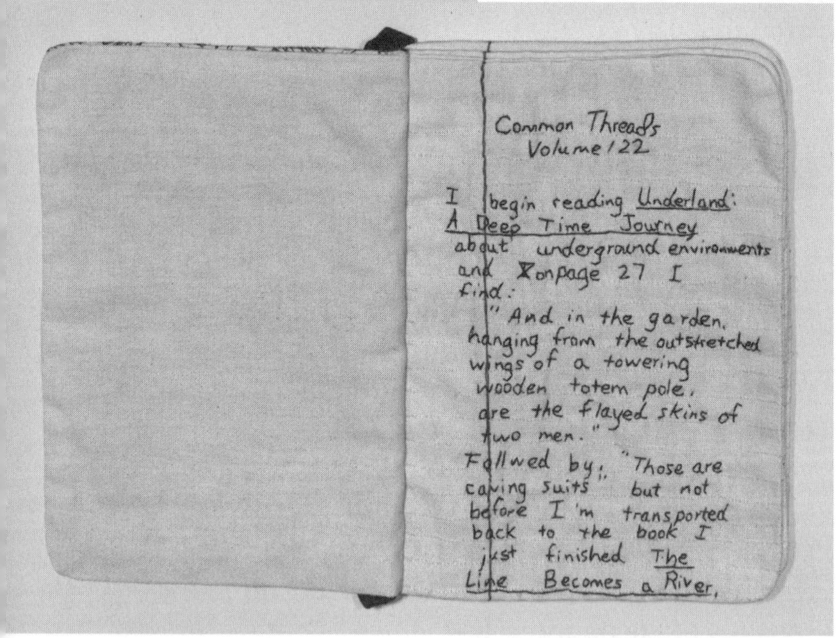

Interior spread of *Common Threads* volume 122, 2020, showing a text correction.

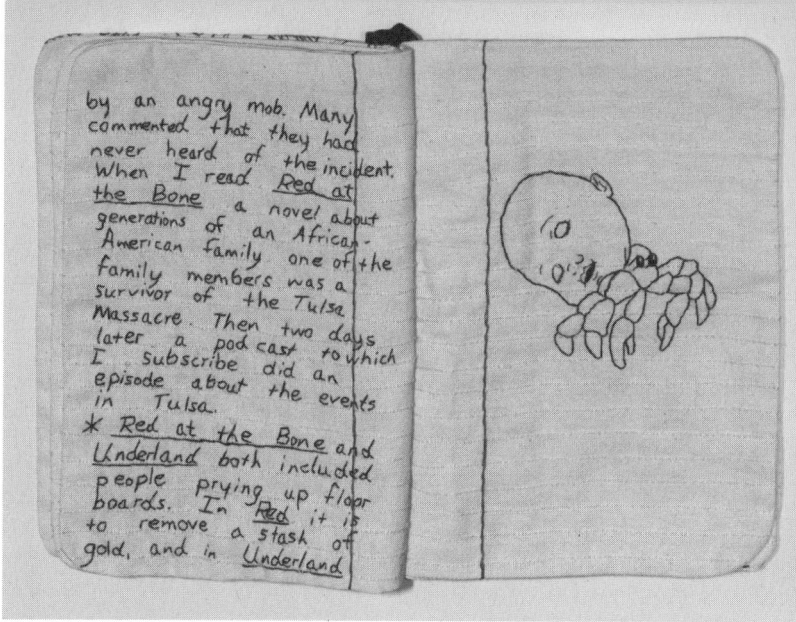

Interior spread of *Common Threads* volume 122, 2020, showing an illustration.

Each book by the artist explores a grouping of "common threads" whether they are strong visuals gleaned from her readings like "candy house" in volume 141, "balls of goat shit" in volume 136, and "hidden object in a chimney flue" in volume 98, or cultural references like Wallace Shawn in volume 119, *Crocodile Dundee* in volume 123, Outkast in volume 107, and the feminist origins of Monopoly in volume 139.[6] Each volume of *Common Threads* serves as an unconventional subject guide and storytelling excursion, and in this sense, emulates the episodic format of podcasts. Through chronological setups and quotes, the reader can learn about each of the selected media objects and publications in turn through minor plot points and micro-details. There is a certain intimacy engendered here, a depth of trust between Hicks and her reader as she invites them on a hunt for profundity.

(1) "Candace Hicks," Booklyn, accessed October 26, 2022, https://booklyn.org/artists/candace-hicks/.
(2) For reading coincidences, see the catalogue entry for "Poet-Saints of July 06."
(3) "Common Threads V.125," Booklyn, accessed October 26, 2022, https://booklyn.org/catalog/candace-hicks-common-threads/.
(4) Adam Smyth, "Commonplace Book Culture" in *Women and Writing C.1340-C.1650: The Domestication of Print Culture*, ed. Anne Lawrence-Mathers and Phillipa Hardman (Woodbridge: York Medieval Press, 2010), 105.
(5) Smyth, "Commonplace Book Culture," 105–6.
(6) Candace Hicks, "Posts," *Instagram*, https://www.instagram.com/candacehicksart/.

Cyberfeminism Index

Seu, Mindy.
Cyberfeminism Index.
Facilitated and gathered
by Mindy Seu, designed
in collaboration with and
developed by Angeline Meitzler,
with front-end support from Janine
Rosen and PDF support from Charles
Broskoski, Arial typeface by Patricia
Saunders and Robin Nicholas, encircled
numbers designed by Laura Coombs.
Premiered October 22, 2020. https://
www.cyberfeminismindex.com/.

Seu, Mindy.
Cyberfeminism Index.
Designed by Laura
Coombs.
Los Angeles: Inventory
Press, 2022. 607 p.; 24 × 17.5
× 4.5 cm.

The sortable, browsable, searchable, "INCOMPLETE and ALWAYS IN PROGRESS" experimental subject bibliography that is the *Cyberfeminism Index* was commissioned by Rhizome and debuted online in 2020 as part of the New Museum's First Look initiative.[1] This robust hub, derived from an earlier "crowd-sourced spreadsheet," is currently made up of 717 numbered entries of "radical techno-critical activism" dating from 1985–2021.[2] The website, facilitated by designer, professor, and researcher Mindy Seu and created with a team of collaborators, is a scholarly work that brings together all manner of voices from the likes of "Cyberfeminism 2.0, black cyberfeminism, xenofeminism, post-cyber feminism, glitch feminism, Afrofuturism, and hackfeministas, transhackfeminism, 넷페미 (netfemi), and 女权之声 (feminist voices)."[3]

An expandable list of open access articles, print monographs, videos, artist's projects, hacktivist websites, and a plethora of hard-to-define resources are displayed in black text on a white background using the font "Arial by Robin Nicholas and Patricia Saunders" which Seu identifies is "one of [the] few system fonts designed by a woman."[4] Each citation in the list leads with an encircled entry number, then year published/created, title, and author.

As a researcher scrolls, it brings the site to life—a neon-green gradient glows in the background then subtly fades to white after a pause. Hover over a citation and the text becomes bright green. With a click, the list item expands to show a short entry. Seu selects an engaging excerpt for readers to get to know each resource (e.g., pulling in a back-cover endorsement, a snippet from an introduction, a summary from the publisher, or an abstract) and adds in external URL(s), additional citation details if needed, and optional images. Using existing texts and paratexts to elucidate the subject and get to the point quickly is both researcher friendly and a smart editorial decision. More on this later. As citations are clicked, their descriptions not only open, they are automatically added to a right-hand "download" column as well. This is one of the coolest features of the site—visitors can build out a personalized reading list or mini-bibliography from Seu's index. Removing a resource from this user-driven compilation is easy too. Hover over its name and when the "x" appears click once to delete it. Clicking on the "download" button generates a PDF of any saved citations with their excerpts and images.

This living collection of cyberfeminism has the possibility of continued growth. The public can suggest additional resources through an online form accessible via a submit button at the bottom of every page. The *Cyberfeminism Index* is an English-language site with some bilingual entries and a few foreign language entries. Seu's project uniquely collates citations to theoretical resources and resources related to the practice of cyberfeminism. She explains:

> Cyberfeminism cannot be reduced to women and technology. Nor is it about the diffusion of feminism through technology. Combining cyber and feminism was meant as an oxymoron or provocation, a critique of the cyberbabes and fembots that stocked the sci-fi landscapes of the 1980s. The term is self-reflexive: technology is not only the subject of cyberfeminism, but its means of transmission. It's all about feedback.[5]

The *Cyberfeminism Index* offers several discovery options for researchers to find materials. The default view for the main list is in alphabetical order by author, but the user can sort resources by date created or alphabetically by title. With so many entries it does takes a while to perform a re-sort, although thanks to the project's developers, the text turns into a set of rogue illegible letterforms while you wait. On other pages in the site, researchers can visually browse a grid of images which will direct them back to a numbered

images

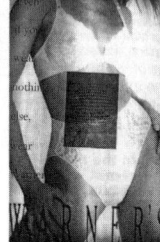

back to top contact submit

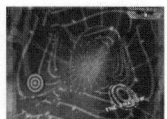

Cyberfeminism Index images page, screenshot.

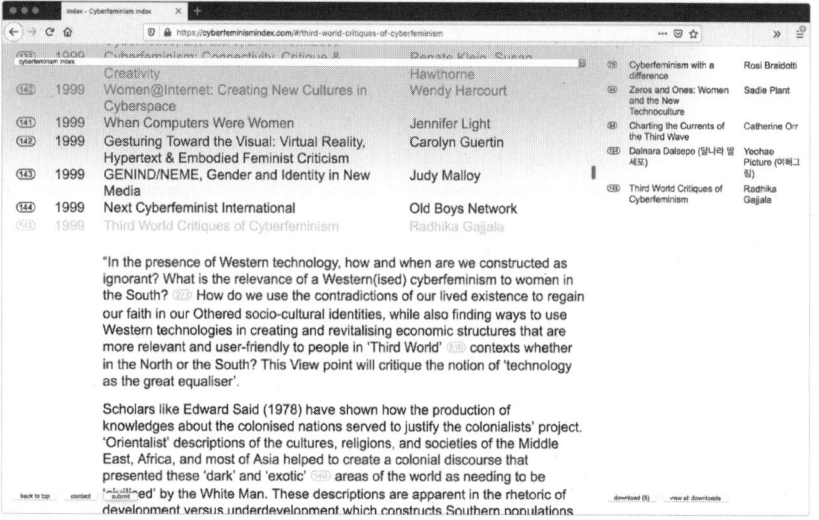

Cyberfeminism Index home page scroll with text drawer, screenshot.

entry on the main page. Users can also navigate to a section named "collections" which are lists guest-curated by other thinkers. A simple keyword search function on another page lets visitors search not only the main title and author entry but the excerpts as well, yielding greater relevancy and more opportunities to discover connections between entries.

The project is a fascinating mix of web bibliography, online publication, an archive of snippets and images, and an index. Typically an index is a list of headings like "a noun or noun phrase—the name of a person, a place, an object, or an abstraction" with corresponding locators to lead the reader to the page, paragraph, or section where its use within a publication occurs.[6] *Cyberfeminism Index* is a bibliographic list at the outset rather than an index of keywords. However, within the world of library science the terms "database" and "index" are used in tandem. Whereas "database" often indicates "aggregate collections of electronic journals, e-books, and articles to which full-text is available," the term "index" is understood to mean "a database of citations, often including information about articles such as abstracts."[7] Library speak: database equals full-text and index equals citations only or citations plus abstracts only. The *Cyberfeminism Index* is an "index" in this sense. That said, there is an inner indexical keyword mechanism at work within the project. Much creative and intellectual labor has gone into selecting the right descriptive passages. Through Seu's careful read, she links certain keywords and phrases out to other citation numbers where they occur in excerpts.

The recently released monograph gathered by Seu and designed by Laura Coombs choreographs the last three decades of global literatures and practices allied to cyberfeminism. The white, acid-green, and black scrollable site becomes a 600-plus-page newsprint directory, visibly hefty but light enough for readers to flip and fan and consider "cyberfeminism's long-ignored origins and its expansive legacy."[8] To speed up the production process going from web to print, Lily Healey has worked some scripting magic on the back end. Edge-to-edge text and full-justified paragraphing signal to readers that this is a reference work while the variance of columns, type sizes, and interspersed images in its section designs invites browsing and skimming. The use of space-saving Arial Narrow instead of Arial (regular) differentiates the book from the website but feels more uptight, and a bit claustrophobic.

Like literary print indexes of the past, Seu guides the reader with an introduction and instructions for use in the front matter. She also stacks the beginning with curated collections by guest experts to offer readers fourteen different paths to explore. The main entries are organized chronologically in this manifestation, starting with 1991 and Donna J. Haraway's "A Cyborg Manifesto." Shorter indexes for titles, people, and images helpfully lead readers back to the main entries. Strangely, the entries have been renumbered from the website so the paperback is not a companion to the website or vice versa. A foreword by Julianne Pierce and afterword by Legacy Russell further contextualize *Cyberfeminism Index* as an important functional, historical, and conceptual work.

(1) Mindy Seu, "about," *Cyberfeminism Index*, text edited by Andrew Scheinman, accessed October 12, 2022, https://www.cyberfeminismindex.com/about/. See also "First Look: Cyberfeminism Index," New Museum, accessed October 12, 2022, https://www.newmuseum.org/exhibitions/view/first-look-cyberfeminism-index.
(2) "Cyberfeminism Index," Inventory Press, accessed October 12, 2022, http://www.inventorypress.com/product/cyberfeminism-index; Mindy Seu, *Cyberfeminism Index* (Los Angeles: Inventory Press, 2022), 12.
(3) Seu, "about."
(4) Seu, "about."
(5) Seu, "about."
(6) *The Chicago Manual of Style*, 17th ed. (2017), s.v. "Components of an Index: Main Headings, Subentries, and Locators," 16.9–16.14.
(7) "Research, Instruction and Outreach," Mississippi State University Libraries, accessed October 12, 2022, https://ask.library.msstate.edu/rio/faq/12493.
(8) Seu, *Cyberfeminism Index*, back cover.

A Die with Twenty-Six Faces

A Die with Twenty-Six Faces, 2019, front cover.

(in order of publication date)

V. by Thomas Pynchon, 1963
Z by Vassilis Vassilikos, 1966
a by Andy Warhol, 1968
B by Eva Figes, 1972
G. by John Berger, 1972
H by Philippe Sollers, 1973
M: Writings '67–'72 by John Cage, 1973
U by Bosse Gustafson, 1973
W ou le souvenir d'enfance by Georges Perec, 1975
O by Leslie Scalapino, 1976
"A" by Louis Zukofsky, 1978
X: Writings '79–'82 by John Cage, 1983
v. by Tony Harrison, 1985
R by Kenne Fant, 1988
S. by John Updike, 1988
C by Arnold Skemer, 1992
D by Arnold Skemer, 1995
S. by Florence Delay et al., 1997
X: Tien dizijnen by Paul Claes, 1997
e by Matt Beaumont, 2000
N. by Ernesto Ferrero, 2000
Q by Luther Blissett, 2000
I. by Stephen Dixon, 2002
K. by Roberto Calasso, 2002
P by Andrew Lewis Conn, 2003
t by Victor Pelevin, 2009
C by Tom McCarthy, 2010
C: Honderd notities van een alleslezer by Paul Claes, 2011
K by Bernardo Kucinski, 2011
Y by Kenneth Jensen, 2012
A by Zach Sodenstern, 2013
F by Antônio Xerxenesky, 2014
J by Howard Jacobson, 2014
M by Acton Das, 2016

A Die with Twenty-Six Faces, 2019, back cover.

Lüthi, Louis. "A Die with 26 Faces."
Bulletins of the Serving Library, no. 3 (2012).
https://www.servinglibrary.org/journal/3/a-die-with-26-faces.

= . = . =

Lüthi, Louis. *A Die with Twenty-Six Faces*.
Design by the author. [Amsterdam]: Roma,
2019. 104 p.: some col. ill.; 20 × 13 × 1.5 cm.

A jaunty serif "L" with an elongated ascender leads the way, filling the blue paper cover of *A Die with Twenty-Six Faces* with intrigue. Isn't an initial punctuated by a period an initial with something to hide? This particular "L" is in fact an "*L.*" A truncation, but of what?

A Die with Twenty-Six Faces is a peculiar kind of bibliography. Written and designed by Louis Lüthi, the work "mix[es] essay and fiction" and includes a fourteen page color insert of alphabet book covers.[1] It is an experiment in writing with the graphic form of typographic letters. A few chapters from the biblio-centric storyline made an early appearance in the online publication *Bulletins of the Serving Library*.[2]

The narrator, who is likely an author proxy for Louis Lüthi and referred to simply as L., has a personal collection of (mostly real) literary works with letters for titles—*G.* by John Berger, *K.* by Roberto Calasso, *C* by Tom McCarthy, etc. His collection is in part inspired by the fictional alphabet books mentioned in James Joyce's *Ulysses* (1922) as well as a desire to survey the "Kells effect" in contemporary literature.[3] Writing in the third person, L.'s chapters unfold with musings on his readings, travels, and experiences, how the initial in an initial title relates to its book, and how the books relate to each other. The narrative of one alphabet book converges with another as L. finds overlaps, symmetries, and kinship between them. He's collected thirty-four volumes so far with triples for "A" and "C" and doubles for "K," "M," "S," "V," and "X."[4]

L. tells the reader that he keeps detailed notebooks about the titles he collects in order of their acquisition. Though the reader is not privy to this order, one understands that *A Die with Twenty-Six Faces* is intended to be a more polished form of these notebooks. On the back cover, the collection appears in a list ordered by publication date and the reader can easily see that these works were all published after *Ulysses*, from 1963's *V.* by Thomas Pynchon to 2016's *M* by Acton Das. An alphabetical list of all the titles appears within the first chapter of the book, where it becomes apparent that "L" is the only isolated title letter missing from L.'s A–Z collection of books. L. without an "L?" Blurring the lines of fiction and reality, the "L." on the cover art for *A Die with Twenty-Six Faces* signifies the narrator's collection gap, while completing his collection. L. as Lüthi as collector and designer took matters into his own hands to solve this alphabetic-bibliographic dilemma drama.

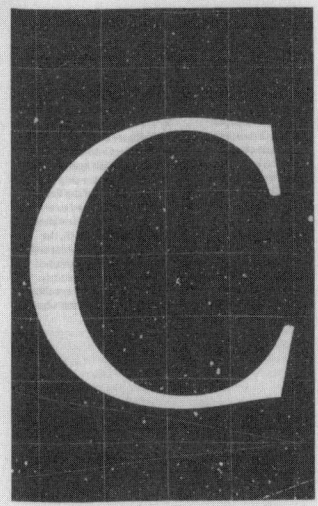

Interior spread of *A Die with Twenty-Six Faces*, 2019.

(1) "A Die with Twenty-Six Faces," Roma Publications, accessed November 10, 2022, https://www.romapublications.org/Roma251-500.html. **(2)** Five out of fourteen chapters from *A Die with Twenty-Six Faces* (2019) first appeared in "A Die with 26 Faces" (2012), although the narrator L. was then the first-person I. Lüthi published another bibliocentric narrative in 2012 as a printed pamphlet. See Louis Lüthi, *Infant A*, vol. 3, *The Social Life of the Book*, edited by castillo/corrales and piecemeal publishing structure and design by Will Holder (Paris: Paraguay Press, 2012). **(3)** Within Ulysses, alphabet books are an idea thought up by the character Stephen Dedalus in an inner monologue. The concept of the Kells effect refers to the "symbolic content" of a decorated initial and its bearing on the surrounding text. Louis Lüthi, *A Die with Twenty-Six Faces* ([Amsterdam]: Roma, 2019), 10–13. **(4)** Lüthi, *A Die with Twenty-Six Faces*, 17–18.

Difficult Times: Every Book About Spirituality I Own

Mills, Mike.
Difficult Times: Every Book About Spirituality I Own. Milan: Gallaria Marella, 2008. Exhibition takeaway for *Something Old, Something New, Something Borrowed, Something Blue*, February 21–May 30, 2008. 12 p.; 15 × 21 × 1 cm.

Mills, Mike.
"Difficult Times: Every Book About Spirituality I Own."
In *The Thing The Book: A Monument To The Book As Object*, edited by Jonn Herschend and Will Rogan, 62–67. San Francisco: Chronicle, 2014. 6 p.: col. ill.; page size: 25.5 × 20.5 cm.

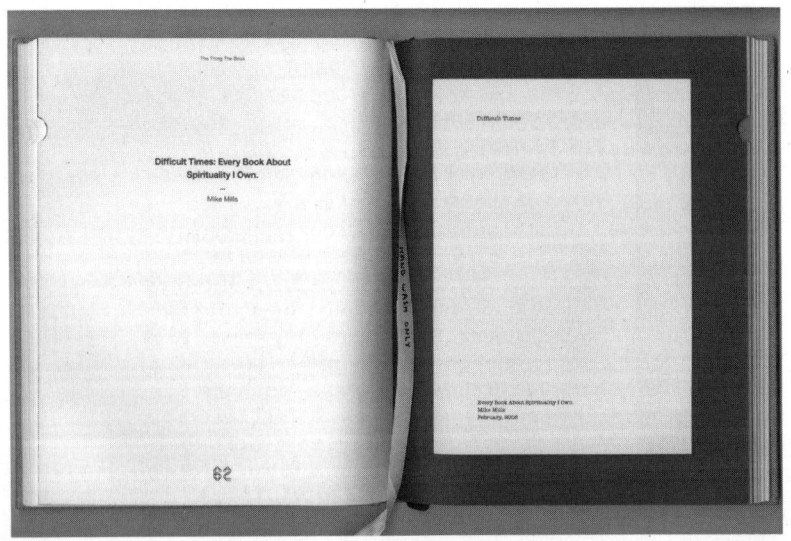

The Thing Quarterly is an object-publication cofounded by Jonn Herschend and Will Rogan. Each boxed issue contains a different limited-run project by an invited artist. Yearly subscribers don't know what will arrive via post: a boomerang by Gabriel Orozco, a bath towel by Ken Kagami, a soccer ball by Michelle Grabner? It's a mixed bag.

The concept behind *The Thing The Book* is an extension of Herschend and Rogan's artist-conceived publishing paradigm. The editors asked over thirty artists to contribute to a book project that examines the codex form and its constituent parts. Each artist received an assignment. Jonathan Lethem was in charge of the footnotes; Miranda July, an errata slip; and Mike Mills, the bibliography. Mills, a filmmaker, graphic designer and artist, submitted "Difficult Times: Every Book About Spirituality I Own," a photographic facsimile of a printed book list, dated February 2008. Ranging from best-selling self-help books to classics to lesser-known works, the bibliography covers multiple traditions including paganism, Wiccanism, New Age spirituality, pluralism, Buddhism, Taoism, and Hinduism. The title "Difficult Times" references a series of events in the artist's life as well as corresponds to two of the bibliography's selections by Pema Chödrön, *The Places That Scare You: A Guide to Fearlessness in Difficult Times* and *When Things Fall Apart: Heart Advice for Difficult Times*.

"Difficult Times" was initially conceived by Mills "as a self-portrait" and given away as a stand-alone pamphlet in a group exhibition at Gallaria Marella, Milan in 2008.[1] There it was shown alongside his work, *Battles, 1000 Hand Painted Rainbows*, a wall installation of watercolor rainbows

Opening spread of "Difficult Times," *The Thing The Book*, 2014, with ribbon bookmark by David Shrigley.

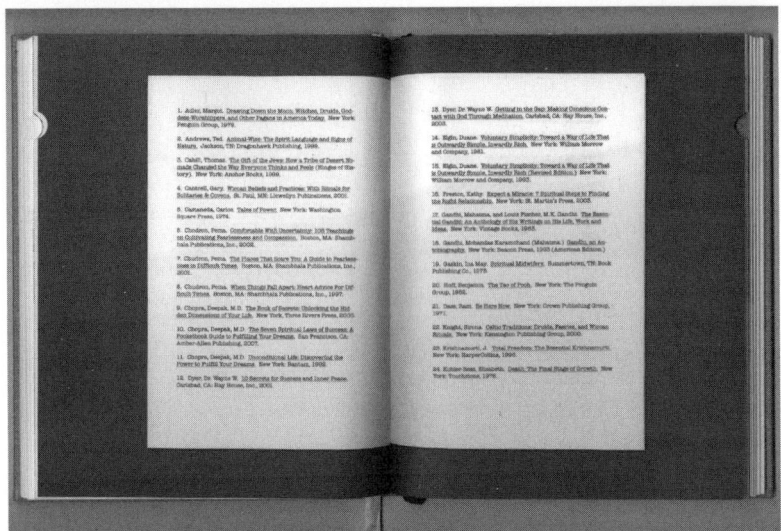

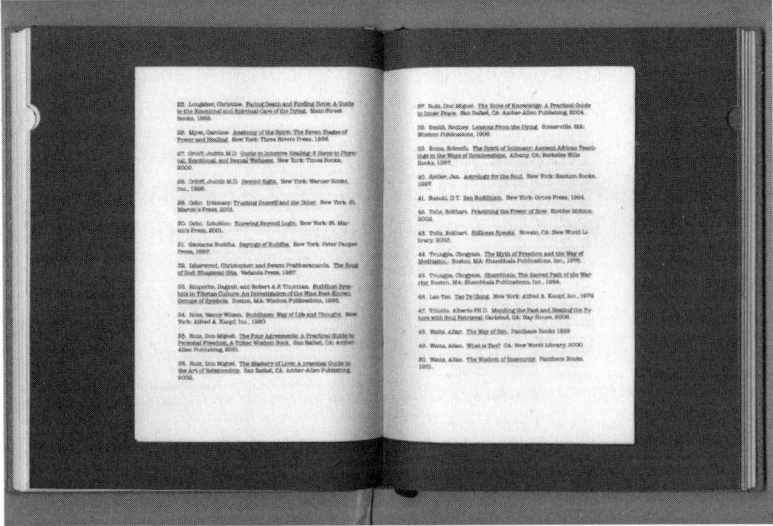

Interior spreads of "Difficult Times" in *The Thing The Book*, 2014.

on paper. Rainbows appear during a rain or after a storm, the mood-boosting reward after a period of grayness. There was a careful optimism to this pairing of publication and "rainbowed" expression.

For *The Thing The Book* the original saddle stitched "Difficult Times" booklet has been re-paginated, printed, bound, scanned, and then displayed full size at 5¾ × 8 inches. This new reworking appears as a book within a book, designed so that the virtual gutter of "Difficult Times" hits the actual gutter of *The Thing The Book*. The reader has a mediated experience of going through the pages of a personal, and sometimes painfully revealing list about finding the right relationship, seeking spiritual guidance, and caring for the dying.

A cheery yellow cover is followed by an enumerated list of fifty titles set in American Typewriter, an upbeat slab serif with unmistakably curly numbers.[2] Even though it's not a long list, exhaustion is implied in the exercise of listing "every book" that the artist owns on spirituality. The visual program of Mills's project fits the accessible, breezy feel of *The Thing The Book* although it seems at odds with the bibliography's contents. But this is his method, a resolutely amicable and vulnerable form of truth-telling.

---

(1) Mike Mills's website, accessed February 17, 2016, https://mikemillsmikemills.com/art-items/gallaria-marella-exhibition-2/.
(2) For other projects in the catalogue that have yellow covers, see "A Final Companion to Books from 'The Simpsons' in Alphabetical Order" and "Kentifrications." Although not particularly relevant here, an anecdote from Gerard Genette remarks, "At the beginning of the twentieth century, yellow covers were synonymous with licentious French books. . . . The signification [of indecency] is certainly the reason Aubrey Beardsley named his quarterly *The Yellow Book*." Gerard Genette, *Paratexts: Thresholds of Interpretation*, trans. Jane E. Lewin (Cambridge: Cambridge University Press, 1987), 24-25.

The El Saturn Research Library

Smith, Cauleen.
>*The El Saturn Research Library*, 2012.
>Installation. Threewalls.

Smith, Cauleen.
>*The El Saturn Research Library*.
>Chicago: Threewalls, 2012.
>Exhibition takeaway for the
>*Journeyman*, September 7–
>October 20, 2012. 1 poster:
>ill.; 87 × 58 cm, folded size:
>23 × 29 cm.

If Cauleen Smith's installation of *The El Saturn Research Library* is read through the lens of bibliography, then this bibliography is a reenactment of a milieu. It shows the constellation of ideas that fascinated members of the El Saturn Research Institute (1945–1993), a secret society of African American scholars and artists on the South Side of Chicago. The Institute, also known as Thmei Research, was started by the musician Sun Ra and his friend and business manager Alton Abraham. The Institute's library allegedly held 15,000 volumes on mysticism, the occult, science, numerology, biblical history, ancient culture, and space exploration.[1] Scholar and gallerist John Corbett writes, "In about 1951, Thmei began writing a dictionary of occult

Installation views of *The El Saturn Research Library*, 2012, at Threewalls.

terms, and they were ultimately interested in following a line of reasoning familiar to Black intellectuals at the time, a quest for independence through the possibility of separatism, rather than integration."[2]

The story of the El Saturn Research Institute is a complicated one to tell. For Smith's exhibition at Threewalls in 2012, she recreated a portion of what may have been in the Institute's library, borrowing over sixty volumes "from the personal library of Sun Ra and Alton Abraham on loan from John Corbett and Terri Kapsalis" as well as contributing a mix of books from her own library that aligned with a reading list that Sun Ra had given out to students at UC Berkeley in 1971.[3] The installation was not meant to be a faithful recreation of a physical, historical library but to revitalize the vibe of an Afro-Futurist atmosphere. In many ways its success as an artwork hinges on the ability to convey the aura of ownership and use-value of specific book objects within the enclosure of a gallery. The decision to show aged books and items with wear-and-tear is part of an overall sensual aesthetic.

In the newsprint takeaway, Smith includes a brief essay about her project, a schematic of the installation, and a bibliography of short citations for each of the books with asterisks marking her personal copies. Gallerygoers and subsequent takeaway readers can inversely identify which volumes had *perhaps* been handled by Sun Ra, Alton Abraham, and members of the El Saturn Research Institute.

The books, 142 volumes in total, were displayed in the gallery cover out, either perched atop an unfinished wood rail and held in place by a piece of wire or secured in a wall-mounted vitrine. The space was set up like a reading room with easygoing handwritten signs delineating sections for Fiction & Poetry, History, Non-Fiction, Reference, Occult

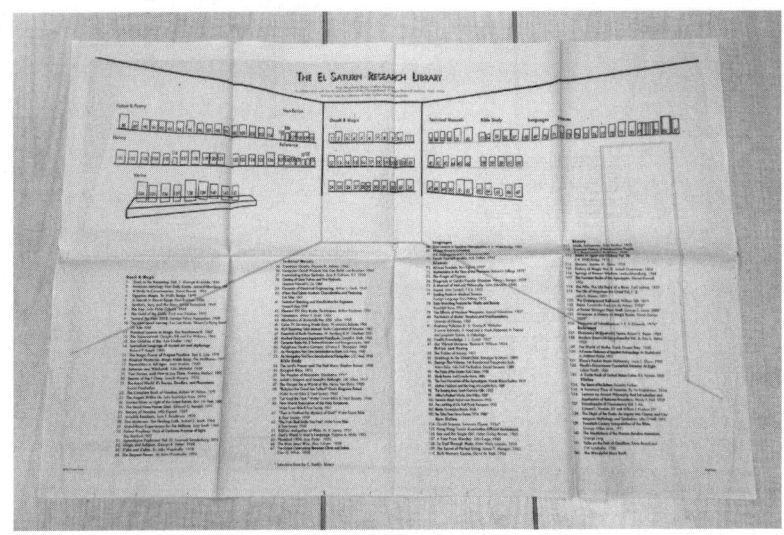

Unfolded interior of *The El Saturn Research Library*, 2012, exhibition takeaway.

& Magic, Technical Manuals, Bible Study, Languages, and Sciences. An oriental rug, a few pieces of wood furniture possibly from the 1950s, and a shiny new record player spinning *Black Utopia: LP*—Smith's album of Sun Ra recordings—occupied the center of the room.

Visually and organizationally mixed messages kept the display from finding a delicate cohesion. Wall texts told gallerygoers not to handle the books, though their tactile qualities and material resonances were promoted. Smith's use of bookstore categories imposed a rigid interpretation on top of a collection of books that had been used by the Institute in inspired and associative ways. Wasn't the point of this library collection to pry ideas loose from codified contexts in order to redefine "the very terms of culture and history?"[4] The mythic was pinned against stark white walls, and the haptic was absent. Rethinking the categories through the lens of Afro-Futurism was a missed opportunity.

But again this is a complex story with a tall order. The artist Cauleen Smith was as much a part of building this library as its Chicago-based Thmei predecessors were a part of constructing theirs. A bibliographic reverberation of the past carried over into the present.

(1) Cauleen Smith, *The El Saturn Research Library* (Chicago: Cauleen Smith, 2012), exhibition takeaway; "Guide to the Alton Abraham Collection of Sun Ra 1822–2008," University of Chicago Library, accessed March 25, 2016, https://www.lib.uchicago.edu/e/scrc/findingaids/view.php?eadid=ICU.SPCL.ABRAHAMA.
(2) John Corbett, "Sun Ra, Street Priest and Father of D.I.Y. Jazz," *Design Observer*, June 22, 2007, https://designobserver.com/feature/sun-ra-street-priest-and-father-of-diy-jazz/5557/.
(3) Cauleen Smith's website, accessed December 20, 2015, http://www.cauleensmith.com/; Smith, *The El Saturn Research Library*, exhibition takeaway.
(4) Smith, *The El Saturn Research Library*, exhibition takeaway.

Exhibition Takeaways

Selection from *Exhibition Takeaways*, 2018–2023.

Rebel, Janelle. *Exhibition Takeaways.* Design by the author. Numbered series of fifteen print publications. Sarasota, FL: Brizdle-Schoenberg Special Collections Center, Ringling College of Art and Design, 2018–2023. Page count varies: ill.; 22 × 18 cm. Open edition.

Rebel, Janelle. *Exhibition Takeaways.* Design by the author. Numbered series of fifteen digital publications. Sarasota, FL: Brizdle-Schoenberg Special Collections Center, Ringling College of Art and Design, 2018–2023. https://ringling.libguides.com/specialcollections/takeaways. Page count varies: ill.

The publication series *Exhibition Takeaways* follows and extends the exhibitions of the Brizdle-Schoenberg Special Collections Center at Ringling College of Art and Design. The series serves as a guide to the collections, a starting point for a topic, an archive of an event, a catalog of afterthoughts, and an opportunity for design. This counter-punctual project relates to the curriculum at the college and the center's collecting interests, including the studies and histories of art, design, communication, media, leisure, and publishing. Fifteen *Exhibition Takeaways* round out the series.

The concept developed out of the exhibition program that Janelle Rebel, the inaugural curator at the Brizdle-Schoenberg Special Collections Center, started in 2017. She uses the opportunity of the exhibition-as-bibliography to intermingle canonical and noncanonical figures, cultural workers operating in different milieus, high and low culture, etc. Each occasion becomes an opportunity to stretch and to try something new while exhibiting the prints, publications, and ephemera in the collection.

The *Exhibition Takeaways* are designed in-house after an exhibition and any exhibition programming have closed. The publication becomes a space where observations on a particular topic can settle or expand into new inquiries. *Exhibition Takeaways* usually, but not always, take their typographic design cues from the exhibition design and their layout changes each issue. Picturing the exhibited objects is important to entice the future reader. Scans of book covers or interiors, photographs of book objects, and/or photographs of the exhibition are included along with any introductory texts, object descriptions, bibliographic checklists that cite local call numbers, and additional essays.

Riso-printed versions are given away free at the center. The ink color rotates between issues and is chosen on press.

Exhibition Takeaways #11–15 for give away, 2023.

Digital versions can be downloaded on the center's website and through the Alfred R. Goldstein Library catalog.

As visual bibliographies, *Exhibition Takeaways* are fundamentally wrapped up in aesthetic play during its research, selection, and compilation processes. The model-making and design investigations of exhibition and publication work feed off and inform one another. The play-worlds they materialize are intended to offer readers an exploratory spark and an entrée to bibliographic networks.

A Final Companion to Books from "The Simpsons"

[Lebrun, Olivier.] *A Pocket Companion to Books from "The Simpsons" in Alphabetical Order: From the Collection of O. Lebrun, Paris.* Zürich: Rollo Press, 2012. [186] leaves: ill.; page size: 17 × 12 cm.

✯✯✯✯✯✯✯✯✯✯✯✯✯✯✯✯✯✯✯✯✯✯✯✯✯✯✯✯✯✯

[Lebrun, Olivier.] *Another Companion to Books from "The Simpsons" in Alphabetical Order: From the Collection of O. Lebrun Paris.* Zürich: Rollo Press, 2013. [352] p.: ill.; page size: 17 × 12 cm.

✯✯✯✯✯✯✯✯✯✯✯✯✯✯✯✯✯✯✯✯✯✯✯✯✯✯✯✯✯✯

[Lebrun, Olivier.] *A Final Companion to Books from "The Simpsons."* New updated ed. Europe: Yellow Pages, 2018. [640] p.: ill.; 18 × 12 × 4 cm.

✯✯✯✯✯✯✯✯✯✯✯✯✯✯✯✯✯✯✯✯✯✯✯✯✯✯✯✯✯✯

[Lebrun, Olivier.] *A Final Companion to Books from "The Simpsons."* Reprint ed. Europe: Yellow Pages, 2019. [640] p.: ill.; 18 × 12 × 4 cm.

A FINAL COMPANION TO

BOOKS

FROM

THE
SIMPSONS

NEW, UPDATED EDITION

A Final Companion to Books from "The Simpsons," reprint edition, 2019, cover.

Lisa Simpson reads *The Joy of Sax* in the backseat of the family car. Marge Simpson consults volume 28 of the *Encyclopedia of Mother's Fears*. Ned Flanders hugs the *Holy Bible* under the night sky. Books make regular appearances as plot points and split-second gags throughout episodes of *The Simpsons*, the long-running animated American sitcom. French graphic designer and publisher Olivier Lebrun seemingly tracks all the books that appear in this drawn universe, paying homage to the show's smallest details.

Lebrun's first compilation of animated frames in book form, *A Pocket Companion to Books from "The Simpsons" in Alphabetical Order*, amassed 174 titles, and his second release, *Another Companion to Books from "The Simpsons" in Alphabetical Order* documented 216 more. Now both out of print, these projects were published by Rollo Press—founded by Urs Lehni, and reproduce black-and-white illustrations on

Spine view of all four editions, plus one that was never released due to technical issues.

golden yellow paper—the signature fleshtone of the Simpson's family. In 2018 Lebrun released *A Final Companion to Books from "The Simpsons"* with Yellow Pages, a book publisher founded by him and Urs Lehni. *A Final Companion* culls from Lebrun's first two projects, bringing a selection of 339 books from *The Simpsons* together on unnumbered pages. Full-bleed stills present books as they appeared within the action of a scene or as close-up object crops.

The index in *A Final Companion* lists the book titles in alphabetical order inside the fold-outs of the front and back covers.[1] Each book is assigned an index number combining the first letter of its title plus a unique identifier 1–339. The handy notational system is used throughout the publication, providing shorthand references to the books in the screenshot and guiding the reader back to the index. This is especially useful when a title in the illustrated frame is hard to read.

Farcical books populate scenes and add visio-verbal humor to the show. In entry A 014, Homer is tucked into bed with a book called *Already-Solved Crossword Puzzles*. In C 045 Lisa pulls *Conservative Women from Queen Victoria to Victoria Jackson* off the library shelf. In G 077 the Flanders family gathers around a volume called *Gentle Tales for Good Boys*.

Textbooks and reference works and Bibles are aplenty. Bart gleefully tosses pages of his math book into a blender in M 142. Lisa is pictured on her bed with a stack of textbooks in E 063. She is reading one simply titled *Extra Credit*. The cover of a *Children's Illustrated Bible* is depicted in C 041 with Jesus jumping on a trampoline with kids on either side of him under a smiling sun.

Then there are numerous books written by the characters themselves: *Homer, I Hardly Knew Me* by Homer Simpson (H 096), *I, Bully* by Nelson Muntz (I 109), *Out of the Mouth*

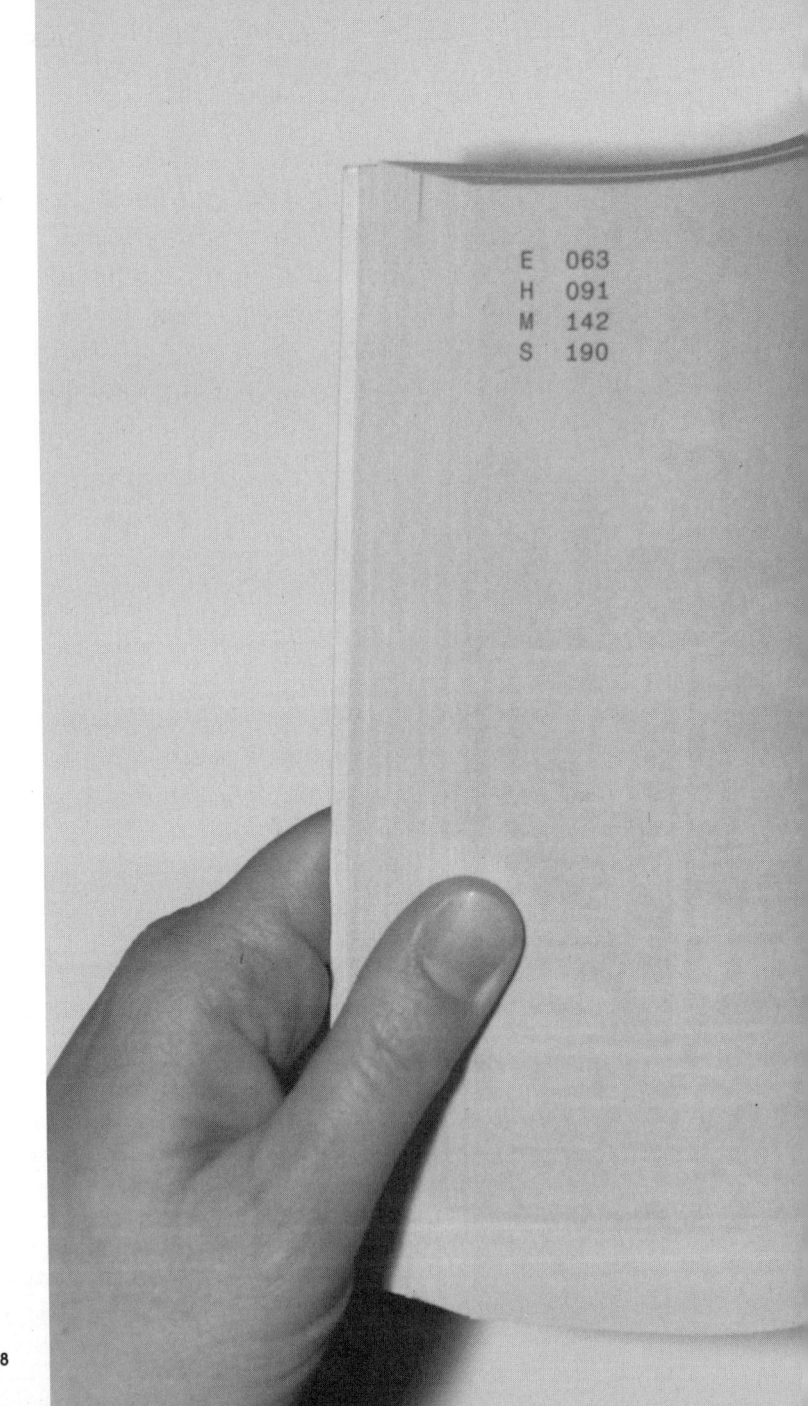

Interior spread of *A Final Companion to Books from "The Simpsons,"* reprint edition, 2019.

of Abe by Marshall Goldman & the late Abraham Simpson (O 163), *Postcards from the Hedge* by Goundskeeper Willie, and *There's a Rainbow in My Basement* by Moe Szyslak (T 296), to name a few.

Contemporary culture and current events directly bleed into the reality of *The Simpsons*. Fake books appear by real people like *Fahrenheit 451,000* by Ray Bradbury (F 065), *Pretending to Like Football* by Mrs. John Madden (P 174), and *Sane Planning, Sensible Tomorrow* by Al Gore (S 174). Real books by real authors are perused by the characters as well. Burns sits in an armchair reading *Bossypants* by Tina Fey (B 034). Marge uses Charles Darwin's *The Origin of the Species* (T 276) to help Lisa. Moe stands behind the bar, halfway through his copy of *Fifty Shades of Grey* (F 068). Lebrun's own book *A Pocket Companion to Books from "The Simpsons" in Alphabetical Order* (A 005) is depicted in an episode for the ultimate in self-referentiality.

A blend of titles real and imagined make up the complex network of *The Simpsons'* biblioverse. With titles and sometimes scant author info displayed, Lebrun's guides may not connect all the dots, but fansites like Wikisimpsons (https://simpsonswiki.com/) or Simpsons Wiki (https://simpsons.fandom.com/) are sure to help the curious reader. A quick Google search will direct you to more information on the episode number or context of the book's appearance. In fact, the publisher includes a special note of thanks on the inside cover to "all *The Simpsons* fans running websites and blogs, and to the readers providing tips—they all helped gathering material for this book."[2] Lebrun's work cleverly identifies and catalogs the growing bibliography created by an ongoing animated television show, and effectively taps into fan cultures for leads.

(1)
Articles like "A" and "The" at the beginning
of titles are not treated as non-filing
characters, so these titles are somewhat
oddly grouped under the sections for
"A" and "T."

(2)
[Olivier Lebrun],
A Final Companion to Books from "The Simpsons"
(Europe: Yellow Pages, 2019),
inside front cover.

Further Listening — Dworkin, Craig Douglas. "Further Listening." In *No Medium*, 141–73. Cambridge, MA: MIT Press, 2013. 34 p.; page size: 23 × 15 cm.

Chapter opening of "Further Listening" in *No Medium*, 2013.

Bibliographies within books are usually relegated to back matter. Not so with Craig Dworkin. He dedicates chapter 8 of his book *No Medium* to the theme of "further listening"—and elaborates on it with a written guide to silent scores, recordings, and performances. The bibliographic concept plays the edge of what seems outwardly ridiculous—how many silent scores could there be?—with an unwavering commitment to instances of creative non-practice. The discography unfolds from John Cage's *4'33"* (1952) and spiders out in all directions to connect genres, decades, technologies, and performers. The oldest piece in Dworkin's survey is a satirical work from 1897, Alphonse Allais's *Marche funèbre composée pour les funérailles d'un grand homme sourd* which begins with a notated silence. The first movement of the piece is "simply nine empty measures, with the tempo marked 'lento rigolando [slowly, jesting].'"[1]

Dworkin's guide to "further listening" is a bibliography that spins out, crisscrosses back and forth through time and visits a myriad of epistemic centers. Sixty-six bulleted, unnumbered entries cluster genealogies of silent projects that are directly or incidentally related to one another. The list requires an attentive reading for the interested, and for the totally immersed there are three additional pages of endnotes. The entries are ordered intuitively by Dworkin rather than chronologically by title or alphabetically by artist. This arrangement doesn't allow the reader to easily scan and compare entries—for example, an artist may have several main entries that do not appear in succession. The publisher's oversized bullets create a distinct visual break between thought clusters, but an organizational symbol-system notation could have offered the reader more navigational possibilities.[2] "Further Listening" is a highly networked narrative that in many ways would work well in a hyperlinked environment. However, when the pages are read linearly as intended by the author, the sequence does yield some sympathetic connections. An entry for an unrealized composition of silent Muzak by John Cage called *Silent Prayer* (1948) is followed by an entry for *Three Minutes of Silence* (1952), a news article about Dick McCann who inserted blank records into the jukeboxes at the student union of the University of Detroit "for the comfort of the silent types."[3] Cage is said to have clipped and saved this article.

The descriptions vary in length and weave in biographical, historical, or production information with Dworkin's critical commentary. He documents his reactions to experiencing the pieces and the reader quickly understands that silence demands a particularly close attention and offers sharp detail in return. In the entry for Peeter Vähi's *Supreme Silence* (1999), Dworkin writes "'supreme' is probably overstating the case" and he is clearly not a fan of Vähi's New Age overtones.[4] But for Yoko Ono and John Lennon's *Unfinished Music 2: Life with the Lions* (1969), Dworkin unravels the reasons for the record's emotional effects, ultimately concluding that it is "genuinely sad."[5] Other materials including *Poemas (in) sonoros* (1969), a visual square record of "inaudible sound poetry" by Edgardo Antonio Vigo, is "mesmerizing"; and John Levack Drever's track "Pastoral Pause" on *A Call for Silence* (2004) is "terrifying," an "ominous, edge-of-your-seat silence recorded on location in Dartmoor."[6]

---

(1) Craig Douglas Dworkin, "Further Listening,"
in *No Medium* (Cambridge, MA: MIT Press, 2013), 147.
(2) *New York Magazine*, for example, loves a good symbol-system shorthand to depict and compare complex information on its pages. Please note that *No Medium* was typeset in-house at MIT Press though no designer was credited specifically.
(3) "The Flip Side: Spin It and Get Acquainted,"
New York Post, January 16, 1952.

(4) Dworkin, "Further Listening," 157.
(5) Dworkin, "Further Listening," 158.
(6) Dworkin, "Further Listening," 160, 171.

Single page of "Further listening" showing entries about John Cage and Dick McCann.

■ Jean-Luc Godard: *Bande à part* (1964). In a moment of boredom, unable to think of how to entertain themselves and too agitated to indulge in a true French *ennui*, Franz (Sami Frey) proposes that the *bande* take "une minute de silence." Godard obliges by cutting the soundtrack (*la bande sonore mise à part*). "Une vraie minute de silence, ça dure une éternité [A real minute of silence can last forever]," Franz notes, but Godard's lasts only 33 seconds. The discrepancy provides an accessible, funny, narrative reprise of the acerbic, mean-spirited abstract silence from the final twenty-four minutes of Guy Debord's *Hurlements en faveur de Sade* (1952). The situationists would denounce Godard's techniques as "tardivement plagié et inutile . . . prétentieuses fausses nouveautés [tardily plagiarized and useless . . . pretentious false novelties]," but they were never known for their sense of humor, and it's really pretty funny.[13] A similar and even shorter composition, presumably by Michel Legrand, accompanies the tabletop finger performance of the film's iconic dance scene, in which Odile and Arthur negotiate the steps they'll soon dance to Legrand's hipster swing number "Le Madison," itself interrupted by parenthetical excerpts from the earlier minute of silence. In mono.

■ John Cage: *Silent Prayer* (1948, unrealized). Hints at the neo-Dada origins of *4'33"* and its latent corporate critique. Cage's plan was to "compose a piece of uninterrupted silence and sell it to Muzak Co. It will be three or four and a half minutes in length—those being the standard lengths of 'canned music.'"[14] Cage, that still unravished *mariée*, would have *mise à nu* canned music—a kind of sonic readymade—and translated it into a Duchampian "hasard en conserve [canned chance]."[15] Always seemed to be playing in the elevator in my old building.

■ Dick McCann: *Three Minutes of Silence* (1952). Just as Cage plotted to insert a blank record into the Muzak playlist, a New York humor columnist imagined blank records inserted into jukeboxes for shy dates who could avoid the latest jump hit by Louis Jordan in favor of discs "that play absolutely nothing, nothing but silence."[16] A follow-up release anticipated ambient minimalist electronica by decades; it was said to incorporate "a beep tone which will sound ever so gently every 15 seconds so that people will know the machine is playing."[17] After his death, it was discovered that John Cage had carefully saved a clipping of the article, which had been published in the same year as *4'33"*.

FURTHER LISTENING 155

Hidden Histories

Strachan, Tavares. *Hidden Histories*. 2018. Series of at least fourteen artworks, dimensions variable.

Written in a stately all caps serif, individual names like GALILEO, COLUMBUS, and SOCRATES are engraved across pairs of limestone bookends that emulate classical entablature. Another set of names in colored neon interrupts and steps forward—[Harriet] Tubman obstructs Galileo, [Oscar Zeta] Acosta obstructs Columbus, and [Winston] Foster obstructs Socrates, respectively—making an unapologetic entrance in a glowing, handwritten script.

The sculptural series *Hidden Histories* formalizes a correction of the Western canon. It is but one expression of Tavares Strachan's extended research into underrecognized and forgotten individuals of historic importance. Such ideas have formalized in interrelated works like the encyclopedia and book-stand sculpture, *The Encyclopedia of Invisibility* (2018 and 2021), as well as the monumental installation and performance at the Carnegie Museum of Art for the

57th Carnegie International, also called *The Encyclopedia of Invisibility* (2018). Strachan's *Hidden Histories* graphically and conceptually offers up an electric knowledge, drawing our attention to the social, cultural, and political contributions of women and minorities through the use of their surnames.[1] Naming is a powerful act. The roster has shifted. The use of surnames for women and minorities is inherently thorny, however, with inescapable connections to patriarchy, colonialism, and slavery. Strachan's project doesn't set out to buck the system—instead, it operates within the logic and folly of the encyclopedia, mimicking its codes.

Sandwiched between each set of bookends is a small curated selection of new, gently-used, or ex-library books, magazines, DVDs, and/or CDs related to each "hidden" figure. For instance, the artwork *Smalls (Hidden Histories)* is about Robert Smalls (1839–1915), an enslaved Black man who heroically gained freedom for himself, his crew, and their families by hatching a plan to pilot a Confederate transport ship to join forces with the Federal Army during the American Civil War. He later became a five-term congressman. For *Smalls (Hidden Histories)*, Strachan inset five volumes—two biographies (one for children and one for adult readers), two reference works that likely have entries about Smalls (one directory and one encyclopedia), and one reprint of a 19th century book that coined the term *eugenics*—to educate the viewer about the life of Robert Smalls and bring the viewer into contact with the worldviews that Smalls was up against. Here the genius of Smalls is set in stark contrast to the racist scientific discourse of the day. In another example, *De Pizan (Hidden Histories)*, the bookends bracket nine books on the life and writings of Christine de Pizan (1364–ca. 1430), a feminist poet and professional court writer active in Europe during the late Middle Ages.

Smalls (Hidden Histories), 2018.

De Pizan (Hidden Histories), 2018.

And in *Foster (Hidden Histories)*, Strachan highlights the life of deejay Winston Foster aka Yellowman (1956–), selecting four books about Jamaican reggae and dancehall music, plus a live show of Yellowman on DVD, and his Christmas album on CD. The artist decorates the covers of each set of resources with vinyl letters and numbers, line drawings and encyclopedic diagrams. Such embellishments create cohesion among the items on the shelf, gives them new purpose, and connects them back to *The Encyclopedia of Invisibility*.

For an install at Regen Projects in Los Angeles, from November 2–December 22, 2018, eight works from the *Hidden Histories* series were presented in darkened galleries with deep, blue-black walls. The names written in neon are manifest, no longer concealed, but the main attraction—albeit still a bit mysterious. The books and media they contain cannot be read or viewed or listened to in such installations. They are stand-ins for ideas and physical representations of what we may know or what little we may know about the life behind each name.

(1) While there doesn't seem to be a specific relationship between the name in neon and the name in limestone, here is the list of works from the series that I've been able to research in alphabetical order:

Acosta (Hidden Histories), [Oscar Zeta] **Acosta** is written on COLUMBUS;
Colvin (Hidden Histories), [Claudette] **Colvin** is written on VOLTAIRE;
De Pizan (Hidden Histories), [Christine] **de Pizan** is written on REMBRANDT;
Du Bois (Hidden Histories), [W. E. B.] **Du Bois** is written on EINSTEIN;
Foster (Hidden Histories), [Winston] **Foster** is written on SOCRATES;
Gentileschi (Hidden Histories), [Artemisia] **Gentileschi** is written on TCHAIKOVSKY;
Henson (Hidden Histories), [Matthew] **Henson** is written on RAPHAEL;
Klint (Hidden Histories), [Hilma af] **Klint** is written on SPINOZA;
Mandela (Hidden Histories), [Nelson] **Mandela** is written on LEONARDO;
Ride (Hidden Histories), [Sally] **Ride** is written on KEPLER;
Selassie (Hidden Histories), [Haile] **Selassie** is written on BEETHOVEN;
Smalls (Hidden Histories), [Robert] **Smalls** is written on DARWIN;
Tubman (Hidden Histories), [Harriet] **Tubman** is written on GALILEO;
Walcott (Hidden Histories), [Derek] **Walcott** is written on NIETZSCHE.

Human_3.0 Reading List 2015–2016

Smith, Cauleen. *Human_3.0 Reading List.* 2015. Series of fifty-seven drawings, graphite, and acrylic on graph paper, 29.5 × 24.5 cm. ◊———◊———◊———◊ Smith, Cauleen. *Human_3.0 Reading List* (blog). Posted on June 15, 2015. https://readinglisthumanthreepointo.wordpress.com/. ◊———◊———◊———◊ Smith, Cauleen. *Human_3.0 Reading List.* 2015. Series of postcards. ◊———◊———◊———◊ Smith, Cauleen. *Human_3.0 Reading List 2015–2016.* Design by David Giordano. Chicago: Corbett vs. Dempsey, 2016. 70 p.: col. ill.; 18 × 13 × 1 cm. ◊———◊———◊———◊ [Smith, Cauleen]. *Cauleen Smith: Human_3.0 Reading List.* [Chicago]: Art Institute of Chicago, 2017. Exhibition takeaway. 4 p.: col. ill.; 18 × 13 cm.

In *Human_3.0 Reading List 2015–2016*, Cauleen Smith exhibits a visual bibliography of fifty-seven book-cover drawings on graph paper—reproduced one per page—followed by a tidy, handwritten numbered list of the titles in alphabetical order by author. Of this selection Smith writes:

> These are some of the books that literally changed my life, saved my life and sustain my life, but also, (fair warning) make it difficult for me to | go along | get along | look the other way | and gets mines.[1]

The book-cover art with the brief end bibliography allows the viewer to place the texts. Here we find a mix of critical theory, poetry, fiction, and art writing that has affected the artist. Writings on Blackness, queerness, history, technologies, and systems that have made the artist. This selection predates 2020 anti-racism lists. This is a 2015–2016 list in the wake of the death of Michael Brown. This is a 2015–2016 list decrying the loss of Black studies departments in higher education, the same Black studies departments that were founded as a direct result of mass campus protests during the civil rights movement. This is also a 2015–2016 Afro-optimist future list. It is precisely a selection of fifty-seven books that the artist has read over a lifetime—during her student days at San Francisco State, her involvement in the All-African Peoples' Revolutionary Party, and in the classroom of Dr. Angela Davis—and that will continue to expand. Many staples of assigned reading in Black studies are present, as well as the quirkiness of Smith's individuality with titles on starfish and sea urchins, kite making, and an issue of the alternative comic *Love & Rockets*.

The drawings themselves, rendered in pencil and watercolor or occasionally acrylic, allow the viewer to encounter

Selection from the *Human_3.0 Reading List* drawings, 2015.

the artist's own books with their creased, torn, curled, or smooth covers. If these are still life drawings, their object energy can hardly be contained, activated by Smith with the frenetic marks of her pencil and color washes that betray their inked outlines. Often one of the artist's hands makes an appearance in the picture plane—holding the book or flexing its spine—simultaneously posing it as a drawing model and holding it out for the viewer to consider: *Here, an offering*. The presence of her hand is a racial signifier too, in communication with the cover art, shifting in shades from honey-toned brown to purplish black. It provides a sense of scale, evident in *The Autobiography of Malcolm X*, a pocket-sized book that rests in her palm. For cover art fans, the face-out visual display provides a clue as to which edition and/or printing she holds dear. Smith's drawings helpfully problematize the cover designs themselves, which in many cases are strangled by visual codes and biases that determine book markets.

In the essay "Human_3.0 Reading List Manifesto," which follows her drawings and handwritten bibliography, Smith produces a provocative, grounded, and brilliant piece of writing in six pages. "BLACK PEOPLE ARE AT WAR WITHOUT THE PROPER ARMOR," she begins.[2] "WE REQUIRE INOCULATIONS THAT REPEL THE SEDUCTIONS OF CORPORATE SERVITUDE."[3] In an argument and proposition poetic and associative, she offers readers three actions: STUDY, CONVERSATION, and RESISTANCE.[4]

Twelve of Smith's original book cover drawings were included in *After Today*, a group exhibition at Gallery 400 curated by Lorelei Stewart, May 8–August 8, 2015. Giveaway postcards for individual titles were distributed at five cafes and one bookshop in Chicago as a part of this project.

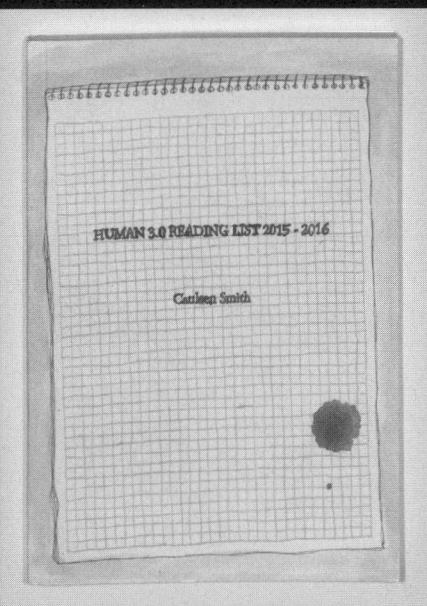

Human_3.0 Reading List 2015–2016, 2016, cover and interior spread.

The full set of fifty-seven drawings debuted in a solo exhibition in the Prints & Drawings galleries at the Art Institute of Chicago, May 27–Oct 29, 2017.[5] A free takeaway version of Smith's handwritten reading list was offered to visitors to accompany the drawings.

(1) Cauleen Smith, *Human_3.0 Reading List 2015–2016* (Chicago: Corbett vs. Dempsey, 2016), 67.
(2) Smith, *Human_3.0 Reading List*, 64. For more on the concept of armor, see the entry for "Africanismus_12469" in this catalogue.
(3) Smith, *Human_3.0 Reading List*, 64.
(4) Smith, *Human_3.0 Reading List*, 66–67.
(5) See "Cauleen Smith: Press Release," Corbett Vs. Dempsey, accessed November 15, 2022, https://corbettvsdempsey.com/exhibitions/cauleen-smith/; and "Cauleen Smith: Human_3.0 Reading List," Art Institute of Chicago, accessed November 15, 2022, https://www.artic.edu/exhibitions/2693/cauleen-smith-human-3-0-reading-list.

Ideal Syllabus

An Ideal Syllabus, 1998, cover with art school library barcode and call number label.

Saltz, Jerry, ed.
An Ideal Syllabus: Artists, Critics and Curators Choose the Books We Need to Read.
London: Frieze, 1998.
62 p.; 16.5 × 11 × 1 cm.

:::

Ideal Syllabus, feature.
Frieze.
few times yearly, May 2008–May 2018.
Typically 2 p.: col. ill.;
page size: 30 × 23 cm.

Back in 1998 critic and educator Jerry Saltz teamed up with the editors at *Frieze* to produce a veritable and portable "list of lists."[1] Saltz, dismayed to discover that the same writings were continually being assigned in art school syllabi, began asking artists, critics, and curators (many of whom were also educators) for their personal reading recommendations. Surely, they would not all have the same locus of references. The resulting pocket-sized book, *An Ideal Syllabus*, brings these findings together, offering an expansive reading guide for art students as well as a bibliographic "self-portrait" of each of the seventy-three contributors in Saltz's circle.[2] The disconnect between the diversity of works that excite artists and art workers and the select few works that funnel through pedagogy is presented as a wide chasm. The project pushes private reading into the light, and the contributors seem to extend nothing but goodwill to unknown readers: *here are a few works to get you started.*

Ideal Syllabus

Eileen Myles discusses the books that have influenced her

Ten years later the idea behind *An Ideal Syllabus* resurfaced within the pages of *Frieze* magazine proper, becoming a recurring series in which the *Frieze* editors solicit curators, artists, and writers to "list the books that have influenced them."[3] Saltz's original project was slightly tweaked, and in the 2008 iteration the language had broadened from "critics" to "writers."

In back-to-back issues, Nicolas Bourriaud and Adrian Piper were the first two contributors to this durational project, in

Eileen Myles's Ideal Syllabus in *Frieze* (November–December 2015).

May 2008 and June–August 2008 respectively. Bourriaud decides on a list of Spanish, French, and English language books providing notes of varying lengths (or no notes at all) for each. He organizes his selections into subcategories: "Novels that are particularly relevant to the beginning of the 21st century," "Theoretical books that somehow invent their objects," "Books for travelling," and "A book for curators."[4] Spoiler: the latter is Raymond Roussel's *Locus Solus* (1914/1984). Bourriaud includes one female writer, Carol Dunlop, who is the coauthor with Julio Cortázar of *Autonauts of the Cosmoroute*.

Piper takes another approach. Thirteen choice picks, ordered by the decade of life in which she read them. She included her first reader in English, Ruth Krauss's *I Can Fly* (1950); a bit of insight into her twenties with *Bhagavad Gita: Song of God* (1944) and Swami Vivekananda's *Karma Yoga* (1896/1955); the Western philosophy of her third and later decades, Immanuel Kant's *Critique of Pure Reason* (1781/1998); and a find in her sixties that rounds out the list, Thomas McEvilley's *The Shape of Ancient Thought: Comparative Studies in Greek and Indian Philosophy* (2001).

In the November–December 2015 issue, the writer and poet Eileen Myles takes on Ideal Syllabus beginning with a confession of procrastination. With the reader's expectations

Gary Panter's
Ideal Syllabus
in *Frieze*
(May 2013).

Ideal Syllabus

Artist Gary Panter draws and discusses the books that have influenced him

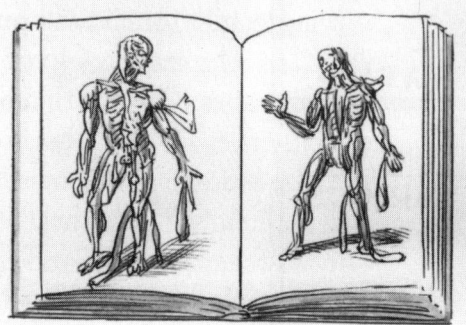

1

Reginald Marsh
Anatomy for Artists
1945

—

Anatomy for Artists was my baby colouring book. My father is a cowboy painter and this was lying around the house throughout my entire childhood. Marsh drew beautiful ink studies of classical drawings and paintings he admired, including tight copies of Andreas Vesalius's flayed corpses, which both terrified and fascinated me.

2

J.G. Ballard
The Unlimited Dream Company
1979

—

Ballard's writing jumped out at me from science-fiction collections in the late 1960s because he wrote about terrain and objects and psychological states and not spaceships. The protagonist in *The Unlimited Dream Company* is named Blake, and the book is hauntingly apocalyptic and paradisiacal.

3

Alexander Cruden
Cruden's Concordance
1737

—

Cruden's Concordance is a topical index of the King James Bible written by Cruden, an English bookseller and Bible enthusiast, and first published in 1737. I received it as a high-school graduation present from our hometown preacher. If I hadn't got the art bug, I might have made a very unhappy Church of Christ preacher. This is a very handy book if you can remember even one word of the biblical thing you are seeking. Ass. Hemp. Brick.

All drawings by Gary Panter, 2013

'Marshall McLuhan and Mad magazine were performing similar functions at the top and bottom of culture, promoting a suspicion of Madison Avenue snake oil.'

4

Donald Barthelme
Sixty Stories
1981
—

Barthelme's *Sixty Stories* really got across to me the magical, image-generating power of prose. If the writer writes it, our brains try to envision it, even if it is a ruby emerald foot on a plane with a bunch of Dunkers. Barthelme, the son of a Modernist architect from Houston, said that he was trying to make the equivalent of abstract painting with his short stories. There is such a good and slightly toxic humour expressed in these maddeningly brilliant stories. Every year, I rip a copy up and give parts of this book to my sophomore narrative classes and hope that they will buy a whole copy some day.

5

Ed Ruscha's books
—

I found Ruscha's books at the Dallas Museum of Fine Art bookshop when I was in high school. I collected as many as I could, I thought they have shaped my taste since. They made me want to make books before I got excited about underground comics. They deliver the goods with the minimal parts one needs to make apparent books: they are beautiful, simple, poetic, bare outsides and insides, are made of paper and ink, and each one expresses a compelling and great idea.

6

Anthony Burgess
The Wanting Seed
1962
—

I read *The Wanting Seed* after *A Clockwork Orange* (also 1962), in a Burgess reading frenzy at college. I was not well educated, so being force-fed a torrent of exotic and arcane words was a very good thing for my mental development. In *The Wanting Seed*, Burgess details – a fat global cultural tome – Catholicism with church and state complicit in perpetuating reports of never-ending wars while marching recruits to a canning factory in Ireland.

7

John Cage
Silence
1961
—

Silence was given to me in 1970 by my painting teacher, Bruce Tibbetts, who put many books and records in my hands. Cage's ideas about democratic vantage point, loud silence, prepared instruments, the use of noises and formal strategies of art-making are still exciting premises.

8

Marshall McLuhan
The Mechanical Bride
1951
—

The Mechanical Bride was also given to me by my teacher Bruce Tibbetts. McLuhan and *Mad* magazine were performing similar functions at the top and bottom of culture, promoting a dawning awareness of the power of media and mediums, suspicion of Madison Avenue snake oil, and the limitless possibilities of a broadminded sense of humour and playfulness in reading and living.

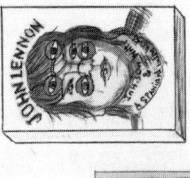

9

Maurice Tuchman
A Report on the Art and Technology Program of the Los Angeles County Museum of Art, 1967–71
1971
—

Tuchman curated a multi-year project in Southern California, pairing artists and corporations with varying results. This is a fascinating document of that project. The book introduced me to the work of Øyvind Fahlström and detailed some very interesting outcomes: Robert Rauschenberg made a bubbling mud pit; Andy Warhol made a bath-like raining fountain with printed flower shower curtain; Roy Lichtenstein is synthetic movie seascape; R.B. Kitaj & model of a minimally white Fahlström collaborated with a sign company to make 'Meat Ball Curtain': a tribute to the work of R Crumb's ZAP comics.

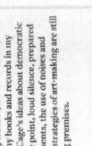

10

John Lennon
In His Own Write
1964
A Spaniard in the Works
1965
—

Lennon's first two books, *In His Own Write* and *A Spaniard in the Works* came out in paperback and appeared at the local drug store when I was in high school. His leaking, mad, punning, caustic prose and loopy drawings transported me to a very free and exhilarating place and, for a few years, I made phoney Lennon poems, which help meow tub truffle and primed me for James Joyce.

11

Josef Augusta
and Zdeněk Burian
Prehistoric Animals
1957
—

In junior high school, I checked this oversized book out at the library would let me. Burian's watercolour and gouache, though loose and apparently handmade, also had a photographic look. Burian and Charles R. Knight's dinosaur renderings were the dominant vision of dinosaurs in illustration, TV and the movies for decades.

12

Artforum
January 1968
—

I spotted this issue of *Artforum* on a newsstand in Oklahoma City and got a brain fever. It was obviously the most amazing humour magazine possible. I still think that. So I got hooked and, in subsequent issues, I learned of Peter Saul, the Hairy Who, Bruce Nauman and Claes Oldenburg, which only turned up the brain heat.

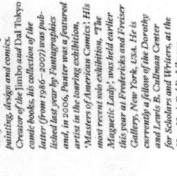

Gary Panter's work encompasses painting, design and comics.

Creator of the Jimbo and Dal Tokyo comic books, his collection of the latter (from 1987–2002) was published last year by Fantagraphics and, in 2006, Panter was a featured artist in the touring exhibition, 'Masters of American Comics'. His most recent solo exhibition, 'The Magnetic Lady', was held earlier this year at Fredericks and Freiser Gallery, New York, USA. He is currently a fellow of the Dorothy and Lewis B. Cullman Center for Scholars and Writers, at the New York Public Library.

effectively tweaked—this is going to be half-assed—Myles then swoops in, gushing over twelve works you need to read right now. Djuna Barnes's *Nightwood* (1936) elicits "this perfect, perfect novel is like a dark echoey growth" and CAConrad's *The Book of Frank* (2009) tugs "whoever you are, it's everything you like."[5] They whirl through a landscape of poetry, novels, novels in verse, and lectures with rhythm.

Throughout its ten year run in *Frieze*, the pulse of Ideal Syllabus varies as the magazine itself cycles through different typefaces and editorial design programs. The feature is usually accompanied by photographs or digital cover art of front-facing book covers, open book spreads, or rows of spine out books. In the May 2013 issue, however, guest contributor Gary Panter broke the mold by drawing and writing about his twelve selections. *Frieze*, who must have a soft spot for Panter, let his Ideal Syllabus span three pages instead of the usual two.

After the May 2018 issue with writer Alexander Chee, Ideal Syllabus disappears from the magazine without fanfare or explanation. *Is it on hiatus? Or has it been retired to pursue other avenues?*

---

(1) Jerry Saltz, ed., *An Ideal Syllabus: Artists, Critics and Curators Choose the Books We Need to Read* (London: Frieze, 1998), 6.
(2) Saltz, *An Ideal Syllabus*, 7.
(3) "Ideal Syllabus" search results, *Frieze*, accessed February 16, 2016, https://www.frieze.com.
(4) Nicolas Bourriaud, Ideal Syllabus, *Frieze*, May 2008, 34–35.
(5) Eileen Myles, Ideal Syllabus, *Frieze*, November–December 2015, 44–45.

Irma Boom: The Architecture of the Book

.. ..

Boom, Irma. *Irma Boom: A Biography in Books: Books in Reverse Chronological Order 2010–1986 with Comments Here and There*. 1st ed. Amsterdam: University of Amsterdam / Grafische Cultuurstichting, 2010. 704 p.: col. ill.; 5 × 4 cm, box size: 15 × 11 cm.

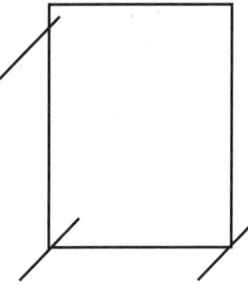

.. ..

Boom, Irma. *Irma Boom: The Architecture of the Book: Books in Reverse Chronological Order, 2013–1986, with Comments Here and There*. 2nd ed. Eindhoven: Lecturis, 2013. 800 p.: col. ill.; 5.5 × 4.5 × 3 cm, box size: 15.5 × 11.5 × 3 cm.

.. ..

Boom, Irma. *Irma Boom: Book Manifest: Books in Reverse Chronological Order, 2022–1986, with Comments Here and There*. 3rd ed. Koln: Verlag der Buchhandlung Walther und Franz Konig, 2022. 999 p.: col. ill.; 7 × 5.5 × 4 cm, box size: 15 × 11 × 4.5 cm.

The first edition of *Irma Boom*, subtitled a "Biography in Books," is a bio-bibliography and retrospective of the Dutch book designer's work. It accompanied an exhibition of the same name at the University of Amsterdam in 2010. Selected projects are included in reverse chronological order. Three years later a second edition revised and expanded the first. Both editions were of course designed by Boom. The second edition displays the first edition *Irma Boom* within its chronology (project number 221 of 265) along with an excerpted lecture by Frits Scholten about the appeal of small things.

The reader suitably has to draw up close to read Scholten's words, as this is itself a very small book. *Irma Boom: The Architecture of the Book* is packaged in a cardboard frame so that it can share a shelf with more conventionally sized books. The extreme miniaturization of the book form imitates prototyping, a practice for which Boom is well-known. She has scale models of her book design projects that date back to 1988. During the design process she makes models to examine things like the sequencing of the project, the scale relationships of text and image, the overall rhythm, and the subject of the book.[1] Instead of creating an amped up retrospective catalog filled with bells and whistles, Boom took the opposite approach adopting a lighthearted and humorous sense of scale. As a printed maquette, the designer sidesteps monumentality and indicates that this accumulating body of work is not final yet.

The contents of her "biography" are similarly humbling. Boom includes the voices of collaborators, commissioners, and scholars alongside her own. Her remarks are brief but include email excerpts and behind-the-scenes descriptions that discuss the challenges and expectations of a project. A biographical timeline called "Highlights" spans fifty-two years in only four pages.

The bulk of the book is focused on displaying and identifying her work. Photographs of printed books and a smattering of other design projects fill the pages, as do digital cover images, typography specimen sheets, and color research. The checklist at the end of *Irma Boom* documents each project with a full citation, plus the page count and size of the book.

The magnitude of work that has gone into compiling this tiny bibliography is astounding. Putting together a book designer's bibliography can be nearly impossible for an outside researcher. For one, a book design credit is rarely captured in the Library of Congress's Cataloging in Publication (CIP) data, a library catalog record, or other bibliographic information. If a book designer is credited, the attribution might appear on the book cover or jacket, on the copyright page, or in an author's acknowledgments. These are difficult searches to conduct without a known title. Irma Boom, who is perhaps a rare exception, is occasionally given an author credit on a book and her publication designs are often promoted in the pages of the design press. For two, who can keep track of a life's worth of titles?[2] Prolific designers rarely find time to break away from a cycle of commissions to process their own archive or update a portfolio site. Good news: a third edition released in 2022 adds Boom's latest decade of work to an ever-evolving archive. *Irma Boom* is an exemplar for designers and design researchers.

---

(1) Irma Boom, *Irma Boom: The Architecture of the Book*, 2nd ed. (Eindhoven: Lecturis, 2013), project 221.
(2) Answer: Johanna Drucker. See catalogue entry for "All."

Juxtaposed

Mike and Maaike.
Juxtaposed: Religion, [2007].
Designed object for blankblank.
Curated by John Simonian.
Reclaimed oak, books,
shelf size: 26 × 91.5 × 20.5 cm.
Edition of 50.
    Mike and Maaike.
    Juxtaposed: Power, [2010].
    Designed object for blankblank.
    Curated by Athmeya Jayaram.
    Reclaimed oak, books,
    26 × 91.5 × 20.5 cm.
    Edition of 50.
        Mike and Maaike.
        Juxtaposed: Religion New Edition, [2017].
        Designed object for blankblank.
        Curated by Athmeya Jayaram.
        Sustainably harvested pine, books,
        27 × 81.5 × 20.5 cm.
        Open edition.

Views of *Juxtaposed: Religion*, [2007].

When Mike Simonian and Maaike Evers of the progressive industrial design studio Mike & Maaike were asked if *Juxtaposed: Religion* was a work of art or design, they replied, "It's a statement . . . a statement that has undergone a design process. We don't claim to be artists."[1] On the studio's website, the *Juxtaposed* series is listed under the furniture category. They are bookshelves. Bookshelves made from reclaimed hardwood or sustainably harvested pine and built around a very specific set of books. They are in actuality curated bookshelves available for purchase. However, as an idiosyncratic bibliographic project, *Juxtaposed* amps up the idea of a core collection and in an odd twist, celebrates the relationship between the organization of books and their attendant shelf systems.

The series is composed of two themed works—*Religion* and *Power*—plus a tenth anniversary edition of *Religion*.[2] Each shelf isolates seven hardcover books in tight proximity, foregrounding a common subject and facilitating a multiple-views shelf conversation. For each iteration, Mike and Maaike worked with specialists to select titles that would bring major traditions of thought together. John Simonian, Mike's brother, has an MA in Theology from Notre Dame and handpicked the books for the religion shelf. Athmeya Jayaram, was a PhD candidate in Political Theory at UC Berkeley when he chose the features for the power shelf.

The books themselves draw attention to their volume and mass, sinking into the wood surface. Each book has a precise notched footprint to call home. The assembled shelf-neighborhood is color orchestrated. The aesthetic arrangement is circumstantial as the books' graphic qualities and stature vary by publisher. It is a departure say, from displaying a set of Penguin Classics or Everyman's Library editions that employ a series design to visually link works.

Here the shelf constitutes the collection. It acts as a leveling podium, aligning the surfaces of the spines as well as the tops of the books. A similar tactic was used by the seventeenth century chronicler Samuel Pepys, who, as rare book curator Terry Belanger reports, "liked all his books to make an even appearance on the shelves of his library. To secure this end he had little high-heels of various heights built which could be set on his shelves under smaller books, in order to bring their tops into the same horizontal line."[3]

For Mike & Maaike's *Juxtaposed: Religion* shelf, the order of books from left to right is: *Bhagavad Gita*, *Holy Bible: New Revised Standard Version*, *The Qur'an*, *The Analects of Confucius*, *Tao Te Ching*, *The Middle Length Discourses of the Buddha*, and *The Torah*. For *Juxtaposed: Power*, the shelf order from left to right is: *The Communist Manifesto* by Karl Marx and Frederick Engels, *Leviathan* by Hobbes, *The Republic* by Plato, *The Federalist Papers*, *Social Justice in Islam* by Sayyid Qutb, *On Liberty* by John Stuart Mill, and *The Conquest of Bread* by Peter Kropotkin. For *Juxtaposed: Religion New Edition* a taller, slimmer edition of the *Bhagavad Gita* is utilized, shifting the shelf order. The colorways shift, too, from taupes, green-grays, and black to navy blues, green, and black.

The entire group of books resides off-center held in place by what seems like a bit of magic. The books stand up perfectly straight without additional supports. The project is visually reminiscent of Rachel Whiteread's *Untitled (Paperbacks)* (1997) that cast the negative space above the shelves of books.

Though the title of Mike and Maaike's series suggests the importance of a *juxtaposition* of ideas, the past tense of juxta*posed* emphasizes a quality of stillness. One holds a pose for the camera. These books, for whatever reason, are staying put. They have demanded their own piece of furniture and are now growing together. This is a bibliography that describes a series of books by literally capturing their impressions.

Juxtaposed: Power, [2010].

Close up of *Juxtaposed: Religion New Edition*, [2017].

(1)
"Interview with Mike & Maaike about Juxtaposed: Religion Bookshelf," blankblank, May 17, 2007, http://blankblank.net/interview-with-mike-maaike-about-juxtaposed-religion-bookshelf/ (page discontinued).

(2)
While this catalogue was in production Mike and Maaike released *Juxtaposed Religion – The Complete Edition* with forty-eight books on one shelf: Mike and Maaike. *Juxtaposed Religion – The Complete Edition*. 2023. Curated by John Simonian. Solid reclaimed oak, books.
27 × 234 × 21 cm.

(3)
Terry Belanger, *Lunacy and the Arrangement of Books*
(New Castle, DE: Oak Knoll Press), 5.

Kentifrications: Convergent Truth(s) and Realities

Hinkle, Kenyatta A. C. *Kentifrications: Convergent Truth(s) and Realities*. Exhibition at Weingart Gallery, Occidental College, February 8–March 11, 2018.

Hinkle, Kenyatta A. C. *Kentifrications: Convergent Truth(s) and Realities.* Designed by Sming Sming Books. Los Angeles: Occidental College, 2018. Col. ill.; 2 booklets + 10 cards, envelope size: 33.5 x 23 cm.

Kentifrications, 2018, installation view at Weingart Gallery.

Artist Kenyatta A. C. Hinkle has been exhibiting segments of her ongoing community and participatory project, Kentifrica, since 2010. Kentifrica is an imagined enterprise—a "contested geography/continent" located between Africa and South America.[1] The project allows participants to critically engage "collective vs. personal histories, Diaspora, migration, immigration, cross-culturalism, and issues of geography."[2]

During an artist residency at Occidental College in 2017–2018, Hinkle expanded this project, installing a Kentifrican study and research room in the College's Weingart Gallery. The artworks exhibited were presented as an archive of Kentifrican objects with particular resonances and histories—an elaborate fiction. Constructed portraits, instruments, and garments mingled with objects of unknown origins on loan from the college's special collections. A standalone bookcase and numerous wall rails were filled with real and invented books that visitors could pick up to read, study, or elicit conversations.

Occidental College published *Kentifrications: Convergent Truth(s) and Realities* designed by Sming Sming Books on occasion of this exhibition. The publication is a large yellow envelope containing an assortment of special items: a glossy exhibition catalogue of installation photos; a handbound *List of Works* which includes the four-page "Kentifrications Reading List;" a screw-post bound *Introduction to Kentifrican Culture*; a stack of postcard-sized book covers of speculative titles for readers to cut and fold; and a flash drive with audio of the Kentifrican alphabet, vocal and instrumental Kentifrican music by Kevin Robinson, and a video excerpt of a cooking demonstration with Isaac DeLamatre.

Here as with Hinkle's gallery installation, the artist and her collaborators have fleshed out Kentifrican identity to detail its origin story, language, geographical features, political history, economics, familial structures, views on sexuality and gender, cuisine, music, and cosmology. The "Kentifrications Reading List" contains writings on race, class and gender, decolonization, the African Diaspora, historiography, contested lands, museology and exhibition-making, cultural memory, and slavery.

With the library and reading list, Hinkle has situated fictitious works on Kentifrica within a specific discourse. The ten imagined titles are well-considered and diverse, an array of literature from advanced scholarship to pop history. The authors have made-up but realistic sounding names and honorifics like Shaw Negraine and Dr. Tenekay Natsatta. Between the titles, author names, and cover art (designed by Adrianna Housman), Hinkle infuses realness into imagined titles. When in situ with the rest of the bibliography, they actualize the ostensible subject (the rediscovery and recovery of Kentifrican culture).

This continual interplay keeps the viewer wondering about truth(s) and realities. It is a tactile and colorful game for deep investigation. As an activity for world-building and sense-making, *what are we able to learn through Kentifrica that we can't see about our own geographies and histories?*

(1) "The Kentifrica Project,"
Kach Studio, Kenyatta A. C. Hinkle, accessed May 21, 2021,
https://www.kachstudio.com/kentifrica.
(2) "The Kentifrica Project."

Kentifrications, 2018, publication.

Lonely Books

MacPhee, Josh.
Lonely Books.
Minneapolis:
Wooden Leg Print & Press,
2016.
[40] p.: ill.;
22 × 14.5 cm.

Lonely Books, 2016,
cover and interior spread.

Lonely Books, a two-color risograph zine, documents the discarded books that Josh MacPhee found in the Park Slope and Gowanus neighborhoods in Brooklyn over the course of a two-year period. He photographs thirty-one solitary books that have been propped up and posed along fence lines and building exteriors as well as publications that stare skyward from sidewalks, stoops, sills, and giveaway boxes. These are books kicked to the curb—some pristine, some a bit worse for wear—trying to find a new reader. Collectively the books give insight into what a community is not reading or rather what a community was reading and is not anymore.

MacPhee includes bibliographic citations below the photographs and interjects a series of questions throughout the sequence to activate some of the titles. For instance, the question "Do ideas ever feel abandoned?" lies opposite the entry for Stephen L. Carter's *Reflections of an Affirmative Action Baby* (1992) and the question "When best sellers are left on the street, do they think about how far they have fallen?" is paired with Lena Dunham's *Not That Kind of Girl: A Young Woman Tells You What She's "Learned"* (2014).[1] The questions pursue a point of view from the books themselves, imagining their feelings and the tragedy of the aloneness that binds them. The books here do feel isolated—printed maroon on a green background—but their overall "sadness" is not compelling. It's a hodgepodge of niche interests and popular works, an assembly by chance of encounter.

The archetypal power of the book as object can form strong emotional ties with casual readers and "book lovers" alike. *Lonely Books* speaks to those desires. Many folx cannot bear to trash or recycle a book even when it is outdated or no longer of use.[2] Such is perhaps the case with the previous owners of McPhee's finds who have offered their books up to the street rather than tie them up in a Hefty bag with the kitchen waste. At the end of the day, somebody still thinks they are special. Someone is still holding out hope that they will find another reader, have another life.

(1) Josh MacPhee, *Lonely Books* (Minneapolis: Wooden Leg Print & Press, 2016), [20], [6].
(2) Many may not be aware of common practices in the US book trades to pulp, recycle, or resell books. For instance, publishers and booksellers regularly pulp inventories of low demand books for tax purposes since the 1979 ruling in *Thor Power Tool Co. v. Commissioner*. Academic and public libraries regularly weed their collections, sending pallets of deaccessioned books to fundraising book sales, underserved communities, and recycling centers.

The Mary Shelley Facsimile Library

★ ★ ★ ★ ★ ★ ★ ★ ★ ★ ★ ★ ★ ★

Werkplaats Typografie.
The Mary Shelley Facsimile Library.
Library project.
2009–.

★ ★ ★ ★ ★ ★ ★ ★ ★ ★ ★ ★ ★ ★

Zenner, Manuel, Yin Yin Wong,
Mathew Whittington, et al.
The Mary Shelley Facsimile Library.
Designed by Manuel Zenner,
Corina Neuenschwander, Ina Meganck
and Noah Venezia.
Arnhem: Werkplaats Typografie, 2011.
142 p.: ill.; 19 × 12.5 × [1] cm.

★ ★ ★ ★ ★ ★ ★ ★ ★ ★ ★ ★ ★ ★

Dähler, Dorothee, and Yeliz Secerli.
www.maryshelleyfacsimilelibrary.werkplaatstypografie.org.
Guide book. Book and typeface designed by
Dorothee Dähler and Yeliz Secerli.
Arnhem: Werkplaats Typografie, 2018.
442 p.: ill.; 30 × 21 × [5] cm.

★ ★ ★ ★ ★ ★ ★ ★ ★ ★ ★ ★ ★ ★

The Mary Shelley Facsimile Library.
Web-based directory.
Website and typeface designed by
Dorothee Dähler and Yeliz Secerli.
Programmed by Magalie Chetrit. 2018–.
https://maryshelleyfacsimilelibrary
.werkplaatstypografie.org/
(site no longer fully functional).

★ ★ ★ ★ ★ ★ ★ ★ ★ ★ ★ ★ ★ ★

Facsimile NV–01 Library	Facsimile YYW–04 Library	Facsimile EP–03 Library	Facsimile VG–01 Library
Facsimile IM–08 Library	Facsimile SF–01 Library	Facsimile MZ–03 Library	Facsimile MW–01 Library
Facsimile NM–03 Library	Facsimile IG–02 Library	Facsimile CHN–01 Library	Facsimile BH–03 Library
Facsimile RV–02 Library	Facsimile LG–08 Library	Facsimile MS–09 Library	Facsimile CN–03 Library

The Mary Shelley Facsimile Library, 2011, cover.

Manuel Zenner

I'm in the process of setting up a plan (diapositif) that will enable me to activate the spaces between the books and essays related to my general practice.

The aim of this working tool is to organize and gather knowledge, but in an open form that can be updated infinitely with time. It is a hybrid and functional form that gathers a linear reading of reference material, from within a net-shaped/atlas projection.

I use the term "bridge" not as a descriptive form for my work but as a term that is both sufficiently suggestive in itself and open enough to further interpretations.

In my opinion, the graphic designer is a medium, a bridge between art and society, or a mediator of meaningful links between the two. In my work I intend to focus on the transition between different media (analogue, digital) as well as the transitions between an idea and its final form. Any reference to the figure of the medium in the mystical sense is intentional: A person that would act as a link between the world of the living and the dead. For me any final form, or fixed end product (in graphic design) results in the death of the process.

Along with the map/plan/device, I have highlighted two kinds of links, bridges between the books and essays:

Hard bridge: Effective and semantic links.
Soft bridge: Intuition, subjective links between different genres and different conceptual typologies

Bridge #1: The road, an open medium connecting two distanced points. (Hard Bridge)
– Regis Debray. *Qu'est ce qu'une route?*, coordinated by Francois Dagognet, Paris: Gallimard, 1996
– Philippe-Alain-Michaud. 'Considering the interval', in *Neutre intense*, Montreuil: Maison populaire, 2008

Bridge #2: The distance between images: The movement of images. (Soft Bridge)
– Philippe-Alain-Michaud. 'Considering the interval', in *Neutre intense*, Montreuil: Maison populaire, 2008
– Yannick Mouren, *Filmer la création cinématographique*, Paris: L'Harmattan, 2009

Bridge #3: Medium on medium, image on image. (Hard Bridge)
– Yannick Mouren, *Filmer la création cinématographique*, Paris: L'Harmattan, 2009
– Rainer Werner Fassbinder, *Warnung vor einer heiligen Nutte*, West Germany: Tango Film, Antiteater-X-Film, Nova International Films, 1971

Bridge #4: Creating "other spaces". (Soft Bridge)
– Michel Foucault. 'Of Other Spaces', Heterotopia, in *Architecture/Mouvement/Continuité*, Paris, 1984
– Yannick Mouren, *Filmer la création cinématographique*, Paris: L'Harmattan, 2009
– Rainer Werner Fassbinder, *Warnung vor einer heiligen Nutte*, West Germany: Tango Film, Antiteater-X-Film, Nova International Films, 1971

Bridge #5: The distance between image and text: an heterotopia? (Soft Bridge)
– Michel Foucault. 'Of Other Spaces', Heterotopia, in *Architecture/Mouvement/Continuité*, Paris, 1984
– Louis Ucciani. *La distance irréparable*, Paris: Les presses du réel, 2009

Bridge #6: Building, crossing bridges. (Soft Bridge)
– Louis Ucciani. *La distance irréparable*, Paris: Les presses du réel, 2009
– Michel Serres. *L'art des ponts*, Paris: Le Pommier, 2006

Bridge #7: Importance and defense of bridges. (Hard Bridge)
– Michel Serres. *L'art des ponts*, Paris: Le Pommier, 2006

Interior spreads of *The Mary Shelley Facsimile Library*, 2011, showing Manuel Zenner's authored entry and images from his working bibliography.

The Mary Shelley Facsimile Library is a library of bootleg editions generated by graphic designers in the Werkplaats Typografie, a two-year masters program in the Netherlands. The facsimile library collects scanned reproductions of books and copies of resources that are pertinent to participants' research interests. Future students at the Werkplaats Typografie can utilize this alternative library and add their own facsimile volumes to the collection. The project reanimates knowledge by capturing "spaces of reading" and individualized systems of notation as well as investigates the creative possibilities of piracy culture.[1]

A catalog was released in 2011 to accompany the library project. This publication, also called *The Mary Shelley Facsimile Library*, contains sixteen thesis bibliographies and a transcription of Paul Elliman's seminar that kicked off the formation of the facsimile library. Elliman's 2009 lecture wends through Mary Shelley's *Frankenstein*, the social life of books, bibliography, and contemporary material culture.

Participants each wrote their own entry for the catalog. Their writing ties their bibliographic picks together and varies in style from first-person to third to imaginative character work. At the end of each participant's authored entry is a textual bibliography in list form, with materials delineated by call number–like tags that abbreviate their selector's name in a display font. For example, Ilke Gers's choices become IG-01, IG-02, and IG-03 and Yin Yin Wong's become YYW-01, YYW-02, and YYW-03. This kind of identification puts the book's reader front and center rather than the subject, author, or title of the work.[2] In the back of *The Mary Shelley Facsimile Library*, the students have correspondingly visualized their working bibliographies, showing scanned covers and the first pages of articles or book chapters labeled with the same call number system, set in the same typeface.

The call number ranges are noted in each designer's unique handwriting and placed vertically on the upper right corner of the page. Representative images of participants' selected materials show handwritten inscriptions, bookmarks and post-its peeking out from the pages, library barcodes, wrinkles, and creased corners.

As Manuel Zenner, one of the designers in the masters program from 2010–2012 notes, "my contribution to *The Mary Shelley Facsimile Library* was actually the beginning of my research."[3] As he continued to think through the creative and expansive possibilities of bibliography, he developed a bibliocentric publication of his own called *Bridge, Medium and Transition: A Taxonomy* and a thesis poster *A Bridge Is a Bridge: A Bibliographical Bridge*.[4] The latter was an annotated bibliographic map that ingeniously stressed the links *between* his selected films, book chapters, and monographs. Zenner theorized nine truisms or reflections about bridges to tease out a personal philosophy of graphic design.

In 2018 Yeliz Secerli who was volunteering as the Werkplaats Typografie's student librarian and fellow master's student Dorothee Dähler saw an opportunity to imagine the next chapter of the Mary Shelley Facsimile Library. After nine years of growth, they thought the collection was "an incredible resource yet unorganized and uninviting for people to explore."[5]

The duo teamed up to initiate a branding, library organization, and website project.[6] Secerli and Dähler arranged the facsimiles by year of publication, rather than by accession date or by participant, in effect intermingling students' research interests by era. From the chronological shelf organization, they developed a ring-bound guide book that collates photocopies of the first page of each facsimile to help users navigate the collection. Within the guide, each

www.maryshelleyfacsimilelibrary.werkplaatstypografie.org,
2018, guide book cover.

cover copy is labeled in a typeface called Library that Secerli and Dähler developed. To accommodate multiple items published in the same year, labels read [year][dingbat]1, [year][dingbat]2, [year][dingbat]3. The adjoining dingbat varies by publication year from a car, to a strawberry, to a crown, etc., and provides readers with a picture aid in addition to the numerical year. The web-based directory *The Mary Shelley Facsimile Library* lists the contents of the library from oldest to newest in short textual citations that begin with title, followed by author, then publication year. The citations flow in one continuous left-hand column. To differentiate entries, each is set in one of Library's five weights for bold, italic, condensed, shadow, and regular. Mousing over a citation brings up a digitized cover scan and the year the work was published to assist researchers navigating the physical library.[6]

The Mary Shelley Facsimile Library is a bibliographic project for fostering design research and a visual bibliography of research in action. It differs from typical institutional thesis collections. It represents the varied interests of a group of international designers and something about the studio environment at the Werkplaats Typografie. The physical facsimile library includes all of the full sources referenced in the participants' thesis bibliographies, including any textual interventions they may have made through underlining, commentary, flagging, and mark making. The facsimile editions are an extension of a personal recommendation and a behind-the-scenes invitation to view research processes. The copies encapsulate the visual traces of readerly interactions.

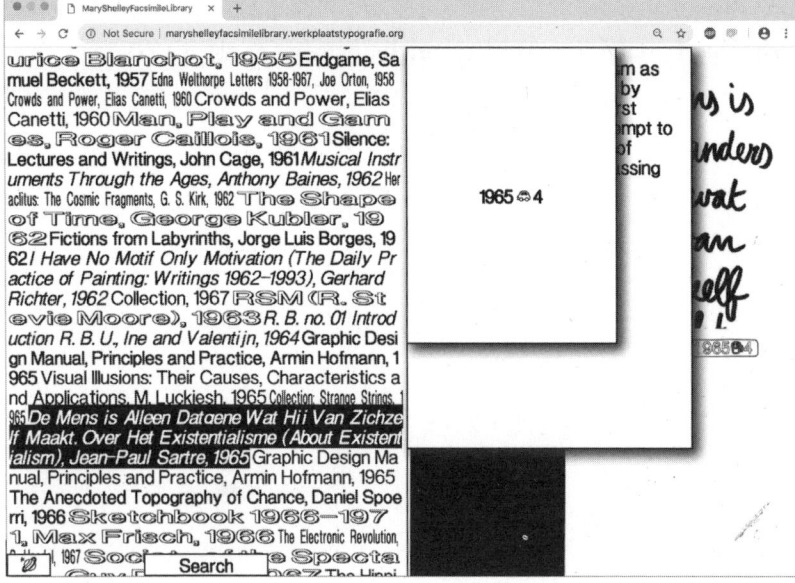

The Mary Shelley Facsimile Library
title entry hover, ca. 2018,
screenshot.

(1) I've taken the phrase "spaces of reading" from a seminar taught by Ann Hamilton, Matthew Goulish, and Lin Hixson. See Ann Hamilton with Matthew Goulish and Lin Hixson, *The Spaces of Reading: Object, Image, Word, Event* (Chicago: School of the Art Institute of Chicago, 2018). On piracy, see Adrian Johns, *Piracy: The Intellectual Property Wars from Gutenberg to Gates* (Chicago: University of Chicago Press, 2009) and Nicolas Maigret and Maria Roszkowska, eds., *The Pirate Book* (Ljubljana: Aksioma, Institute for Contemporary Art, 2015).
(2) For example, Library of Congress and Dewey Decimal call numbers begin with a subject classification sequence followed by a unique cutter number derived from creator name, title, and date of publication.
(3) Manuel Zenner, email message to author, December 14, 2022.
(4) Zenner, email, December 14, 2022.
(5) Yeliz Secerli and Dorothee Dähler, email message to author, January 31, 2023.
(6) Secerli and Dähler, email, January 31, 2023.
(7) The website https://maryshelleyfacsimilelibrary.werkplaatstypografie.org/ is no longer fully functional.

Meanwhile,
the Surrogate for the Presently Absent Gets a Proxy

Rebel, Janelle. *Meanwhile, the surrogate for the presently absent gets a proxy*, 2016. 20 books (various heights) + 1 shelf (30.5 cm long).

Rebel, Janelle. *Meanwhile, the surrogate for the presently absent gets a proxy*, 2016. Installation. On the occasion of the group exhibition *Making Out* at Defibrillator Gallery, Chicago.

Meanwhile, the surrogate for the presently absent gets a proxy, 2016, installation view at Defibrillator Gallery. *A Prehistory of the Cloud* located second from the right.

When an item goes missing from a circulating library, its absence is not necessarily visible on the shelf. Library workers continually tighten rows of books to make way for incoming titles, closing any spatial gaps within the stacks in due time. However when an item is discovered to be missing from its shelf location, the status is often noted within the details of its catalog record. For the time being, the item record which is also referred to as a digital surrogate, takes on a new importance. Suddenly, though quite discretely, the surrogate for the presently absent has additional representational responsibilities, standing on its own, no longer serving as a representation for another.

The set of book objects *Meanwhile, the surrogate for the presently absent gets a proxy* negotiates between analog and digital library collections, materializing a group of titles culled from the missing items list at the School of the Art Institute of Chicago, Flaxman Library.[1] Twenty books resembling decorators' chop props stand together to constitute an alternative shelf: the shelf of missing items. Titles are reconstructed from catalog descriptions, however standardized and incomplete, which list one physical dimension (the height of the book rounded to the nearest centimeter) and an often incorrect page count (numbered pages rather than total pages).[2] No depth dimension is recorded.[3] These proxies don title, author, location, call number, and item status details on their spines. Yellow, black, and green circles and lozenges proliferate on the spines as well, imitating the language of library label and color-coding systems.

As an inverse bibliography, the display reflects the reading interests at an art and design school: Rosalind Krauss's *Perpetual Inventory* (2010), Trevor Paglen's *A Compendium of Secrets* (2010), Anthony Elms and Steve Reinke's *Blast Counterblast* (2011), and Paul Ricoeur's

Rule of Metaphor (1977). It also provides a snapshot of the collecting priorities of the library, which is heavy in Ns (Fine Arts), Ps (Language and Literature) and Ts (Technology and Photography). But more so, because these books vanished without a trace, one might wonder what these missing items are doing now.[4] *Are they presently part of an alternative system of circulation? Or taking up new residence in a private collection? Will they at any point make their way back to the library shelves?* While Rebel was fabricating her set of phoney books, one title *A Prehistory of the Cloud* (2015) unexpectedly turned back up at the Flaxman Library. This sudden change altered her planned installation at Defibrillator Gallery. Instead of removing this proxy from the shelf of missing items, she showed it fore-edge out to visualize its change of status.

(1) The "missing" designation denotes that the item was not attached to a patron account when it was moved from its shelf location. It is essentially off-the-grid, unlike "lost" items which can be traced back to particular users or user groups.
(2) The odd number of pages that is documented in a catalog record would otherwise be impossible to reconcile. Pages come in twos. One leaf = two pages. Similarly unnumbered pages like the blank pages that fill out the last signature of a book are not noted. All that to say, these are slim proxies.
(3) Librarians are concerned with knowing the height of the shelf needed rather than the depth.
(4) And perhaps as Josh MacPhee might ask, are they lonely? See catalogue entry for "Lonely Books."

The Missing Pieces

Lefebvre, Henri. *The Missing Pieces*. Translated by David L. Sweet. Designed by Hedi El Kholti. South Pasadena, CA: Semiotexte, 2014. 86 p.: ill.; 20.5 × 14 × 1 cm.

Margin to margin, full-justified texts flow in solemnity. A list of unknowable or partial cultural works—unfinished, lost, stolen, destroyed—fill the pages, crisscrossing through examples from literature, art, music, and film to people, places, and events. From ancient past to near present, *The Missing Pieces* is a staggering paper-memorial-as-chapbook imprinting the unsettled, the dead and lost who do not rest in peace, who exist in the rumor mill, who persist in our collective memory.[1] Henri Lefebvre tracks these in varying

HENRI LEFEBVRE • THE MISSING PIECES

TRANSLATED BY DAVID L. SWEET

Murder, The Hope of Women, a twenty-five minute opera composed in 1919 by Paul Hindemith • The novel *Theodor* by Robert Walser • The letters of Milena Jesenska to Franz Kafka • Heinrich von Kleist burns the manuscript of *Robert Guiscard, The Duke of the Normans* and attempts to enlist in Napoleon's army when the poet Wieland informs him of his admiration for this text • Missing, the poems of Robert Creeley, which littered the hardwood floor of Brautigan's house in Bolinas, on drunken nights; Brautigan would gather them in the morning and put them in a bowl on the piano, "for posterity," he'd say • The *Journal* of Annemarie Schwarzenbach, destroyed by her mother • *La Confusa*, a comedy by Miguel de Cervantes • In 1933 and from 1937 to 1938, Jean Giono shot fragments of poetic films without characters; none of the works exist any longer • The contents of a telephone conversation between Stalin and Pasternak after the arrest of Osip Mandelstam • Pierre Guyotat's head of hair • Jerome David Salinger since 1959 • The "line" of Apelles • Because his editors refused to publish *Stephen Hero*, James Joyce threw the manuscript into the fire in 1905; at the cost of some burns, his companion, Nora, saved a fifth of the text

semiotext(e)

The Missing Pieces, 2014, cover.

detail through written phrases and sourced quotations. Each entry is separated by a bullet point to compile a narrative via clerical list that is administrative *and* ecclesiastical. Truncated and thwarted lives run together page after page. *What propels the reader? What makes this project so compelling?* Despite its serious facade, it is a gossipy tell-all.

Some entries overtly speak to taboos:

> In her film *Scarlet Diva*, Asia Argento requires non-simulated sex from her actors and then cuts the scenes during the editing[2]

and

> *Biathanatos* was never seen by its contemporaries; In it, John Donne supported the thesis that Jesus Christ committed suicide, but refused to publish the book during his lifetime.[3]

Others are legendary turning points,

> In 1964, Marcel Broodthaers destroys the fifty unsold copies of his book of poems, *Pense-Bête*, by dipping them in some plaster; his first sculpture[4]

bewildering mistakes,

> A text by Jenny Holzer, created for the 1982 Documenta exhibition at Kassel and painted on the facade of a building, is erased in May 2002 when the new owner of the building decides to have the facade restored; he did not know it was a work of art[5]

or unsolved mysteries:

> No one knows why Donald Goines, Black American novelist, was assassinated in October 1974.[6]

The list is not without its nuggets of humor. There are hidden callouts to the unpublished and lost bits of the author's own life and work:

> *The List of Transparencies*, text by Henri Lefebvre and linocut by Marie-Noëlle Gonthier[7]

and

> We no longer know why Henri Lefebvre fell out with Guy Debord.[8]

The entries—while not formulaic in structure—are pithy fragments, well mixed and well paced. Just like navigating any subject bibliography, the more names, places, and works you are familiar with, the fuller your reading experience will be. No doubt each reading of *The Missing Pieces* will yield different points of interest, laughter, and curiosity, depending on what you've just watched, read, and absorbed.

The subject matter points to larger questions too. *What kind of space should missing works occupy in the realm of ideas? Are they fighting for disappearance? Or longing for acknowledgment, validity, or even substantiality? In an information age overwhelmed by an abundance of data, isn't it nice to have some things that don't survive? Isn't it necessary for the process of cultural renewal, at some level? Or should we attempt to archive as much as we can?*

Published posthumously by Semiotexte, the collection of stuff Lefebvre has assembled here is stuff with cultural traction, stuff that has, at least for the time being, a societal memory that persists. This stuff won't die. It fuels the chatter of fanatics. It fascinates us. Haunts us. Propels us. Lives a life beyond the author.

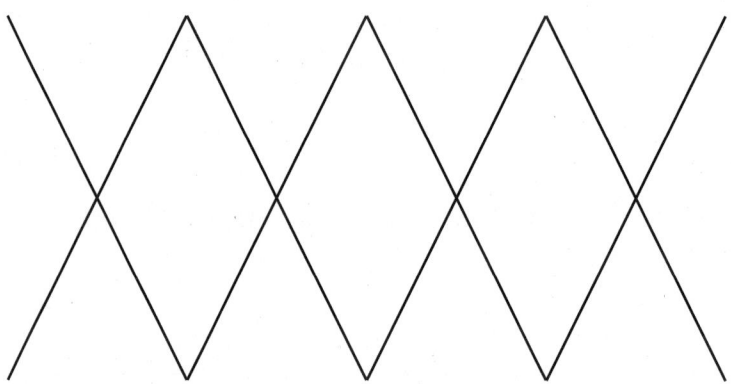

(1) Compare to Thomas Browne's seventeenth century project, the *Bibliotheca Abscondita*.
(2) Henri Lefebvre, *The Missing Pieces* (South Pasadena, CA: Semiotexte, 2014), 29–30.
(3) Lefebvre, *The Missing Pieces*, 40.
(4) Lefebvre, *The Missing Pieces*, 23.
(5) Lefebvre, *The Missing Pieces*, 25.
(6) Lefebvre, *The Missing Pieces*, 35.
(7) Lefebvre, *The Missing Pieces*, 17.
(8) Lefebvre, *The Missing Pieces*, 34.

A People on the Cover

◉ Ligon, Glenn. *Artist-in-Residence: Glenn Ligon*, 2000. Installation. Andersen Window Gallery, Walker Art Center, Minneapolis. In partnership with the Givens Collection of African American Literature at the University of Minnesota and the Walker Art Center Teen Arts Council.

▯ Ligon, Glenn. *A Guide to Glenn Ligon's Exhibition of Books from the Givens Collection of African American Literature*. Designed by Santiago Piedrafita. Edited by Pamela Johnson and Kathleen McLean. [Minneapolis]: Walker Art Center, 2000. 1 accordion-folded sheet (12 p.); folded: 25.5 × 11.5 cm.

▯ Ligon, Glenn. *A People on the Cover*. Designed by Joseph Logan with the assistance of Rachel Hudson. London: Ridinghouse, 2015. 140 p.: col. ill.; 24 × 17.5 × 1.5 cm.

◉ *Source Material: Glenn Ligon at the Walker*, 2018. Curated by Alexandra Nicome. Best Buy Aperture, Walker Art Center, Minneapolis.

A People on the Cover, 2015, cover.

Maybe it was his lifelong love of reading or his fascination with book covers, but something clicked when Glenn Ligon was in the stacks at the Archie Givens, Sr. Collection of African American Literature at the University of Minnesota. While he was an artist-in-residence at the Walker Art Center from 1999–2000, Ligon decided to look at the covers of trade books and academic titles written by or about African Americans, conducting an informal survey of black representation in the mid to late-twentieth century. He prepared an installation of sixty racially coded books, showing volumes from the Givens Collection supplemented by titles from his personal library and the Walker Art Center Library. Intermixed within the book display are his commentary and selected quotes from notable figures, along with historically situated magazine covers and popular music from the same time period. Ligon organized the books under five observational headings: Beauty, Synecdoche, The revolution will not be televised, Graphic, and Post-. An accordion-fold pamphlet accompanied the installation showing a panoramic photograph of the books spine out.

A People on the Cover is an outgrowth of this early exhibition and takeaway, and acclimates easily to book form. Ligon has made a few selection changes, narrowing the number of books to fifty-two, but has kept the original headings intact. Each of the sections opens with a short text by Ligon who invokes the likes of James Baldwin, Stuart Hall, Jean Genet, Hilton Als, and Sun Ra via Kodwo Eshun to tease out his themes. Notably in the section "Graphic," the artist talks about how seeing the "bold red text" on the cover of James Baldwin's *The Fire Next Time* first made him "conscious of the power language has to convey ideas and emotions when it is used as an image."[1] He went on to explain: "The use of text in all of my paintings and prints

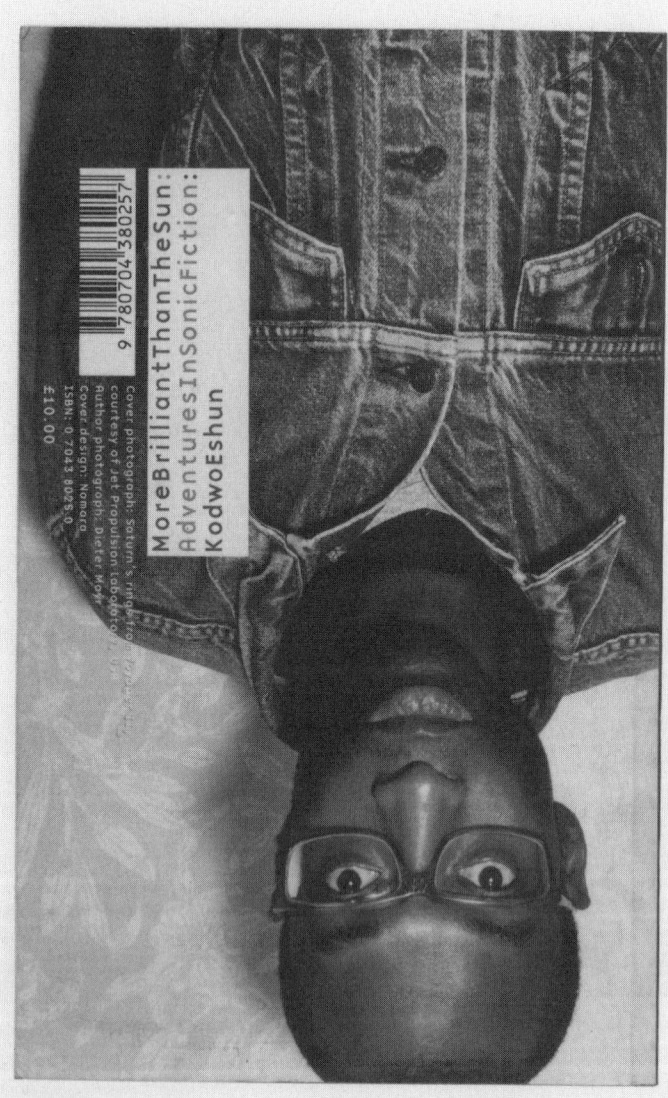

MoreBrilliantThanTheSun:
AdventuresInSonicFiction:
KodwoEshun

Cover photograph: Saturn's rings...
courtesy of Jet Propulsion Laboratory...
Author photograph: Dieter Mohr
Cover design: Nomora
ISBN: 0 7043 8025 0
£10.00

Interior spread from "Post-" in *A People on the Cover*, 2015.

came out of thinking about the relationship between that book's cover and its content."[2]

As a bibliography of representation, this book is filled with images of book covers that date from the 1930s to the 1990s. The front covers are printed large on the recto, and the back covers, if included, are displayed on the verso of the same spread. A list of book citations appears at the end of each section. The information includes the author, title, and facts of publication as well as the cover design and cover image credits. The latter credits are an interesting add that in context neither shame nor praise the visual makers. The attentive reader may find autobiographical nuggets. *The Adventures of Maud Noakes* was designed by Andy Warhol, one of Ligon's influences; and one of Ligon's collaborations with Byron Kim, *Rumble Young Man Rumble (Version #2)* is the cover image for the Duke University Press book, *Race and the Subject of Masculinities*. Readers can no longer determine which volumes are borrowed from what collection as they could in the original exhibition pamphlet. *A People on the Cover* intentionally deals with mass market books at the manifestation level rather than exact copies at the item level. The selection embraces all genres and for the most part is not made up of rarefied publications but works that have circulated in popular culture and academic circles.

What is particularly curious about Ligon's investigation is that the entries are not arranged chronologically but thematically. Within each theme he continually shuffles forward and backward in time to complicate what effect these racial codes have on the present. He does not say what he thinks or feels about this or that cover design or why it is included. A sequence in "Synecdoche" begins with photographic covers primarily from the '60s that display part of the black body: several show isolated hands, a few crop in close to the eyes. Eight covers deep, the reader suddenly sees a full-body illustration of Sambo from the 1931 edition of *The Story of Little Black Sambo*. Ligon's suggestions and juxtapositions are left open for interpretation. Readers will be more familiar with some titles than others and bring their own backgrounds and sensibilities to reading these cover designs. In some instances, readers may want to flex their own ability to judge a book by its cover while at the same time feel conflicted about doing so. *A People on the Cover* is a visual archive that shuffles and re-sorts a bibliographic past to confront a present reality. Its own cover is, however, devoid of any images, choosing a non-representational strategy—a plain white canvas.

In 2018, Alexandra Nicome, an interpretation fellow at the Walker Art Center, revisited Glenn Ligon's 1999–2000 community-based residency projects by going through documentation held by the Walker Library and Archives. She re-presented a version of Ligon's book cover display as part of an exhibit called *Source Material: Glenn Ligon at the Walker*.

(1) Glenn Ligon, *A People on the Cover* (London: Ridinghouse, 2015), 99.
(2) Ligon, *A People on the Cover*, 99.

Interior spread from "Beauty" in *A People on the Cover*, 2015.

The Perverse Library

Dworkin, Craig Douglas. *The Perverse Library*. York, England: information as material, 2010. 175 p.; 20 × 13 × 1.5 cm.

Poet, editor, and literary historian Craig Dworkin is amused by the idea of the pinacographic bibliography—the cataloging of a library, or in his case, the cataloging of a personal library. *The Perverse Library* contains an extensive essay, "Pinacographic Space," followed by two bibliographies.

The longer of the two bibliographies, "A Perverse Library," fills over one hundred pages and inventories the books in Dworkin's home library at the time. This intriguing bibliography is ordered alphabetically by publisher and then by oldest date to correspond to his shelf arrangement. Years earlier he had grouped his books by trim size to pack boxes during a move. Sorting by format incidentally reordered the books into groupings by press, which in Dworkin's collection is a mix of radical small press publishers alongside academic imprints, literary trade publishers, and galleries and museums. When he unpacked his library he adopted this new organization for his shelves. Later a colleague, upon seeing these bookshelves, admonished: "This is a very perverse library."[1] As Dworkin recounts, "I wasn't sure at first if he were referring to the collection, or to its organization. Either way, I was pleased and took it as a compliment."[2]

In "A Perverse Library" the citations begin with the name of the publisher in small caps followed by the place and date of publication in parentheses, and include the edition size or number in the edition, if applicable, at the end of each entry. These edition numbers are important to Dworkin as he believes they connect him to "a community of other actual, individual readers" rather than to a club of "exclusivity."[3] No physical dimensions are given though this would be an interesting revision to further tie into the shelf arrangement.

This long list serves as the spatial (architectural) and conceptual backbone to the short bibliography called "The Perverse Library." This five-page inventory, also ordered by publisher and date, is entirely dedicated to a "phantom shelf," that is, of "all the volumes that ought, ideally, to be assembled in a single place."[4] It delineates the titles that feel absent from Dworkin's home library. Libraries are not static entities, he emphasizes, but defined by their desire for growth and often evaluated and perceived by what they lack. Dworkin writes:

> The organization of a library immediately invokes the absent volumes that would confirm, complete or contradict its categories: other books by a given author; missing titles in a series; issues from the same press; books published in the same year; or in the same format; or, more slippery and expansive still, the genres and subgenres that are themselves defined by affinities.[5]

Dworkin envisions an abstract annex for his home library within the pages of "The Perverse Library," introducing forty new publishers to his existing collection (e.g., Editions Hansjörg Mayer and Horse in a Storm Press), filling in scarce issues here and there (e.g., of *Aerial* and *Dark Ages Clasp the Daisy Root*), and individual choice titles (e.g., Lyn Hejinian's *A Border Comedy* and Janet Zweig's *The 336 lines currently expurgated from Shakespeare's Romeo and Juliet in ninth grade textbooks*). The wished-for entry under the publisher known as information as material cites *Bibliomania 2000–2001*.[6] To gain insight into the logic of this theoretical bibliography, one needs to flip a few pages to compare it to the longer shelf list. For instance, Dworkin has accounted for sixteen titles published by information as material in his library, including, miraculously, the one you are reading: *The Perverse Library*.[7]

The Perverse Library, 2010, cover.

As Italo Calvino suggests, libraries have great influence upon the books in their catalog: "Within these systems each work is different from what it would be in isolation or in another library."[8] Dworkin's bibliographic project reveals the private library and organizational system of a bibliophile-collector and discerning reader. He makes his search for missing and elusive resources public, allowing others to both visualize and scrutinize the shelves of his ideal library.

(1) The full anecdote is succinct and enjoyable.
Craig Douglas Dworkin, *The Perverse Library*
(York, England: information as material, 2010), 40.
The book-length text is also accessible through
"Craig Douglas Dworkin," Eclipse, accessed
December 28, 2022, http://eclipsearchive.org/Editor/.
(2) Dworkin, *The Perverse Library*, 40.
(3) Dworkin, *The Perverse Library*, 25.
(4) Dworkin, *The Perverse Library*, 24.
(5) Dworkin, *The Perverse Library*, 12–13.
(6) See the catalogue entry for "Bibliomania."
(7) Dworkin was on information as material's
editorial team from 2006 to 2018.
(b) Italo Calvino, "Literature as Projection of Desire:
On Northrop Frye's *Anatomy of Criticism*"
in *The Uses of Literature*, trans. Patrick Creagh
(San Diego: Harcourt Brace & Company, 1986), 60.

Pile of Books

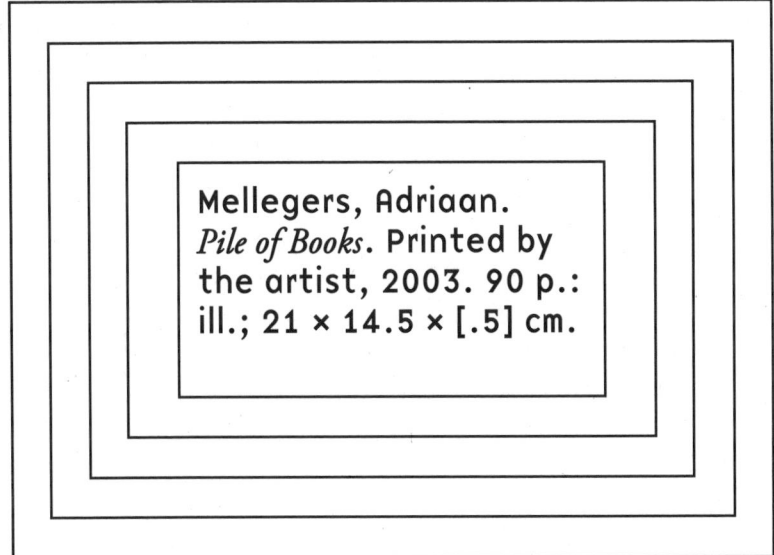

Mellegers, Adriaan. *Pile of Books*. Printed by the artist, 2003. 90 p.: ill.; 21 × 14.5 × [.5] cm.

Before Adriaan Mellegers finished up his BA in graphic design at the Academy of Art and Design in Hertogenbosch, Netherlands, he produced a photographic bibliography of "all the books he could collect in one day."[1] He stacked the books by size in his workspace to create a tapering tower, and photographed every book from above, working his way down the pile. The collection of design-related titles is a working collection of books for the studio. He assembled them into a black-and-white publication bound at the top edge. Thus, the page-turning action is from bottom to top rather than from right to left. The reader moves the pages away from their body to reveal each title. The experience is akin to sifting through a pile of books one at a time.[2]

This bibliography not only captures a particular subject—the reference books in an active studio at a particular moment in time—but adds details about the books themselves. The photographs record the cover artwork and design, the choice and use of typography, and any particulars printed on the cover regarding the title, author, and/or publisher. Book covers provide a wealth of information at a glance and sometimes astutely represent the contents of a book. Despite the tired maxim that you should never judge a book by its cover, in Mellegers's bibliographic project you can and absolutely should. In a similar vein, the stack arrangement exposes knowledge about a book's relative size and its proportions—information that is typically not given, for instance, in a library catalog entry. In the physical description portion of a MARC record—the MAchine-Readable Cataloging standards used by libraries—only a book's height is stated in centimeters, rounded to the nearest whole number. Height and width proportions are commonly not stated unless the width of the item is greater than the height. In *Pile of Books* materiality is not overlooked and the book is acknowledged as a visual and structural entity.

(1)
Robert Klanten and Matthias Hübner, eds.,
Fully Booked: Cover Art & Design For Books (Berlin: Gestalten, 2008), 34.

(2)
As a photobook, it is also reminiscent of Kenneth Josephson's
Bread Book (1973) in which the reader moves slice
by slice through a full loaf.

PM Tables, Visitor Tables, Your Tables

Printed Matter. PM Tables, Visitor Tables, Your Tables. Website feature. Designed by Linked by Air. 2013–. https://www.printedmatter.org/catalog/tables.

In the late 1990s and early aughts, brick-and-mortar bookstores began expanding onto the World Wide Web, developing consumer-friendly interfaces for searching their inventories and looking for ways to offer virtual book browsing experiences.[1] A bookseller may merchandise their wares in store through a variety of rotating front-table picks, timely topical displays, endcaps of book-award winners, staff recommendations interfiled in the stacks, and so on to get their customer's attention. As some of these forms of book-centric knowledge, marketing, and hospitality trickled online, they've been reimagined as annotated lists with embedded links, bookshelf-like grids of thumbnail images, and the ever-popular image carousel of book covers.

Enter Printed Matter, "the world's leading non-profit organization dedicated to the dissemination, understanding and appreciation of artists' books and related publications."[2] They were not the first online bookseller certainly—they had a placeholder web page from 1998–2001 before they established a website proper in 2002. But by December 2013, Printed Matter had debuted a major redesign of their website, doing away with a previous section of content called Curated Lists and replacing it with a novel segment of interactive, subject bibliographies called Tables or PM Tables. The website and Tables were both designed by Linked by Air, a Brooklyn-based design and technology firm, to foster ecommerce and art interactions.[3]

The Tables have continued to evolve and currently include three tabbed categories to facilitate discovery of artists' books and zines from Printed Matter's active inventory and archive. PM Tables are selected by Printed Matter staff and special guests; Visitor Tables, by the public; and Your Tables, by you and automatically generated by your online purchases.

The PM Tables which now exceed 550 groupings, are filled with curated gift guides, new arrivals, staff picks, and fundraising editions.[4] Some PM Tables focus on a single artist or collective, publisher, serial, or book fair, while others hone in on a particular subject of the curator's interest. For example, there are tables titled "I Love You Earth," "Architectures of Language & Sound," "Collective Action/Imagining Utopia," and "Police State." Certain topics can be especially tricky to keyword search in any catalog. Tables like "New Latin Wave" and "Celebrate Black Artists" have gathered items around identity-based themes and "Innovative Forms" explores a variety of unconventional book structures.

The Visitor Tables continue to grow with nearly two hundred sets of resources chosen by Printed Matter's customers.[5] In this tab, users will find wish lists, tables showing off recent purchases, and a variety of creatively conceived topics. A user with the screen name "meggles_dabomb" devised an original selection of publications called "friendsenemieslovers."[6] In the synopsis they write, "friends to lovers? enemies to lovers? no, we all know the best romantic trope is friends to enemies to lovers. the dedication. the betrayal. the reconciliation."[6] Visual research is on public display here too with guides called "lines and swirlies" and "Book Project."

The section called Your Tables is private, accessible with a login. Your Tables are populated with books from past orders or you can create and name your own. To add books to a new table, users select the button for "add to table" below any item in the catalog. In the table editing mode, you can further customize your bibliography by adding linked subject tags from a list of suggested labels, writing an introductory description or curator's remarks, and/or annotating individual items. You can choose to keep the list private for your own research or publish it to the Visitor Tables.

Visually, the tables are a solid color, a customized backdrop chosen from a palette of fifty-one vibrant and pastel screen colors. In the editing mode, a draggable interface allows scaled versions of book cover images to be arranged and grouped any way a curator-shopper chooses, whether lined up in neat rows or loosely stacked in piles of overlapping shapes. To further make sure visitors feel the full table-likeness of these tables, creators may select and add stock objects to their virtual surfaces as well—think a houseplant, watch, set of keys, or an apple. These emulate an environment that is homey and domestic rather than a commercial retail space, and subtly help shoppers visualize these surrogates in their homes.

| Printed Matter, Inc. | | OPEN **Main location** 231 11th Ave, NYC Today until 7 pm | Closed **St Marks** NEW! 38 St Marks Pl, NYC Open tmrw at 2 pm |

PM Tables Visitor Tables Your Tables

Holiday Promotion - 25% off of select Fundraising Editions
BY PRINTED MATTER

Animals
BY CHRISTINA MARTINELLI

Riso Revolution!
BY PRINTED MATTER

New Arrivals ~ Winter 2022
BY PRINTED MATTER

In a Bind?
BY PRINTED MATTER

Selections from NYABF '22
BY PRINTED MATTER

Myth, Magic and all in between: a table by Rin Kim
BY PRINTED MATTER

Shanzhai Lyric NYABF Window
BY PRINTED MATTER

Karen Lamassonne
BY PRINTED MATTER

Word and image and emoji: zines and prints by Ivy Zheyu Chen
BY PRINTED MATTER

we web keepers: a bookshelf by Lukaza Branfman-Verissimo
BY PRINTED MATTER

End of Summer
BY PRINTED MATTER

Heresies: A Feminist Publication on Art and Politics
BY PRINTED MATTER

NYC Art & Performance 1970s-1980s: Live and Cover Magazines
BY PRINTED MATTER

Journals of Artist Writing: 1970s-1980s
BY PRINTED MATTER

Main directory of "PM Tables, Visitor Tables, Your Tables," screenshot.

| Printed Matter, Inc. | | OPEN | Main location
231 11th Ave, NYC
Today until 7 pm | Closed | St Marks NEW!
38 St Marks Pl, NYC
Open tmrw at 2 pm |

PM Tables   Visitor Tables   Your Tables

I Love You Earth

by Printed Matter PM

Facebook   Tweet   Embed

Agriculture   Earthwork   Environment

Checklist

Print checklist

1. Kurt Johannessen
   Moon
   Bergen, Norway: Zeth Forlag, 2004
   700
   $30.00

2. Anca Benera and Arnold Estefan
   Debrisphere: Landscape as an Extension of the Military Imagination
   Bucharest, Romania: PUNCH, 2018
   Out of stock

3. Gunnar Harrison
   Lake Effect
   Salt Lake City, UT: GD4 LLC, 2020
   Out of stock

4. Brett Bloom
   BREAK DOWN WORKBOOK #4: SONIC MEDITATIONS: IMMERSIVE ECOLOGICAL ENTANGLEMENT
   Auburn, IN: Breakdown Break Down Press, 2018
   Out of stock

Interactive table "I Love You Earth" curated by
Printed Matter staff, screenshot.

285

The soft sales pitch: you could have just as much fun playing with real books.

While in the viewing mode, the book covers move slightly when hovered over with a mouse, activating the surface of the table. Users can click on any image to bring up its corresponding product page or scroll down to read an introduction, summary, or short essay by the curator, if available. This information is followed by an image-text inventory containing author, title, facts of publication, edition size, and either a price or an "out of stock" note. The titles are enumerated in the order they were added to the table, like an accession list. Site visitors also have options to embed a PM Table into a website, send it to Facebook or Twitter, or print the checklist.

Whether users prefer sifting and clicking through book-cover images on a virtual surface or scrolling through a more traditional checklist, this bibliographic project allows users the freedom to choose how they navigate a table and stumble upon resources that might otherwise be difficult to unearth in a catalog search. The ability to customize your own tables allows the user to actively participate in the interpretation and historicization of artists' publications.

The Tables are linked to Printed Matter's vast active online inventory as well as their archive of out of stock items. (In the case of the latter, visitors will rarely encounter a broken link.) This is a great feature for the longevity of the Tables. Key materials that are not currently for sale can help flesh out topics of interest.

Printed Matter Tables have not yet eradicated the image carousel, but, by God, they've been demonstrating sound alternative possibilities for nine years.

(1) A quick search for independent booksellers in the Internet Archive Wayback Machine shows that the Seminary Co-op launched a website in 1996, Powell's Books in 1998, and The Strand in 2000.
(2) "Mission & History," Printed Matter, accessed October 27, 2022, https://www.printedmatter.org/about/mission-history.
(3) See "Online," Linked by Air, accessed December 19, 2022, https://www.linkedbyair.net/projects/format/2-online.
(4) As of October 27, 2022, there are 562 PM Tables.
(5) As of October 27, 2022, there are 191 Visitor Tables.
(6) meggles_dabomb, "friendsenemieslovers," Printed Matter, last updated 2/22/2021, https://www.printedmatter.org/catalog/tables/20299.
(7) meggles_dabomb, "friendsenemieslovers."

Poet-Saints Of July 06

[Rebel, Janelle]. *Poet-Saints of July 06*. 2013. https://foldtocenter.com/projects/poet-saints/index.html.

The Poet-Saints of July 06 is a bibliographic website that assembles books of poetry by eighteen authors into a reading guide of mini-lists. The project, initially exploring unorthodox uses for database search features and an uncanny reading coincidence, locates all of the poets that died on the bibliographer's birthday.[1] The text-based website, created somewhat anonymously by Janelle Rebel, is entirely designed and written with the featureless accommodations of TextEdit and Notepad. It contains one repeating photograph of an ikebana arrangement on the index page. The philosophy of ikebana—*the life of a flower is very short*—anchors the theme of the bibliography.

The resulting list of authors, displayed by surname in the website's header, is a sequentially and geographically disparate group.[2] It is, as Italo Calvino defines, an "improbable shelf," one "containing books that we do not usually put side by side, the juxtaposition of which can produce electric shocks, short circuits."[3] As it happens, the poets are not entirely disconnected from one another. For instance, one of the strongest affinities is that the American poet Kenneth Koch wrote the epic *Ko; or, A Season on Earth* (1960) influenced by the Italian Renaissance poet Ludovico Ariosto's work, *Orlando Furioso* (first edition 1516). Koch and Furioso share the same date of death separated by 469 years. In another curious case, Chicago-based poet Scharmel Iris who was working at the beginning of the twentieth century, "proved to be a plagiarist and [a] forger."[4] Iris, it seems, could have ripped off any of the poet-saints that came before him.

Each of the reading lists focuses on books of poetry written by a single author. This guideline helps narrow what might otherwise be a set of unwieldy bibliographies. Exceptions to this rule have been made for Judith Sargent Murray, whose work is primarily uncollected, and Helene Johnson, whose poetry is mainly found in anthologies. Of the international authors included in the guide, only English-language translations have been cited, which means that some author pages have no entries. This is a publicly accessible guide that is paradoxically driven by private selection criteria and the bibliographer's own reading habits.

(1) "All of the poets" is relative. The eighteen included are those figures who have been identified as poets and recorded as such in major literary reference sources.
(2) As noted in the catalogue entry for "Hidden Histories," the use of surnames alone may be problematic, esp. for women and minorities.
(3) Italo Calvino, "Whom Do We Write For? or The Hypothetical Bookshelf" in *The Uses of Literature*, trans. Patrick Creagh (San Diego: Harcourt Brace & Company, 1986), 82.
(4) This archival finding aid is surprisingly gossipy. "Scharmel Iris Papers," The Newberry Library, Chicago, last modified 2008, https://mms.newberry.org/repositories/2/resources/207.

Poet-Saints of July 06 index page, screenshot.

Julia de Burgos (February 17, 1914 – July 06, 1953)
/ Puerto Rican-born poet

Editions in English

Roses in the Mirror. Translated and edited by Carmen D. Lucca. San Juan: Mairena, 1992.

A Rose Made of Water. Translated by Rafael Ramos Albelo. San Juan: 1994.

Song of the Simple Truth: The Complete Poems of Julia de Burgos. Translated by Jack Agüeros. Willimantic, CT: Curbstone, 1997.

Suggest additions and corrections to the Project Editor, 2013.

Mini-bibliography for Julia de Burgos from *Poet-Saints of July 06*, screenshot.

The Queen's English

Syms, Martine, with Cat Roif and Jeff Cain. *The Queen's English*. Exhibition and reading room at the Armory Center for the Arts, Pasadena, CA, July 13–August 29, 2014.

Big City Forum (BCF), an interdisciplinary program championed by Leonardo Bravo, invited LA-based artist-instigator Martine Syms to exhibit in their mezzanine-turned-reading-room at the Armory Center for the Arts. *The Queen's English* was one of three exhibitions presented by BCF in a series of events in 2014 called *City of Hope, City of Resistance: Research and Actions at the Urban Level*.

Inspired by a used bookstore find, Syms produced a bibliographic reenactment of librarian J. R. Roberts's *Black Lesbians: An Annotated Bibliography* (1981). The artist presented over thirty books along a wall rail in the reading room. The titles were culled from the pages of *Black Lesbians*—"from authors such as Audre Lorde, Toni Morrison, Pat Parker, Diane Bogus, and Red Jordan Arobateau."[1] Surrounded by Jeff Cain's wood furniture and several poster-sized diptychs

View of *The Queen's English* exhibition and reading room at the Armory Center for the Arts.

CITY OF HOPE
CITY OF RESISTANCE

CITY OF HOPE, CITY OF RESISTANCE: RESEARCH AND ACTIONS ON THE URBAN LEVEL

BIG CITY FORUM IN RESIDENCE

MEZZANINE

Big City Forum, founded in 2008, is an interdisciplinary, conversation based, curatorial research project that explores the intersection between design-based creative disciplines within the context of public space, the built environment, and social change. City of Hope, City of Resistance: Research and Actions on the Urban Level is Big City Forum's 15-month, three-part residency at Armory Center for the Arts; it brings together the creative forces of numerous participants across the fields of architecture, urban design, contemporary art, new media, and social and community activism.

Los Angeles is at a pivotal moment of transition and transformation. Social fragmentation and isolation is giving way to a celebration of plurality and difference; identities and communities are coalescing around collective, design-based solutions. City of Hope, City of Resistance: Research and Actions on the Urban Level explores, discusses, and produces various forms of social space from community-based initiatives; new physical and social architectures; individual and collective actions that have affected public civic engagement; and ideas and actions that will influence life in the region in constructive, positive ways.

This residency project features three distinct phases. January through June 2014 Big City Forum directors Leonardo Bravo and River Jukes-Hudson focused on research and planning, developing programs that include a series of exhibitions and events in the Armory's Mezzanine Galleries, which are unfolding from July through December 2014; the ideas generated throughout 2014 will be consolidated into a publication, to be released in spring 2015.

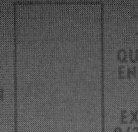

MEZZANINE

MARTINE SYMS
CAT ROIF
JEFF CAIN

7/13–

THE QUEEN'S ENGLISH

EXHIBIT 8/31

THE QUEEN'S ENG- LISH

THE QUEEN'S ENGLISH is an exhibition and reading room by Los Angeles–based artist Martine Syms. Inspired by the distributions of knowledge within the radical, black feminist community in the 1970s, The Queen's English uses text as homage to form an intergenerational dialogue about language and representation.

Syms describes her work as an "excursus from a primary text," one that takes imaginative liberties with the past in order to make it work for the future. Black Lesbian Caucus, Christopher Street Liberation Day Parade, 1973 recasts protest messages as commercial signage. The Dedication pieces connect the words of each author to a new audience, while For Nights Like This One, 1979, a series of prints made collaboratively with photographer Cat Roif, suggests a fictional character and narrative that draws from the source materials on view.

Modeled after JR Roberts' 1981 book Black Lesbians: An Annotated Bibliography, the first published collection of black lesbian literature, the project also gathers a selection of pulp paperbacks, novels, biographies, and chapbooks from authors such as Audre Lorde, Toni Morrison, Pat Parker, Diane Bogus, and Red Jordan Arobateau, among many others.

The Queen's English is the latest manifestation of Syms' ongoing inquiry into the role of the reader as a position of power. Through researching, collecting, archiving, and remembering, the project enacts the ways that information circulates within subcultures, forging a continuity between her practice and the radical tradition.

Exhibition signage and furniture for *The Queen's English*.

created by Syms with the photographer Cat Roif, the books were reactivated in a contemporary art space.

When Roberts's seminal guide was published, it gathered a rich body of work written by a twice-overlooked community. In the foreword by Barbara Smith, the aim of *Black Lesbians* was to circulate the knowledge of the existence of this literature as well as to correct the "overwhelming whiteness of lesbian research specifically and women's studies research generally."[2] It contributed to a long line of projects in Black bibliography from *A Select Bibliography of the Negro American* (1901) by W. E. B. Du Bois to *Black American Writers Past and Present* (1975) by Theressa Gunnels Rush, Carol Fairbanks, and Esther Spring Arata. The individual titles in *Black Lesbians* struck a chord with Syms who understands that finding, reading, and remembering literature written by and about Black lesbians is a way of participating in an "intergenerational dialogue."[3]

Roberts's original bibliography had six chapters: "Lives and Lifestyles," "Oppression, Resistance, and Liberation," "Literature and Criticism," "Music and Musicians," "Periodicals," and "Research, Reference, and Popular Studies." *The Queen's English* draws on "Literature and Criticism" and displays an array of "pulp paperbacks, novels, biographies, and chapbooks" for gallerygoers to peruse.[4] Syms is transparent about the catalyst for her inspiration and offers her audience more than bibliographic snippets. The work of *Black Lesbians* is physically manifested as an interactive reading room for a new generation of readers.

(1) *The Queen's English,* 2014, exhibition signage.
(2) Barbara Smith, foreword to *Black Lesbians: An Annotated Bibliography*, by J. R. Roberts (Tallahassee, FL: Naiad Press, 1981), ix.
(3) "The Queen's English," Martin Syms's website, accessed March 20, 2016, http://martinesyms.com/the-queens-english/. Archived at https://web.archive.org/web/20160328041427/http://martinesyms.com/the-queens-english/.
(4) *The Queen's English*, 2014, exhibition signage.

Reading Trayvon Martin

Syms, Martine. *ReadingTrayvonMartin.com*. Last article February 5, 2014. Accessed March 25, 2016. http://readingtrayvonmartin.com. Archived at https://web.archive.org/web/20160312064206/http://readingtrayvonmartin.com/.

To follow the events that transpired after the tragic shooting of African American teenager Trayvon Martin in 2012, artist and "conceptual entrepreneur" Martine Syms spun up a web bibliography. She considers reading a position of power and started building a list of links to articles, videos, essays, blog posts, and primary documents related to the investigation of Martin's death and the subsequent trial of his shooter, George Zimmerman.

ReadingTrayvonMartin.com is a personal bibliography that is publicly available, commissioned by Rhizome and exhibited online with the New Museum in 2013.[1] It collects seventy-seven links listed by article title or article title with publication name, and includes sources from major news outlets, alternative news organizations, and personal blogs. The order of entries is not immediately discernible though it is likely the order in which Syms herself read and discovered the articles. The site roughly configures a reverse chronological trajectory through the national media debate with pieces like *Truthout's* "Hoodie Politics: Trayvon Martin and Racist Violence in Post-Racial America" and the *New Yorker's* "George Zimmerman, Not Guilty: Blood on the Leaves."

A black hoodie, an Arizona iced tea, and a bag of Skittles hovers over the list. As the user scrolls through the entries, the titles are partially obscured by the shapes. The images propagate the media symbols that came to be associated with Martin and, at the same time, interrupt the media voices from which they sprang.

From the outset *ReadingTrayvonMartin.com* was designed as a durational project, a site that would remain open until media attention dwindled. The web bibliography provides a wily cross-section of serious and click-bait news coverage.

By publishing the site online, Syms assumes that there is an audience beyond herself that might engage with these picks. To use the site as a reading path however is cumbersome. Article links open in the same window rather than in a new tab. With one click, the reader is *poof!* directed away from ReadingTrayvonMartin.com's list of selected documents and thrown into the hyperframe of this or that news site.

ReadingTrayvonMartin.com performs best as a narrative that records the arcs of Martin's case, rather than as a guide to explore specific sources. The stream of headlines can be seen at a glance, creating a time-lapse effect. As the story unfolds, the Trayvon Martin case devolves into the George Zimmerman story. The latest and presumably last entry is an article from January 31, 2014, hyping the possibility of a celebrity boxing match between Zimmerman and the rapper, The Game. At this point Syms drops off, presumably losing interest or moving on to other pursuits. The durational selection thus gradually ceases and the site itself remains an accessible archive of events.

(1) See "Martine Syms: Reading Trayvon Martin," New Museum, accessed November 6, 2022, https://www.newmuseum.org/exhibitions/view/reading-trayvon-martin-by-martine-syms.

Saints & Guides

Nonnus Studio. *Saints & Guides*.
A Little Lord. [1st print-on-demand ed.]
Wheaton, IL: Nonnus Studio, 2010.
88 p.: ill.; 17.5 × 11 × 1 cm.

Nonnus Studio. *Saints & Guides*.
A Little Lord. Wheaton, IL: Nonnus, 2010.
https://issuu.com/nonnus/docs
/saints?e=1838034/2295880.
88 p.: ill.

Are Not Books & Publications.
Saints & Guides. A Little Lord.
2nd print-on-demand ed. Wheaton, IL:
Are Not Books & Publications, 2013.
88 p.: ill.; 17.5 × 11 × 1 cm.

Saints & Guides looks deceptively simple, an inviting pocketbook with three parts. It is a bibliography of multiple persons, a set of new canonical figures that will provide "secular guidance for a Godless era."[1] It is a bibliography for reading as much as it is for consulting, written and designed by Nonnus Studio, now published by Matt Smith at Are Not Books. In the first two parts, each of the twenty-seven saints selected has their own spread. Every saint name bears a one to four word summary-heading set in the thin, French

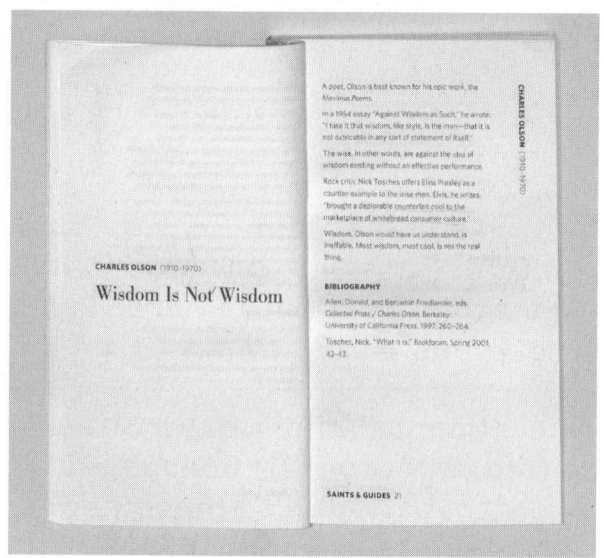

Interior spread of part 1 in *Saints & Guides*, 2010.

characters of Enlightenment-era Didot. A sans-serif running head is placed vertically in the top-right margin and a running footer is situated horizontally in the bottom-left margin to define the edges. This tidy promenade provides the ground to romp through a series of discordant juxtapositions.

The figures are plucked from the tenth century to the present day, and allied in no perceptible order. They are a disparate list of raconteurs, thinkers, mystics, critics, and artists. Occasionally the headings are linguistically playful. For example, the entry for Titus Burckhardt reads "Religion Is Not Sacred," which is followed by entries for Thomas Frank, "Business Is Not Culture," and Charles Olson, "Wisdom Is Not Wisdom." The headings in part 1, like those mentioned above, tend to indicate a key idea that is embodied or championed by the figure of the saint it describes. In part 2, the entry headings take on a different function, attempting to straightforwardly identify who the person is. Art Tatum is thus, "The Performer" and Gloria Steinem, "The Feminist." The language has a more authoritative ring, as if there is only one performer and one feminist, and Tatum and Steinem are it. Part 3 is curiously titled in the table of contents as "Portraits of the Guides; Icons, or Windows into the Secular Heaven." It contains a series of black-and-white illustrations that do not recognizably correspond to the saints and guides mentioned in parts 1 and 2. In fact, some of the drawings are not human figures at all. There is a puppet, a bird, a grand piano, a ladder. A great obfuscation.

The written entries are thoughtful and satisfying, a few focused paragraphs in length each. The writing draws out a tantalizing idea or a set of ideas related to each figure, sometimes extolling one of the minor philosophies of a major figure that is relevant to contemporary times. The descriptions expose something about why this or that saint is so compelling to the book's writers—"a group of artists who work in close collaboration."[2] There is a short list of references, a mini-bibliography, for each entry. These recommendations are imaginative—referring readers to films, artist's publications, scholarly works, and periodicals—as well as an exercise in restraint. These little bibliographies bring together a group of central and tangential readings that are sure to enrich the reader whether they are well-versed about the saint or not. The entry for Quentin Crisp refers readers to his well-known autobiography *A Naked Civil Servant* (1968) but also swerves to Max Weber's *The Protestant Ethic and the Spirit of Capitalism* (first English translation, 1930).[3] The spread designated for Moses Maimonides calls attention to one of his major works *The Guide for the Perplexed* (c. 1190) and in the same breath points readers towards Jacob Needleman's *Money and the Meaning of Life* (1991).[4]

The book is filled with conceptually sharp transitions

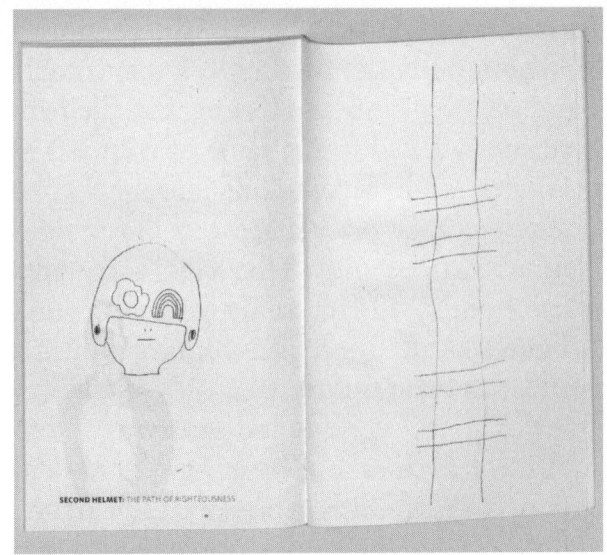

Interior spread of part 3 in *Saints & Guides*, 2010.

and is designed to encourage the reader to keep exploring. It does require a bit of trust on the part of the reader to open *Saints & Guides*, but its variety of figures is assembled to provoke and to lead the way. The publication proffers guidance for the devout and the seeker.

(1) Are Not Books & Publications, *Saints & Guides*, A Little Lord (Wheaton, IL: Are Not Books & Publications, 2013), back cover.
(2) Are Not Books & Publications, *Saints & Guides*, [88].
(3) In *Saints & Guides*, the copies listed are those examined by the author(s): *A Naked Civil Servant* (Penguin Classics, 1997) and *The Protestant Ethic and the Spirit of Capitalism* (Scribner, 1958). I've cited the dates of first publication to show the historical range.
(4) *The Guide for the Perplexed* noted in the *Saints & Guides* entry is to a Dover edition from 1956.

Someone Else – A Library of 100 Books Written Anonymously or Under Pseudonyms

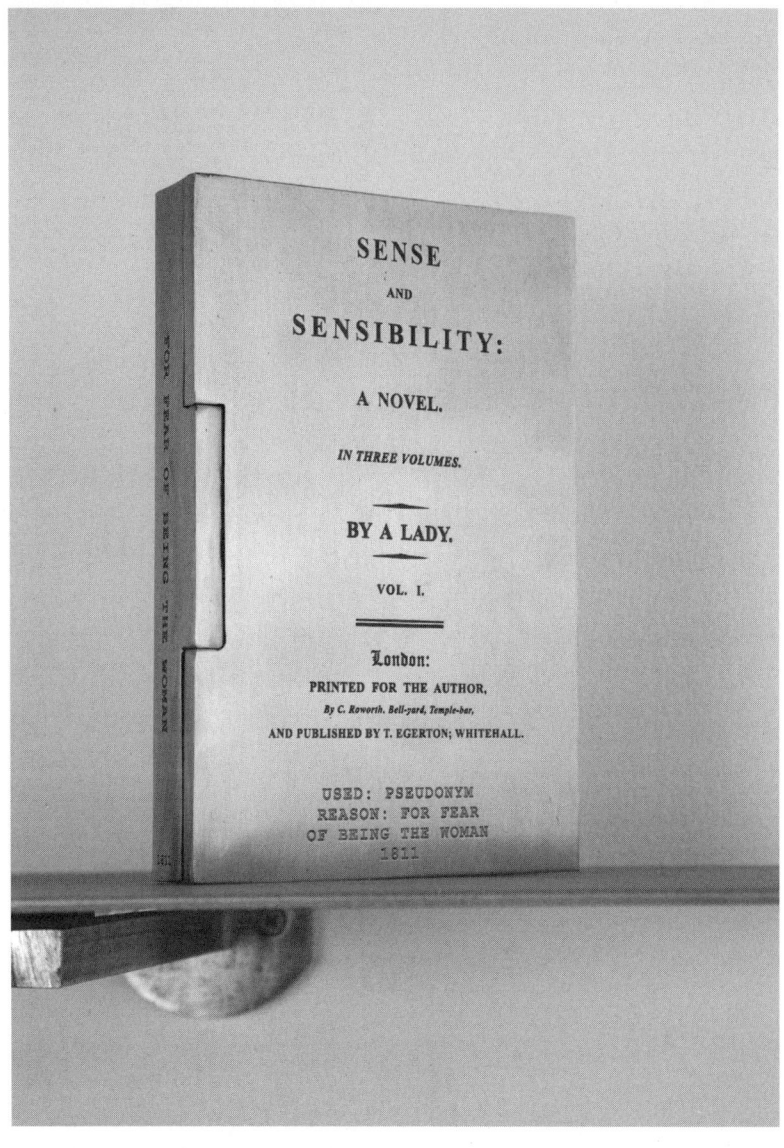

Close-up of *Someone Else – A Library of 100 Books Written Anonymously or Under Pseudonyms*, 2011.

Gupta, Shilpa. *Someone Else – A Library of 100 Books Written Anonymously or Under Pseudonyms*, 2011. Installation with stainless steel etched books and mild steel shelves, 488 × 22 × 190 cm.

Gupta, Shilpa. *Someone Else – A Library of 35 Books Written Anonymously or Under Pseudonyms*, 2011–2012. Installation with stainless steel etched books and mild steel shelves, 244 × 22 × 189 cm. Edition of 3.

Gupta, Shilpa. *Someone Else – A Library of 100 Books Written Anonymously or Under Pseudonyms*, 2012. Library installation in English at Bristol Central Library, Bristol.

Gupta, Shilpa. *Someone Else – A Library of 100 Books Written Anonymously or Under Pseudonyms (With Turkish Authors)*, 2012. Library installation in Turkish and English at Dr. Riza Nur Public City Library, Sinop.

Gupta, Shilpa. *Someone Else – A Library of 100 Books Written Anonymously or Under Pseudonyms (With Portuguese Authors)*, 2013. Library installation in French at Fondation Calouste Gulbenkian Délégation en France, Paris.

Gupta, Shilpa. *Someone Else – A Library of 100 Books Written Anonymously or Under Pseudonyms (With Dutch Authors)*, 2014. Library installation in Dutch and English at Permeke Library, Antwerp.

Gupta, Shilpa. *Someone Else – A Library of 100 Books Written Anonymously or Under Pseudonyms (With Spanish Authors)*, 2016. Library installation in Spanish and English at Villena Public Library, La Habana.

Someone Else – A Library of 100 Books Written Anonymously or Under Pseudonyms (With Turkish Authors), 2012, installation at Dr. Riza Nur Public City Library, Sinop.

In *Someone Else – A Library of 100 Books Written Anonymously or Under Pseudonyms,* artist Shilpa Gupta gathers a curious array of literature. In a multipart project that began in 2011, she unravels some of the personal, social, and political reasons that writers across time periods and geographies have not published under their own names.

Someone Else – A Library of 100 Books Written Anonymously or Under Pseudonyms, 2011.

As a stark ode to restrictions on self-expression, Gupta's project bonds a surprising array of authors together who would otherwise be scattered across different sections of a library or bookstore.

One facet of *Someone Else* is intended for a museum or gallery. It is a stainless steel sculpture of one hundred life-sized etched book covers—namely a selection of popular titles—set across five long shelves. The likes of Anne Rampling [Anne Rice], George Orwell [Eric Arthur Blair], J. K. Rowling [Joanne Rowling], and John le Carré [David John Moore Cornwell] are all here, as are well-known titles first published anonymously—e.g. Jane Austen's *Sense and Sensibility: A Novel* (1811) written "by a lady" and Edgar Allan Poe's *Tamerlane and Other Poems* (1827) written "by a Bostonian." Each metal cover is a proxy, literally a shell of a book. The covers stand up stiffly on their own either face out or spine out, or rest flat against the shelves. Visually, it is a library that is only half full, at most, with generous spacing between the titles. Each front cover bears the line-art version to simulate a particular edition's cover art or title page layout, plus some short deets announced in an all caps slab serif on why the author published anonymously or under a pseudonym. This reason is repeated in the same typewriter-style font on the spine, e.g. "TO WRITE FREELY IN MULTIPLE GENRES," "TO KEEP HIS DAY JOB," "FOR FEAR OF CENSORSHIP BY THE COLONIAL STATE," "TO CONCEAL HER GENDER," etc.

Another facet intended for the art collector is *Someone Else – A Library of 35 Books Written Anonymously or Under Pseudonyms*, an editioned work with five shelves only half as wide, supporting thirty-five book covers. Similar to the larger version, ephemeral book jackets and covers all are fixed in the permanence of stainless steel and carefully arranged. The viewer can contemplate and explore the titles in these metal libraries without touching.

The third facet of this project is a public engagement piece where viewers can browse, read, and even check out the real titles that Gupta has researched and aggregated. She has created different interventions within public libraries and special libraries in England, Turkey, France, Belgium, and Cuba. For these renditions of *Someone Else*, the artist places informational black-and-white signage in the stacks or out on tables next to the books being referenced. The appearance of these framed signs in the stacks draws attention to the prevalence of authors who do not use their own names to publish and raises visibility to pseudonyms which the reader may not have known. The framed pieces combine a photo or intentionally blurred photo of the pseudonymous or anonymous author respectively, the typographic setting from the book's title page, and the usage and rationale written in the common language or languages spoken in that library's community. This is similar to the kinds of thematic displays that librarians design to recommend titles to their readers, albeit Gupta's has an extra aesthetic finesse. It is a sensitive and adaptable work too—for instance, in the library installation in Sinop, Turkey, the artist highlights books by Turkish authors, no doubt mining that local collection.

Understandably, writers have sought safety for themselves, better social reception, creative freedom to write as another persona, etc. Gupta's bibliographic project uncovers a literary history of whispers and alternate identities. It draws attention to the perennial problems that plague authorial freedom in a modern era, all the while piquing the viewer's interest into learning more about the [unnamed] writers themselves.

---

(1) For another project that uses three-dimensional proxies, see catalogue entry for "Meanwhile, the Surrogate for the Presently Absent Gets a Proxy."

Sorted Books

Katchadourian, Nina. *Sorted Books*, 1993–. Ongoing project with 13 series of artworks, to date, plus 1 series in progress.

+

Katchadourian, Nina. *Sorted Books*. San Francisco: Chronicle Books, 2013. 176 p.: col. ill.; 16 × 21 × 2 cm.

The Castrati in Opera
from the series
Special Collections Revisited,
1996/2008
(*Sorted Books* project, 1993–).

Nobody has paid more attention to spine typography than Nina Katchadourian. She works within the stacks of personal libraries and institutional collections to make sortings for her *Sorted Books* project. For thirty years she's been finding spirited associations between books. Usually working with anywhere from two to nine volumes at a time, she creates messages using the spine titles. Sometimes Katchadourian photographs her arrangements of sorted books, and develops them as C-prints. Other times she exhibits them as sculptures. Her practice is site-specific and hands-on, exploring the spatial, topical, and visual dimensions of books and libraries.[1] Her bibliographic compilations are considered and spontaneous, an instantiation of tacit knowledge.[2] Each sorting is unique. The gatherings represent "a cross section of the larger collection" from where they came and often draw out a library's main themes.[3] An edition published by Chronicle Books in 2013 also called *Sorted Books* collects and distinguishes eight distinct series from the first twenty years.[4] Each series acts as a portrait of a particular collection.

In her first two series, *Composition* (1993) and *Reference* (1996), Katchadourian flips the books on the shelf so that the spines read consecutively from bottom up, left to right. The surrounding books are shelved fore edge out to isolate a word string, for instance: *Macbeth / Trust Me / You Are Not the Target / For Whom the Bell Tolls.* Her three-dimensional writing comes together to form a sentence, a poetic fragment, a monologue or dialogue, or some other form of word play. The size, weight, style, and color of the typefaces vary the pace and inflection as you read across the spines.

From *Special Collections Revisited* (1996/2008) and forward, she starts stacking the books horizontally and aligning the title typography rather than the edges of the book. The reading goes left to right, top to bottom. It's a conversational shelf—humorous: *The Castrati in Opera / The Story of Organ Music* and contemplative: *Why Spiders Spin / The Memory of All That / Bitter Music*.

She breaks away from displaying the spines on occasion. In the series *Once Upon a Time in Delaware/In Quest of the Perfect Book* (2012) she places the books face-out, full cover to show off the decorative publisher's bindings (c. 1870–1920) held by the Helen Farr Sloan Library and Archives at the Delaware Art Museum. She uses a similar cover-out placement in *What I Know About Magic* (2022), working with the H. Adrian Smith Collection of Conjuring and Magicana held by the John Hay Library at Brown University. The effect in these series is not as fluid or punchy. Reading left to right, there is a longer pause between each title. The eye has more to take in, set adrift by gilt ornamentation, botanical framing devices, and other cover graphics.

What's interesting about the *Sorted Books* project in general is the implication that if the books are now sorted through Katchadourian's intuitive intervention, then whatever state they were in previously was an unsorted one.[5] This shelf arrangement is of a new kind, reliant on the title of the book, its spine artwork, and its ability to resonate with nearby volumes. It's different than Aby Warburg's famous classification system extolling the law of the good neighbor and a far cry from the subject entry points of the Dewey Decimal or Library of Congress classification systems. When looking at the photographs of her sortings, they not only reflect who acquired them—one may wonder why such a book was purchased or for what purpose—but also something stranger. Maybe these books do belong together. What if you were to read them in her order? William Stafford's book of poetry *The Way It Is* would be followed by artist Richard Long's *Walking in Circles* and concluded by Jon Kabat-Zinn's scientific mindfulness *Wherever You Go, There You Are*.

Walking in Circles
from the series
BookPace, 2002
(*Sorted Books* project, 1993–).

(1) Nina Katchadourian, *Sorted Books* (San Francisco: Chronicle Books, 2013), 15. Though Katchadourian is typically hands-on, she worked remotely on the *Noguchi* (2021) series during the pandemic. See Nina Katchadourian, "'Sorted Books' at The Noguchi Museum," accessed December 19, 2022, https://www.noguchi.org/isamu-noguchi/digital-features/sorted-books-at-the-noguchi-museum/.
(2) Richard Shiff defines tacit knowledge "as a type of intuitive or fast thinking." Richard Shiff, *Doubt* (New York: Routledge, 2008), 156.
(3) Katchadourian, *Sorted Books*, 14.
(4) Although eight series were completed when the Chronicle Books publication came out, Katchadourian is at present working on series number fourteen, called "Look Who's Talking." Nina Katchadourian, email message to author, December 17, 2022.
(5) If they were previously "sorted" then the artist's project would be one of "re-sorting" or "resorting."

A Stack of Books, A Book of Stacks

Tamm, Triin.
A Stack of Books, A Book of Stacks. Zürich: Rollo Press, 2011. 109 p.: ill.; 11 × 17.5 × 1 cm.
Tamm, Triin.
A Stack of Books, A Book of Stacks, 2011. Installation. On the occasion of *If It's Part Broke, Half Fix It* at the CAC Vilnius, Vilnius, Lithuania.

Estonian artist Triin Tamm created a small but bewildering book of books for *If It's Part Broke, Half Fix It* at the CAC Vilnius in 2011. The book has two titles on the cover *A Stack of Books* and *A Book of Stacks*, plus two ISBN barcodes. She installed a single pallet of books on the gallery floor, ready to peruse or purchase.

Each softcover book is a network of excerpts with newsprint pages reminiscent of the Scholastic Book Fair. The front flyleaf is stamped with a waddling penguin bookplate that announces "This book belongs to Triin" and the inside back cover bears a yellow sticker that emphatically states "PLEASE CIRCULATE." The table of contents presents an orderly list of thirty-five titles arranged alphabetically, though the system is only a ruse, an empty signifier. The arrangement disorders the material through a guise of civility. Similarly, the visual program of *A Stack of Books* has an air of credibility, containing a simple citation (author, title, publisher, date) beneath a photo or digital rendering of each of Tamm's book selections. A sample from each book's interior, one to seven pages in length, follows. It's like the Surprise Me! feature in Amazon's book previews, only these excerpts, images, and puzzles give the reader choice among deliberately enigmatic picks rather than machine random picks. For instance, opposite the anonymously authored *The History of the Origin of All Things* is a dialogue between two characters explicating every word of a nonsense poem, while Hugo Vermer's *The Winter Journey* is paired with a scan of a blank page damaged by burrowing bookworms. Books from 2011 are placed next to books from the early twentieth century. The nonlinear narrative of the bibliography weaves in and out of topics like reading, languages, technology, and hoaxes.

Are these Tamm's recent acquisitions of plays, poetry, stories, prose, and games? Partway through the book the reader finds a self-published title by Tamm, *If It Ain't Broke, Break It* which is an address to the exhibition's theme and a clue to the riddle. *A Stack of Books* is a bibliography that spans from "existing and semi-existing books to non-at-all-existing [*sic*] or soon-to-be-existing ones."[1] The reader may identify familiar authors, titles, or publishers, but not know what has been fabricated. Tamm plays with the legitimizing technology of the book and the bibliography, and disorders the reader's usual means of addressing a text. In doing so, she creates a *real* tangle of associations between books, fake and actual.[2] Only the reader with the right touch will intuit these bonds.

(1) "Triin Tamm: A Stack of Books," Rollo Press, accessed March 25, 2016, https://rollo-press.com/#guest-publication-a-stack-of-books.

(2) See the catalogue entries for "Kentifrications," "A Final Companion to Books from 'The Simpsons' in Alphabetical Order," and "Strike and Riot."

Strike and Riot

Lee, Chris.
"Strike and Riot: A Possible Syllabus."
"Hieroglyphs of the Anti-Commodity."
Special issue, *Counter Signals* 2
(Fall 2017–Winter 2018): 162–79.

Lee, Chris.
"Strike and Riot."
In *Extra-Curricular,* edited by Jacob Lindgren,
118–49. Eindhoven: Onomatopee, 2018.
Ill.; page size: 22 × 15.5 cm.

Lee, Chris.
"Strike and Riot."
Neshan 45 (Autumn 2018–Winter 2019).
http://www.neshanmagazine.com/Article
.aspx?l=2&Id=418.

Chris Lee's "Strike and Riot" project is a speculative reading list for a graphic design program if it was embedded in an anarchist college, specifically the long defunct Tolstoy College at University at Buffalo SUNY (active 1969–1985). Iterations of Lee's project have appeared in several places, including in print within an issue of *Counter Signals*, a multiform journal of design and politics, as well as within the pages of *Extra-Curricular*, a monograph on alternative pedagogical practices and programs for graphic design.

While the backdrop may sound complex, Lee was rooted in a particular place and time. He was concerned with questions of historiography while teaching graphic design history at University at Buffalo SUNY:

> What was graphic design made with, by whom and to what ends? What were its canonical practitioners concerned with and what were they not concerned with? Who and what counts as part of graphic design history and how does that history affect what these students believe they will become?[1]

And he was intrigued by the history and legacy of Tolstoy College on campus.

This combination of interests presented an opportunity. With "Strike and Riot," Lee clearly marks out what this project is and what it aims to do—infuse radical theory and the study of oppression into the graphic design curriculum and challenge the disciplinary boundaries that limit the realm of graphic design to client-driven, aesthetic decision-making.

Under the guise of a fictional book publisher called Strike & Riot, he conceives of a list of twenty-three titles, real and speculative. In addition to editorially developing the list, he visually actualizes it through new cover art and spine designs to digitally wrap each book and demarcate an original series. Within *Extra-Curricular*, black-and-white renderings of dimensional books are paired with each bibliographic entry, giving the reader an indication of their shape and thickness. Each book is frozen in movement on a black background, seen hovering, perching, leaning, or rocking back.

For each selection, Lee indicates the subject area to which it belongs, documents its title and author, and contributes a short description to tie the book into the series. About half of the titles already exist as published works, for example, *Discipline & Punish* (1975) by Michel Foucault, *Imagined Communities: Reflections on the Origin and Spread of Nationalism* (1983) by Benedict Anderson, and *The Undercommons: Fugitive Planning & Black Study* (2013) by Stefano Harney and Fred Moten. The rest are speculative titles that theoretically or hypothetically could exist as published works, for example, by authors long dead but known for a certain subject (*The Disciplines* (n.d.) by Jeremy Bentham and Willey Reveley), by an act of translation into English that hasn't yet occurred (*Posrednick: Mediator* by Leo Tolstoy), or by an apparent dissertation in process (*Poids et Mesures: The Renovation of the Bastille Prison—A Monument to the Metric System* by Cabelle Ahn).

"Strike and Riot" captures a range of intriguing readings from the eighteenth to the twenty-first century on typography, law, architecture, social structures, education, geopolitics, and, of course, graphic design. It functions as an innovative and challenging syllabus and an ideal publisher's list.

(1) Chris Lee, "Strike and Riot," in *Extra-Curricular*, ed. Jacob Lindgren (Eindhoven: Onomatopee, 2018), 119.

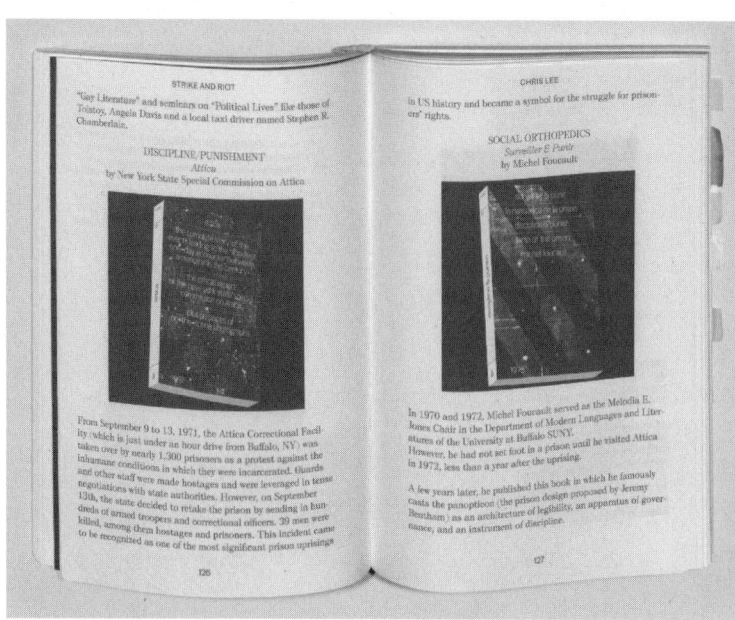

Interior spread of "Strike and Riot" in *Extra-Curricular*, 2018.

Study Room Guides

Study Room Guides, 2005–, selected cover designs.

Study Room Guides. [London]: Live Art Development Agency, 2005–. Ongoing series of thirty-eight commissioned digital publications, to date. https://www.thisisliveart.co.uk/resources/study-room-guides/. Variously 8–146 p.: some col. ill.

Study Room Guides. [London]: Live Art Development Agency, 2005–. Ongoing series of thirty-eight commissioned print publications, to date. Variously 8–146 p.: some col. ill.; page size: 30 × 21 cm.

The Study Room at Live Art Development Agency (LADA) in London, opened in 1999, and is now one of the largest libraries in the world dedicated to "live art," an umbrella term that includes "a huge range of practitioners, from those working at the edges of theatre, dance, film and video, to performance writing, socio-political activism and the new languages of the digital age."[1] In 2005, while cofounder Lois Keidan was director of LADA, the *Study Room Guides* launched online and in-print to help visitors navigate the Study Room's noncirculating reference collections, tap into live art networks, and spur dialogue in the realm of event-based art.

LADA commissions practitioners and writers to devise bibliographic guides on their area of specialty citing books, periodicals, DVDs, VHS tapes, CD-ROMs, or digital files available in the Study Room, as well as web resources or materials that LADA should consider acquiring. The inaugural issue was *The Body in Performance* (2005) by Franko B. Since then, one to four new guides have been published each year, with a print edition added to the Study Room and a digital edition posted online.[2] The next guide in the works is on Southeast Asian live art. The organization's decision to seek out the recommendations of others through commissioned projects helps them resist their own recommendation ruts, blind spots, and biases.[3]

These inventive *Study Room Guides* take on a different mode each issue, ranging from the condensed eight-page list in *Performance, Politics, Ethics & Human Rights* (2006) by Adrien Sina to the 146-page book-length primer *Performing Borders* (2016) by Alessandra Cianetti. A range of writing dictates how one would navigate each guide, as each has its own internal logic. In some cases, the guides include charts of recommended resources, an essay by the commissioned artist, essays by their colleagues, artist interviews, project reviews, and/or stills, as well as spillover into extra-publication content like toolkits, audio recordings, and websites. Some guides are more designed than others and a few of the most recent releases have a named designer. Bibliography is exemplified here as a creative act of care, where one's personal research path and embodied knowledge can enlighten others.

Three *Study Room Guides* are particularly meta when it comes to thinking about possibilities for experimental subject bibliography. One early issue to wrest from the typical form of a library subject guide was John Jordan's seventeen-page *In the Footnotes of Library Angels: A Bi(bli)ography of Insurrectionary Imagination* (2006). In it, Jordan writes a personal letter to the reader about the shift in his own practice from socially engaged art to direct-action movements. Words and phrases from the letter are copiously footnoted to tease out references to persons, events, and theories at the intersection of art and activism. The footnotes are "an equal partner," taking up as much space (or more) on each page as the body of the letter, and are intended as "walking guides to take us through the resources and books in this library and elsewhere."[4] All together, this is a conversational, approachable, and informative read that injects annotated bibliography with new life.

Charlotte Cooper's extensive twenty-eight page guide *Tantalising Glimpses* (2020) mines the Study Room for resources related to the intersection of fatness and performance as well as analyzes what artists are *not* found within LADA's Study Room. To address the latter, Cooper designates a section called "The Missing Study Room," an alphabetical listing of fat live artists from the UK, North America, and Europe that has been collectively assembled by her and her friends. She

Study Room Guides, 2005–, selected cover design.

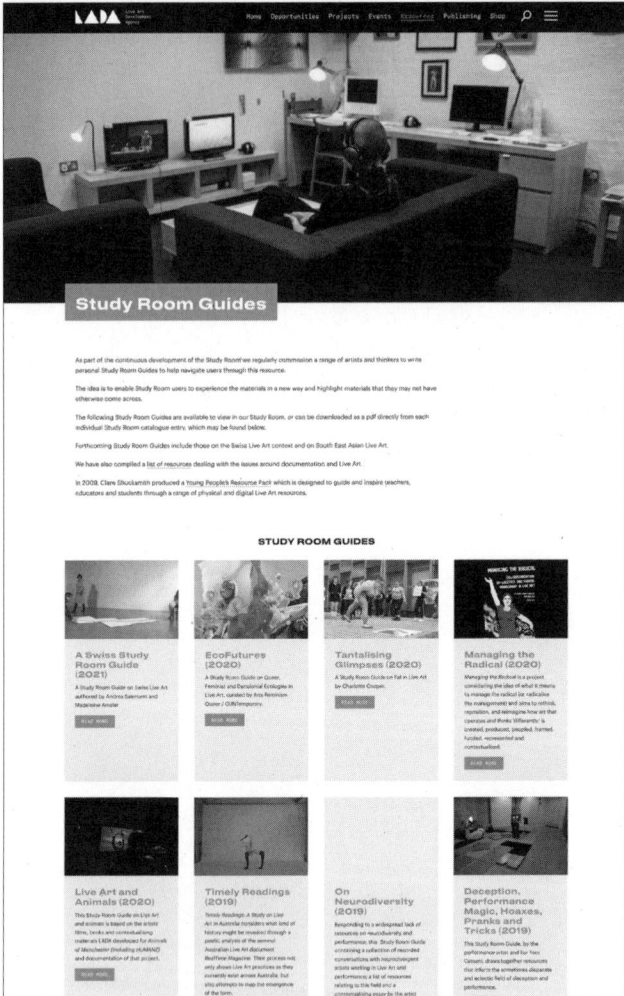

Study Room Guides online directory, screenshot.

doesn't describe each performer, just offers the invitation, "Maybe you'd like to find out more about them?"[5] It's an imaginative bibliography for a future-forward organization looking to expand the diversity of its ideas and to solicit institutional critique.

Another guide that charts new territory is *(W)reading Performance Writing* (2010), compiled and written by Rachel

Lois Clapham with twenty contributors. Clapham closes the sixty-three page guide on performance writing with a piece called "Touchstones OR FINGER / ing a historical lineage (Pointing literally and literarily)." She photographed her hand touching pages from four works at the British Library. She gives a brief citation for each work with author and title, e.g. "Mallarmé *Un Coup de Dés Jamais N'Abolira Le Hasard*," along with where and when the touching took place, how she felt touching the book, and what the book felt like. In brief descriptions she documents the experience of interacting with historical examples, creating a touchy-feely mini-bibliography within a bibliography.

The *Study Guides* are a catalyst to action. They are a hub of diverse knowledge objects that expand the bibliographic networks of live art. They are a town crier enunciating various subtopics of performance in performative ways. While no doubt useful to LADA's own Study Room researchers, the guides can be accessed anywhere with an Internet connection and thus can reach an expanded live art readership.

(1) *Are We There Yet?: Study Room Guide on Live Art and Feminism* ([London]: Live Art Development Agency, 2015), [7], https://www.thisisliveart.co.uk/wp-content/uploads/2020/02/Arewethereyet_Final.pdf; "What is Live Art?," Live Art Development Agency, accessed October 23, 2022, https://www.thisisliveart.co.uk/about-lada/what-is-live-art/.
(2) Two exceptions: no guides were released in 2007 or 2022.
(3) See *Are We There Yet?*, [8]. For guest curated lists, see also catalogue entries for "Cyberfeminism Index" and "PM Tables, Visitor Tables, Your Tables."
(4) John Jordan, *In the Footnotes of Library Angels: A Bi(bli)ography of Insurrectionary Imagination* ([London]: Live Art Development Agency, 2006), 2, https://www.thisisliveart.co.uk/wp-content/uploads/2020/02/IntheFootnotes_Final-copy.pdf.
(5) Charlotte Cooper, *Tantalising Glimpses* ([London]: Live Art Development Agency, 2020), [25], https://www.thisisliveart.co.uk/wp-content/uploads/2020/07/Tantalising-Glimpses-Charlotte-Cooper.pdf.

Wherein the Author Provides Footnotes and Bibliographic Citation for the First Stanza Drafted after a Significant and Dangerous Depression Incurred upon Being Referenced as a "Hack" Both by Individuals Unknown to the Author and by Individuals Whom the Author Had Previously Considered Friends[(*)(†)(‡)(§)]

⑥
Verlee, Jeanann.
 "Wherein the Author Provides Footnotes and Bibliographic Citation for the First Stanza Drafted After a Significant and Dangerous Depression Incurred Upon Being Referenced as a 'Hack' Both by Individuals Unknown to the Author and by Individuals Whom the Author Had Previously Considered Friends[(*)(†)(‡)(§)]."
 Rattle 36 (Winter 2011): 51–52. ⑥
 ⑥
Verlee, Jeanann.
 "WHEREIN THE AUTHOR PROVIDES FOOTNOTES AND BIBLIOGRAPHIC CITATION FOR THE FIRST STANZA DRAFTED AFTER A SIGNIFICANT AND DANGEROUS DEPRESSION INCURRED UPON BEING REFERENCED AS A 'HACK' BOTH

BY INDIVIDUALS UNKNOWN TO THE AUTHOR AND BY INDIVIDUALS WHOM THE AUTHOR HAD PREVIOUSLY CONSIDERED FRIENDS[*][†][‡][§].*" Rattle*, September 3, 2012. https://www.rattle.com/wherein-the-author-provides-footnotes-by-jeanann-verlee/.

Verlee, Jeanann.
  "Wherein the Author Provides Footnotes and Bibliographic Citation for the First Stanza Drafted after a Significant and Dangerous Depression Incurred upon Being Referenced as a 'Hack' Both by Individuals Unknown to the Author and by Individuals Whom the Author Had Previously Considered Friends[*][†][‡][§].*"
  In *Said the Manic to the Muse*, 69–73. Edited by Jon Sands, Adam Falkner, Angel Nafis, and Ian Khadan. Interior layout by Andie Flores. Austin, TX: Write Bloody Publishing, 2015. 5 p.; page size: 21.5 × 14 cm.

What is Jeanann Verlee's poem "Wherein the Author Provides Footnotes and Bibliographic Citation for the First Stanza Drafted after a Significant and Dangerous Depression Incurred upon Being Referenced as a 'Hack' Both by Individuals Unknown to the Author and by Individuals Whom the Author Had Previously Considered Friends[*][†][‡][§]?" It is a poem about an episode of depression, yes, "by 35, when madness has overcome her."[1] It is an in-progress poem, one that the title indicates has just begun, "the first

Interior spread of "Wherein the Author Provides Footnotes and Bibliographic Citation . . ." in *Said the Manic to the Muse*, 2015.

Wherein the Author Provides Footnotes and Bibliographic Citation for the First Stanza Drafted After a Significant and Dangerous Depression Incurred upon Being Referenced as a "Hack" Both by Individuals Unknown to the Author and by Individuals Whom the Author Had Previously Considered Friends (*)(†)(‡)(§)

by 35[1], when madness[2] had overcome her[3]; when her body[4]
sloshed[5] like[6] rubbery meat[7] in the softest swells
of armsag[8] and stomach fold[9];
when the night brought[10] marching ants[11] to her[12] pillow[13]
and[14] wailing[15] teapots[16] swarmed in the kitchen[17];
when the cannibals came[18] wearing eyeliner and capped teeth[19];
when the flock of birds erupted from her throat[20],
leaving her mouth a clog[21] of feathers[22],
she paced the apartment[23], a fury[24]. a yowling beast[25].
caged rhinoceros[26], severed horn[27] in its bloody[28] maw[29, 30]. (¿)

---

[1] "by 35" | References author's own age. Mercy Hospital, Denver, Colorado, March 1974.
[2] "madness" | Term used to reference mental illness, specifically within the manic phase of Manic Depression.
[3] "had overcome her" | Happenstance of exact quotation, discovered after drafting stanza: Yeats, *On Baile's Strand*, Character: Fool, Page 23.
[4] "when her body" | Happenstance of exact quotation, discovered after drafting stanza. Chivers, "Ceratioid Anglerfish," Line 24.
[5] "her body sloshed" | Similar use of verb root, discovered after drafting stanza: "The train sloshes." McDaniel, "St. Theresa of the 6," Line 3. (Formula: [article/pronoun] [noun] slosh/es/ed.)
[6] "like" | Colloquialism in Southern California, most American High Schools, and various Skateboard Parks across the United States, often used to fill silence in conversation, replacing the more common terms, "uh" or "um." Also used in employment of similes, meaning "similar." Preposition.
[7] "rubbery meat" | The quality of overcooked flesh. Hirsh, "Microwaves no longer make rubbery meat."
[8] "armsag" | Term fabricated by author. Concept credit: 1. "sweatdrop." Bonair-

stanza drafted after a significant and dangerous depression." It is a poem directly spurred on by an incident that caused said depression, the devastating occurrence of "being referenced as a 'hack'" by both strangers and those she knew personally. It is a feminist reaction, owning the weakness of the body, the fallibility of the mental self, while addressing her critics. It is the manifestation of a desire to outwit and outsmart. It is therefore a heavily footnoted poem, and as Verlee herself notes, in the tradition of, for example: "1. Tolson, 'E. & O. E.' 2. Gottleib, *selected poems*. 3. Fabri, 'The Word-Lover's Miscarriage.'"[2] A forty-three-word title directs you to four footnotes. One eight-line stanza yields thirty footnotes with superscript numbers emphasizing and interrupting words and passages. The footnotes which contain shortened citations are further elaborated by a full end bibliography, just in case you were to doubt the author's academic prowess. Though the sprawling footnotes and bibliography are set in a smaller type size than the title and stanza, they overwhelm the partial poem, becoming essential to the poem itself, nay, the main attraction.

Verlee has dissected her own poem. She discovers instances of phrases that occur happenstance in another's work—for example, "had overcome her" is footnoted to also appear in a work by Yeats and the use of "and" is footnoted to have been included in the *Holy Bible*, Genesis 1:1.[3] Phrases that are allegedly direct quotes may nest a footnote inside a footnote. For example, the phrase "wearing eyeliner and capped teeth" is apparently a direct reference to an "eHow.com article, 'How to Make a Jack Sparrow Costume.' (1. Character from 'Pirates of the Caribbean: Curse of the Black Pearl.')."[4] She cites definitions for individual words and in the case of "armsag" tells the reader that she's invented the term, giving a list of examples of conjoined words created by published and self-published poets.[5] Many such footnotes are humorous with a bent towards the absurd, but the soberness of a struggle with depression comes through too. Footnote 15 reads, "'wailing'|Author here draws a parallel between the whistle of a heated tea kettle and the sound commonly emitted during the act of weeping. Definition: prolonged, inarticulate, mournful cry. Verb" and footnote 24 reads, "'fury'|References rage. Rage is a function of Manic Depression."[6]

Jeanann Verlee's poem "Wherein the Author Provides Footnotes and Bibliographic Citation . . ." is a power poem to the haters; a tragicomedy about depression, research, and writing; and a bibliography of low-brow and high-brow literature skillfully woven together.

---

(1) For ease of reading, Verlee's embedded citation numbers have been omitted here. Jeanann Verlee, "Wherein the Author Provides Footnotes and Bibliographic Citation for the First Stanza Drafted After a Significant and Dangerous Depression Incurred Upon Being Referenced as a 'Hack' Both by Individuals Unknown to the Author and By Individuals Whom the Author Had Previously Considered Friends[(*)(†)(‡)(§)]," in *Said the Manic to the Muse* (Austin, TX: Write Bloody Publishing, 2015), 69.
(2) Verlee, "Wherein the Author," 71.
(3) Verlee, "Wherein the Author," 69–70.
(4) Verlee, "Wherein the Author," 69–70.
(5) See Verlee, "Wherein the Author," 69–70.
(6) Verlee, "Wherein the Author," 70.

Works From Stack 655

Desjardin, Arnaud.
Works from Stack 655,
2012.
Installation.
Curated by Susan Johanknecht
and Finlay Taylor.
Camberwell Space,
Camberwell College of Arts,
London.

Arnaud Desjardin, artist, bookseller, and author of *The Book on Books on Artists Books* (2011), was invited to participate in BookMare to "explore how artists have used books as concepts and components in their practice with disquieting results."[1] The weekend exhibition and event series was curated by fellow book artists Susan Johanknecht and Finlay Taylor at Camberwell Space, London in July of 2012.

For *Works from Stack 655*, Desjardin created a wall shelf to display twenty-five books about books that he hand-picked from the Camberwell College of Art Library. The language of libraries—that is, the glare of polyester book jacket covers and white spine labels—was on full display. The books were available to browse, shelved cover-out on two rows. The shelf order changed as visitors handled the books. Because *Works from Stack 655* took place in a gallery rather than a library, its tactility, for attendees, would have been a novelty in an atmosphere where looking but not touching is the norm. The selection of books provided an abbreviated view of the library's holdings and the school's interests in making, preserving, and describing books. The three-dimensional bibliography included *Phantoms on the Bookshelves* by Jacques Bonnet, *Principles of Bibliographical Description* by Fredson Bowers, *A Book of the Book: Some Works & Projections About the Book & Writing* edited by Jerome Rothenberg and Steven Clay, and *Typographica* by Rick Poynor. Some book choices related to other works in the exhibition. For example, *Bookworms: The Insect Pests of Books* on Desjardin's shelf corresponded to the exhibition of Finlay Taylor's one-of-a-kind book *East Dulwich Dictionary*, a book that had been consumed and altered by snails.

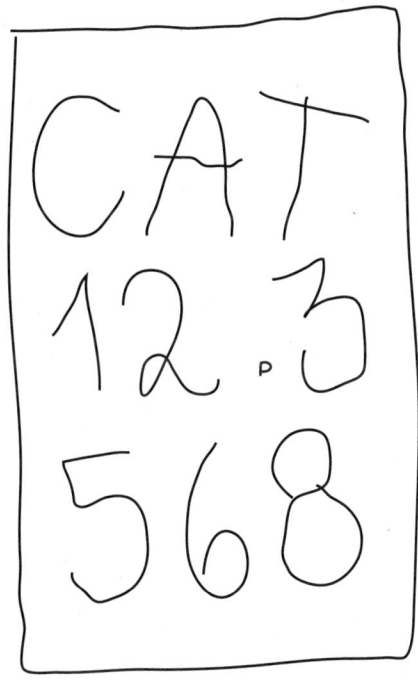

ACKNOWLEDGMENTS

The best acknowledgments perhaps I've ever read appear in the front of Felipe Ehrenberg's *Codex Aeroscriptus Ehrenbergensis* (Atlanta: Nexus Press, 1990). In eight short paragraphs, twelve sentences in all, he is gracious without descending into mere flattery and sprinkles in the right amount of unexpected truthy details. While my prose cannot compare, here is my expression of appreciation in eight short paragraphs and twelve sentences.

First my gratitude goes to the individual creators, collaborators, and featured organizations whose work is central to this book. Studying your projects has made going into a writing hole challenging and enjoyable in the best ways.

Thanks are due in no small part to all those who listened, conversed, and offered insightful feedback as I have attempted (and continue to attempt) to articulate my ideas around visual bibliography and experimental subject bibliography.

Since *Bibliographic Performances & Surrogate Readings* started as an idea for a master's thesis while I was in the Visual and Critical Studies program (2014–2016) at the School of the Art Institute of Chicago, I especially want to thank my thesis advisor Joseph Grigely and committee members Patrick Durgin and Johanna Drucker for their subject knowledge, insights, and project recommendations.

Then as now I'd like to recognize my family, friends, and colleagues near and far for their words of encouragement, phone calls, home-cooked meals, and social excursions which motivated me during this research, writing, and publishing process.

I am grateful for the day-to-day support of current and former colleagues especially Kristina Keogh, Alexandra Vargas-Minor, and Claire Powell who allowed me workplace flexibility when our employer awarded and then reneged my sabbatical.

Thank you to the makers, thinkers, libraries, galleries, and arts organizations who have kindly responded to questions, provided scans and images, and fostered this research over the years.

Searching for and applying to publication grants was an eye-opening experience and exposed me to the current conditions of art publishing. Special thanks to the Design History Society (UK) for being the first to take a chance and award me a Research Publication Grant, as well as to the College Book Art Association for a Member Support Grant, ARLIS/NA for the H.W. Wilson Foundation Research Award, and SECAC for the Artist's Fellowship Honorable Mention Award. I am humbled to count these professional organizations as project backers.

Last I want to extend my fondest admiration to the publishing team of Arnaud Desjardin as publisher and Margherita Sabbioneda as designer at The Everyday Press in London, and to Jon Boggs as editor in Knoxville, Tennessee. In addition to being a delight to work with, thank you for your patience, inventiveness, and guidance to make what I would say has become a damn sexy book.

REPRODUCTION CREDITS

Unless otherwise specified, copyright on the works reproduced lies with the respective creators. Certain credits appear at the request of the creator or creator's representatives.

82–83	Scans used with permission of Kathy Slade.
86, 88	Courtesy of Tania Prill, Alberto Vieceli, and Sebastian Cremers.
91	Courtesy of Jamal Cyrus and Inman Gallery.
93	Screenshot used with permission of Johanna Drucker.
96	Courtesy of Sternberg Press and The Book Lovers (Joanna Zielińska and David Maroto).
99	Scans used with permission of The Book Lovers (Joanna Zielińska and David Maroto): Interior spread showing *Espahor Ledet Ko Uluner!* by Guy de Cointet (Qei no mysxdod, pseud.) (published by author, 1973), photo: © Marc Domage, courtesy of Air de Paris, Paris; interior spread showing *At Battle of Drosabellamaximillian. Seeing Glandelinians Retreating Vivian Girls Grasp Christian Banners, and Lead Charge Against Foe* by Henry J. Darger (Chicago: mid-twentieth century). Watercolor, pencil, and carbon tracing on pieced paper, 19 × 47 3/4". Collection American Folk Art Museum, New York, 2002.22.1b. © Kiyoko Lerner, photo: James Prinz.
101	Courtesy of Mousse Publishing and The Book Lovers (Joanna Zielińska, and David Maroto), photos: Anna Azzali.

102	Scans used with permission of Heidi Neilson.
105-6, 109	Courtesy of Aaron Krach.
111, 113	Courtesy of Scott Blake.
114, 117	Scans used with permission of Ferenc Gróf / Société Réaliste.
120, 124-5	Courtesy of Tan Lin and Westphalie.
127	Screenshot used with permission of Tan Lin.
131	Courtesy of Janelle Rebel.
135, 136	Courtesy of Simon Morris, photos: Ricky Adam.
138-9, 141	Courtesy of Simon Morris.
145, 147	Courtesy of the Sitterwerk.
156	Courtesy of Laura Davidson, photos: John Polak.
160, 162-63	Scans and screenshot used with permission of Stuart Bertolotti-Bailey and David Reinfurt.
166	Screenshot used with permission of Ann Hamilton Studio.
168	Courtesy of Ann Hamilton Studio and The Fabric Workshop and Museum, photo: Carlos Avendano.
174-75	Scans used with permission of Candace Hicks.
180-81	Screenshot of *Cyberfeminism Index* images page courtesy of Mindy Seu, 2021, Firefox v76.0.1 on Mac OS 10.13.3; https://cyberfeminismindex.com/images.
182	Screenshot of *Cyberfeminism Index* home page scroll with text drawer courtesy of Mindy Seu, 2021, Firefox v76.0.1 on Mac OS 10.13.3, https://cyberfeminismindex.com/#/third-world-critiques-of-cyberfeminism.
185-86, 189	Scans used with permission of Louis Lüthi.
190, 192	Scans used with permission of Mike Mills, Jon Herschend, and Will Rogan.
195	Courtesy of Cauleen Smith.

197	Photo used with permission of Cauleen Smith.
199, 202	Photo and scans courtesy of Janelle Rebel.
205, 208-9	Scans used with permission of Olivier Lebrun.
206	Courtesy of Olivier Lebrun.
212-15	Scans used with permission of Craig Douglas Dworkin.
218	*Smalls (Hidden Histories)* courtesy of the artist and Marian Goodman Gallery, photo: Tom Powel Imaging.
218	*De Pizan (Hidden Histories)* courtesy of the artist and Regen Projects, photo: Joshua White.
223	Courtesy Cauleen Smith and Corbett Vs. Dempsey.
225	Scans used with permission of Cauleen Smith and Corbett Vs. Dempsey.
237, 241	Courtesy Mike & Maaike, photos: Mike & Maaike.
240	Courtesy Mike & Maaike, photo: Dwight Eschliman.
242	Courtesy Kenyatta A. C. Hinkle and Sming Sming Books, photo: Michael Underwood.
245	Courtesy Kenyatta A. C. Hinkle and Sming Sming Books, photo: Sming Sming Books.
246-47	Scans used with permission of Josh MacPhee.
251-52	Courtesy of Manuel Zenner, photos: Manuel Zenner, book design: Manuel Zenner, Corina Neuenschwander, Ina Meganck and Noah Venezia.
255, 257	Courtesy of Dorothee Dähler and Yeliz Secerli.
258-59	Courtesy of Janelle Rebel.
263	Scan used with permission of Semiotexte.
268, 270-71, 273	Scans used with permission of Glenn Ligon.
276	Courtesy of Craig Douglas Dworkin.
284-85	Screenshots used with permission of Printed Matter.

291	Courtesy of Janelle Rebel.
293-95	Courtesy of Armory Center for the Arts, photos by Jeff McLane.
302, 304	Scans used with permission of Are Not Books & Publications.
305, 308-9	Courtesy of Shilpa Gupta, photos: Anil Rane.
307	Courtesy of Shilpa Gupta, photo: NA.
312, 315	©Nina Katchadourian, courtesy of the artist, Catharine Clark Gallery, and Pace Gallery.
321	Scan used with permission of Chris Lee.
322, 325	Digital covers used with permission of the artists and Live Art Development Agency.
326	Screenshot used with permission of Live Art Development Agency.
330-31	"Wherein the Author Provides Footnotes and Bibliographic Citation..." by Jeanann Verlee appears in *Said the Manic to the Muse* (Write Bloody Publishing, 2015) and originally appeared in *Rattle* (2011). Scan used with permission of Jeanann Verlee.

INDEX

- alphabetical order, 76, 188, 207, 275, 316
- annotations, inventive or poetic, 131–34, 162–64, 168, 213–215, 264–65, 302–4, 323–27
- Are Not Books & Publications: *Saints & Guides*, 301–4
- artist's archive, 38–40, 44–45
- artist's book, 43–45, 80–83, 102–4, 122, 150, 154–55, 172–76. *See also* photobook; zine.
- artwork, 89–91, 216–20, 258–61, 305–15. *See* artist's book; drawing; installation (art); performance.
- auto-bibliography. *See* bio-bibliography.
- Bertolotti-Bailey, Stuart, Angie Keefer, and David Reinfurt: *Bulletins of the Serving Library*, 159–64
- bibliography: as activism, 178, 224; author emphasis in, 105–113, 305–11; book cover design, 53–54, 185–89, 222–24, 243–44, 272–73, 280, 314, 319–20 (*see also* typography); and conceptualism, 16, 30n20, 35–36; by multiple contributors, 135–43, 228, 250–57, 323; hybridity of page and screen, 110–13, 120–25, 144–48, 159–71; interaction with historical record, 89–91, 117, 131–34, 154–58, 177–84, 194–98, 216–20, 242–45, 298–300, 305–11, 318–21; and literary anthology, 60–61, 71n37, 114–19; as literary narrative, 50–51, 114–25,

185–89, 212–15, 313; as paratext, 51–52, 324, 328–33; and pedagogy, 59–61, 71n36, 142, 227–32, 250–57, 318–21; portrait of bibliographer(s), 82, 94, 120–25, 135–43, 172–76, 191, 221–26, 228, 274–78, 288–91; portrait of collector(s), 154–58, 187–88, 191, 274–78, 313; portrait of community, 194–96, 248, 250–57, 260–61, 279–80; public participation in creation of, 144–48, 165–71, 179, 210, 246–49, 282–84; as social commentary, 89–91, 210, 217–19, 236–41, 298–300

- bibliopsychology, 153
- bio-bibliography, 92–94, 234
- Black bibliography, 57–59, 89–91, 194–98, 217–19, 221–73, 292–97
- Blake, Scott: *Barcode Cornel West*, 110–13; *Barcode Oprah*, 110–11
- books, symbolic status of, 36–38, 89–91, 249
- bookworms, 317, 335
- Boom, Irma: *Irma Boom*, 233–35
- call numbers and classification systems, 39, 81, 140, 145, 207, 253, 257n2
- chronological order, 76, 80–81, 94, 114–23, 234, 254, 299
- coincidence(s), 172–76, 289
- commonplacing and commonplace books, 62–68, 165–76
- Cyrus, Jamal: *Africanismus_12469*, 89–91
- database, 22, 58, 76, 92–94, 97, 117, 137, 182, 289
- Davidson, Laura: *The Bookshelf Project*, 154–58
- Desjardin, Arnaud: *Works from Stack 655*, 334–35
- drawing, 37, 154–58, 206–7, 221–26, 230–32, 303–4

- ★ Drucker, Johanna: *All*, 92–94
- ★ Dworkin, Craig Douglas: "Further Listening", 212–15; *The Perverse Library*, 274–78
- ★ excerpts, 65, 97–98, 118–19, 167–70, 172–76, 178–83, 317
- ★ exhibition(s), 97, 190–93, 194–98, 199–203, 224–26, 234, 242–45, 316, 334–35. *See also* libraries and archives, as curatorial space; gallery-turned-reading room.
- ★ feminist bibliography, 157, 177–84, 217, 296, 332
- ★ film, 65, 175, 217–19, 264, 303, 323
- ★ *Frieze* magazine: Ideal Syllabus, 227–32
- ★ furniture, 236–41, 283, 292–97
- ★ gallery-turned-reading room, 40–42, 292–97, 334–35
- ★ Gupta, Shilpa: *Someone Else...*, 305–11
- ★ Hamilton, Ann: *cloth • a commonplace*, 166–69; *(habitus • cloth • a commonplace)*, 165–71
- ★ Hicks, Candace: *Common Threads*, 172–76
- ★ Hinkle, Kenyatta A.C.: *Kentifrications*, 242–45
- ★ imaginary or speculative books, 47–50, 188, 206–10, 244, 317, 319–320
- ★ installation (art), 46, 107, 170, 194–98, 242–43, 305–11
- ★ intuitive or associative order, 144–48, 172–76, 213, 314–15
- ★ Katchadourian, Nina: *Sorted Books*, 312–15
- ★ Krach, Aaron: *The Author of This Book Committed Suicide*, 105–9
- ★ LADA. *See* Live Art Development Agency.
- ★ Lebrun, Olivier: *A Pocket Companion to Books from "The Simpsons" in Alphabetical Order*, 204–6; *Another Companion to Books from "The Simpsons"*

  in Alphabetical Order, 204–6; *A Final Companion to Books from "The Simpsons"*, 204–11
★ Lee, Chris: "Strike and Riot", 318–21
★ Lefebvre, Henri: *The Missing Pieces*, 262–66
★ libraries and archives, as curatorial space, 38–40, 105–9, 154–58, 305–15
★ Ligon, Glenn: *A People on the Cover*, 267–73
★ Lin, Tan: *Ambient Fiction Reading System 01*, 121–22; *Bib*, 121–22; *Bib., Rev. Ed.*, 120–25; *Bibliographic Sound Track*, 126–30; *The Ph.D Sound*, 126–30
★ Live Art Development Agency: *Study Room Guides*, 322–27
★ Lüthi, Louis: "A Die with 26 Faces" / *A Die with Twenty-Six Faces*, 185–89
★ MacPhee, Josh: *Lonely Books*, 246–49
★ Maroto, David: *The Artist's Novel*, 98–101
★ Maroto, David, and Joanna Zielińska: *The Book Lovers*, 95–97; *Artist Novels*, 95–99
★ Mellegers, Adriaan: *Pile of Books*, 279–80
★ Mills, Mike: "Difficult Times: Every Book About Spirituality I Own" / *Difficult Times: Every Book About Spirituality I Own*, 190–93
★ Mike and Maaike: *Juxtaposed*, 236–41
★ Morris, Simon: *Bibliomania*, 135–43; *Bibliomania 2000/2001*, 135–43
★ Morris, Simon, and Helen Sacoor: *Bibliomania*, 135–37
★ music, 58, 129, 212–15, 217–19
★ Neilson, Heidi: *Atlas of Punctuation*, 102–4
★ new technology, 144–48, 281–87
★ Nonnus Studio. *See* Are Not Books & Publications.
★ performance, 65, 80–83, 126–30, 213, 322–27
★ photobook, 84–88, 267–73, 279–80.

See also artist's book; zine.
- Prill, Tania, Alberto Vieceli, and Sebastian Cremers: *336 Pages 336 Books*, 84–88
- Printed Matter: PM Tables, Visitor Tables, Your Tables, 281–87
- publishing and book collecting, 45–46, 185–89, 274–78
- Queer bibliography, 67, 222, 292–97
- reading room guide(s), 43, 144–48, 199–203, 250–57, 322–27
- Rebel, Janelle: *Bibliography of Architecture Theory*, 131–34; *Exhibition Takeaways*, 199–203; *Meanwhile, the surrogate for the presently absent gets a proxy*, 258–61; *Poet-Saints of July 06*, 288–91
- Saltz, Jerry: *An Ideal Syllabus*, 227–32
- Seu, Mindy: *Cyberfeminism Index*, 177–84
- Sitterwerk: *Bibliozines*, 144–48
- size and scale of books, 157, 224, 238–39, 260, 280, 283, 320–21
- Slade, Kathy: *52 Transactions*, 80–83
- Smith, Cauleen: *The El Saturn Research Library*, 194–98; *Human_3.0 Reading List 2015-2016*, 221–26
- Société Réaliste: *The Best American Book of the 20th Century*, 114–19
- Strachan, Tavares: *Hidden Histories*, 216–20
- Syms, Martine: *The Queen's English* (with Cat Roif and Jeff Cain), 292–97; *ReadingTrayvonMartin.com*, 298–300
- Tamm, Triin: *Bookcatalogtest*, 149–53; *A Stack of Books, A Book of Stacks*, 316–17
- television, 12, 172, 204–11
- text mapping, 102–4, 114–19
- thematic order, 94, 153, 169, 196–97, 269, 282–83

- typography, 84–88, 102–4, 139, 178–83, 185–89, 201, 302
- unpublished books, 48, 92, 262, 317
- Verlee, Jeanann: "Wherein the Author Provides Footnotes . . .", 328–33
- web bibliography, 92–94, 97, 177–84, 254–57, 281–91, 298–300
- Werkplaats Typografie: The Mary Shelley Facsimile Library, 250–57
- Zenner, Manuel, Yin Yin Wong, Mathew Whittington, et al.: *The Mary Shelley Facsimile Library*, 250–54
- zine, 146–47, 246–49. *See also* artist's book; photobook.

AUTHOR BIO

Janelle Rebel's post-medium activities span artist's publications, experimental bibliography, critical graphic design, theoretical writing, performance, and inclusive exhibition making. Recent projects include the feminist digital art project and web archive of intercepted political polls *Dear Vern* (2020–2023); the pandemic video performance collab with Wes Kline *Humid Trance Distance* (2020–2021); the three-volume artist's book *Feminisms of the Upper Air* (Are Not Books, 2019); a scholarly article examining bibliographic models and design research, "Unrecognized Creative Labor: A Critique of the George Wittenborn Memorial Book Award" (*Art Documentation* 38, no. 2, Fall 2019); a theory of special collections in ten slides, "*Synthetic Fabric*, Neckties, Diableries" (2018); a dialogue on collaborative curating in *Freedom of the Presses: Artists' Books in the 21st Century* (D.A.P./Booklyn, 2018); and an exploratory chapbook, *From Where: A Reverie on Digital Surrogates* (Kenning Editions, 2016). She studied visual and critical studies at School of the Art Institute of Chicago, library and information science at Dominican University, and fine arts and graphic design at Ball State University. She was the curator and head of the Brizdle-Schoenberg Special Collections Center at Ringling College of Art and Design from 2016 to 2023. Janelle is currently the Seymour Adelman Director of Special Collections at Bryn Mawr College.

©
Janelle Rebel

Published by
The Everyday Press
2024

Designed by
Margherita Sabbioneda

Printed by
Tallinna Raamatutrükikoda

ISBN
978-1-912458-20-2